first PEOPLES *first* CONTACTS

This publication was made possible

by a generous grant from the

Eugene V. and Clare E. Thaw

Charitable Trust, Santa Fe.

first PEOPLES

first CONTACTS

Native Peoples of North America

J.C.H. KING

Published for The Trustees of

The British Museum by

BRITISH MUSEUM PRESS

© 1999 The Trustees of the British Museum

First published in 1999 by British Museum Press
A division of The British Museum Company Ltd
46 Bloomsbury Street, London WC1B 3QQ

A catalogue record for this book is available from
the British Library

ISBN 0 7141 2546 6 (cased)
ISBN 0 7141 2538 5 (paperback)

Designed by Harry Green
Typeset in Baskerville and Gill
Printed in Slovenia by Korotan

CONTENTS

North America divided into the general areas covered in chapters 2–10.

PREFACE

First Peoples, First Contacts: Native Peoples of North America
has been written to coincide with the introductory display of
the British Museum's collections in the Chase Manhattan
Gallery of North America. The book is constructed from a
number of narratives intended to juxtapose a museum perspective with Native accounts and to present an idea of Native
culture in the context of a turbulent and contested history.
While much of this is entirely conventional – the focus is on
art and material culture rather than ideas – it seeks also to
reflect the multiplicity of approaches available for interpretation.
Oral, public and national histories are integrated into the
narratives, the Native voice offering a counterpoint to more
usual interpretations.

In Europe understanding of Native North America is
mediated by distance, by the often unapparent divisiveness of a
common language and by the European stereotypes alternative
to, but in some respects more firmly rooted than, those in
Canada and the United States. The book reflects the historical
and cultural approach taken in this North American Gallery. It
provides a series of vignettes starting with the pre-European
contact period in North America generally and following in a
spiral around the continent, from the historic Northeast, clock-
wise through the Southeast, to California, the Northwest Coast,
the Arctic and the Subarctic, to end in the centre on the Plains
and in the American West. It is hoped that this approach will
temper the romantic mesmerizing curiosity of Europeans about
Native America with a sense of realism.

The intention is to emphasize the multiplicity of cultures

and the diversity of cultural influences in Native North America, and to supersede the predominant image of all Indians as the feather-bonneted warriors of the Plains with an idea of the complexity of North America. Before European contact some 25 per cent of all world languages were Native North American; today English, with French and Spanish, predominates. It should also be noted that narratives of exploration and points of contact are less an indication of boundaries between differing cultures than new centres of interchange between different peoples. Contact between Europeans and Native Americans is not something that happened once in 1492, when Columbus arrived in the Bahamas, but instead a long process, lasting many hundreds of years, of gradual interaction between strangers across the continent. The role of women, as significant hunters as well as creators of most of the artefacts shown here, must be emphasized. Most significant of all was the underwriting of European colonization by Native women, who in New York and New England, as in the Appalachians, Hudson Bay, the Upper Missouri and Alaska, contributed their labour to the preparation of skins and furs. Finally, and perhaps most important of all, it must be recognized that art and material culture are only one aspect of Native expressive culture. Most Europeans in early encounters with Indians noted, for instance, the magnificence of Indian oratory as much as, if not more than, the splendour of Indian architecture and costume.

Collecting Native North America

Although the British Museum was founded in the eighteenth century, its traditions are largely rooted in the nineteenth. So it would be reasonable to expect that the Museum was the regular recipient of collections from imperial grandees such as the Governors-General of Canada, who continued to be British until the 1940s. Yet there is only one such collection, that of a couple of dozen artefacts sold to the Museum by Lord Lorne in 1887 (see p. 250). Instead, the paradigms governing the creation of the North American collections are associated with eighteenth-century Enlightenment ideas of knowledge and learning. North American ethnography was accumulated in a random and indeterminate manner by seemingly minor people engaged in the professional task of collecting natural history artefacts. Similarly, while British archaeologists have worked in many if not most parts of the world, little serious archaeology has been undertaken from the United Kingdom in North America. The collections that exist in the British Museum are therefore mostly ethnographic, acquired as souvenirs and trophies rather than in the form of balanced collections of indigenous art and manufactures obtained in the field.

The Museum was founded in 1753 under the will of Sir Hans Sloane, an insatiable collector, physician and scientist, sometimes known for the introduction of the Nahuatl chocolate drink to London. As part of his scientific collection, he acquired a group of what he termed 'Miscellanies', 2,000 objects that did not fit easily into any of his other categories and were an appendix to his collection of natural history specimens. Amongst these are items of major historical importance, comprising the only or earliest surviving examples of several types of artefact. They include, for instance, what may be the earliest article made by a named Indian (fig. 34).

For the first century, until the 1850s, the Museum was primarily a passive recipient of ethnographic collections made by explorers collecting for natural scientific purposes; only incidentally were ethnographic materials collected. Expeditions, such as Cook's Third Voyage of 1776–80 or that in which George Vancouver heroically mapped the coast between Santa Barbara, California, and Anchorage, Alaska, in 1791–5, generated collections which, after passing through laborious channels, were deposited in the British Museum. In this respect the ethnographic collections were an aspect of science, so-called 'artificial curiosities'. They were intended, for instance, as indicated in instructions from the naturalist Sir Joseph Banks (1743–1820), to include samples of textiles for Europeans to examine. 'Curiosity' in its late twentieth-century meaning suggests oddity, rather pejoratively; in the eighteenth century curiosity implied 'worthy of scientific interest' and therefore of preservation. This museum function of receiving collections from official voyages of exploration continued in the nineteenth century up until the 1870s, when another half a dozen, mostly Arctic collections were deposited in the Museum.

In the eighteenth century the primary focus of the Museum was on the Pacific, with the creation of a South Seas Room in 1780, which included western and northwest America, and this remained the case until at least the 1860s. In the 1860s the focus changed because of the bequest of a collection made by Henry Christy (1810–65), a banker and industrialist with two main claims to commercial fame. He introduced, at the 1851 Great Exhibition, the concept of looped pile towels – the kind we all use today – which he had copied from those he saw in Turkey. He also brought to his textile business the use of silk for top hats to replace the matted beaver felt imported from Canada. Christy's initial interest in the diversity of textiles seems to have developed into a more general interest in material culture. This included the investigation of the French Palaeolithic with the then curator of the Department of Antiquities and Ethnography, A.W. Franks. After Christy's death Franks, with great taste and, perhaps more importantly, with the necessary funds and generosity, augmented Christy's collection. Initially, he acquired 'Esquimaux' objects, for instance, from people who included, in 1871, the Canadian Admiral of loyalist American descent, Sir Edward Belcher. These were used as comparative materials for the European Palaeolithic, vital for the construction of evolutionary development schemes.

From this base A.W. Franks established a collection, largely through osmosis, which came to include Native North American materials from all over the continent.

In this century collections largely derived from the acquisitive habits of private collectors, who recirculated materials acquired by administrators, military and naval personnel, fur traders and the like. These had often been deposited in small local museums, which from the turn of the century began to de-accession and dispose of materials not significant to their immediate interests. Most famous of the collectors and benefactors was an American, Sir Henry Wellcome, from Wisconsin and Minnesota, who by marketing the newly invented 'tabloid' (tablet or pill) acquired the wealth to indulge his scientific collecting instincts. As a boy he had seen the effects of the Santee Sioux uprising of 1862 (see p. 255), and later became passionately interested in and wrote about the missionary efforts of William Duncan, a strong-willed Anglican Missionary who established an ideal community in what was to be the only reservation in Alaska. From the 1970s onwards contemporary collections, of art as well as more traditional material culture, have been acquired through fieldwork, particularly from the Arctic, Northwest Coast and Northeastern Woodlands.

Nomenclature

No other aspect of contemporary Native North America is so contentious and also, in its own way, so interesting as the naming of peoples. In a sense nothing is more important than the ability of individuals, peoples or nations to maintain their own name, or self-designation – ethnonym – for themselves rather than accept those imposed by outsiders in North American or European English. Yet in North America there has been little consensus as to what these names should be. And for Europeans it is important to use familiar terms, if only to avoid confusion. In general, where the self-designation is widely accepted, then that term is used here; otherwise the earlier name is retained. So, for instance, the Nootkas of Vancouver Island are here called by their modern name 'Nuu-Chah-Nulth'. 'Iroquoian' is used to refer to all peoples speaking an Iroquoian language, and 'Iroquois' to the Five (later Six) Nations: Senecas, Cayugas, Onondagas, Oneidas, Mohawks and Tuscaroras. Similarly, 'Algonquian' refers to people speaking an Algonquian language.

Indians are Indians because Columbus thought he had arrived in India rather than, in reality, the Bahamas. In North America Asian Indians are often referred to as 'South Asians'. Conversely, in England if 'North American Indian' is not used, the unacceptable 'Red Indian' is still sometimes employed, along with *peaux rouges* in France. The red originally came less from the natural colour of the skin than from the ochre pigment painted on and liberally used, for instance, by the Beothuks, the 'Red Indians' of Newfoundland, in annual spring ceremonies of renewal. No doubt, for the Beothuks, as for the Cherokees and other peoples, red was a sacred colour. The most reasonable and most generally used term for the indigenous population of North America, adopted here, is 'Native', as in 'Native American'. Yet in the United States Natives often, if not usually, refer to themselves as 'Indians', or rather 'Indian people'. Indian is also much in use in titles, as in the Native newspaper *Indian Country Today*, and it still has an important meaning in contrast to Eskimoan peoples, while, on the other hand, one advantage of Native is that it combines both Indian and Eskimoan populations. A Canadian alternative is 'aboriginal', or in Francophone contexts, *amérindien*, or more usually *autochtone*. But 'native' is a term with its own complexities. The phrase 'native American', for instance, arose in the nineteenth century to refer to old stock European-Americans, in opposition to the German and Irish influx of the 1840s. Later, native was adopted by the eugenics movement in the United States with this same meaning. In some states with significant new inflows of population, native is employed to mean 'born in the state': a Florida politician may call him/herself a 'native Floridian', meaning that he or she is not a 'snow-bird', that is a recent arrival from the cold north. Perhaps William Apess, the nineteenth-century Pequot historian, might be allowed the last word: 'The proper term which ought to be applied to our nation, to distinguish it from the rest of the human family, is that of *Natives* – and I humbly conceive that the natives of this country are the only people under heaven who have a just title to the name…'

In Canada the preferred term is 'First Nations', as in the 'Assembly of First Nations', the national Canadian Native political umbrella group, which may nonetheless be about to be renamed. In common – actually professional, closed-circuit – use 'First Nation' is often replaced by 'Native', 'indigenous' or 'aboriginal'. And other widespread terms, particularly 'tribe', are similarly lost in a mêlée of contradictions. While apparently unacceptable and negative in African English, 'tribe' is still used in reference to entities in Canada for instance, where a 'tribal' council will group together in an organization a number of bands sharing geography, language and culture. In general in North America, however, tribe is gradually being replaced by nation, as, for instance, in the designation 'Navajo Nation'.

The use of 'Eskimo' also illustrates problems in naming. Originally it seems likely to have come, circuitously, from the term used for 'snowshoe netter' by the Algonquian-speaking Montagnais on the St Lawrence estuary. This century, however, the term has usually been liberally translated as 'raw meat eater', which, while in a sense correct as an epithet, arose because of a similar word in Ojibwa with this meaning but in use to the west. The self-designation of the Canadian Eskimo, *Inuit*, or 'people' in Inuktitut, is now preferred for Eskimo. The campaign for the change was spearheaded from 1971 by Tagak Curley with the umbrella group, the Inuit Tapirisat of Canada. The success of the ethnonym arose in conjunction with the development of Inuit art on the multicultural international stage, enabling Inuit to assert a name of their own choice. Some North American dictionaries, however, such as Webster's, employ Inuit inclusively to designate the Eskimoan peoples in Alaska, although Alaskans often retain the word Eskimo, and the Yu'pik- and Inupiaq-speaking peoples of that state use their own self-designations, 'Inupiat' and 'Yuiit', rather than Inuit. In addition, Arctic peoples use the self-designation of their own particular community, so that individuals know exactly where they come from. In Greenland the term 'Greenlander' is employed, seemingly to cover all inhabitants including those of mixed descent, while in Labrador the mixed or white population, originally from Ireland and the west of England, is termed 'settler'. Further difficulties arise in the use of singulars and plurals; it is now said to be demeaning to employ terms in the singular, yet Inuit is already plural and the singular 'Inuk' would confuse, while 'Inuits' is incorrect. Plurals have often been used here, although we may still talk of the British and French rather than 'Britishers' and 'Frenchies'.

Most vexed of the terminologies are those which describe people of bicultural or mixed ancestry. The terms 'half-breed', 'breed' and 'full blood' have disappeared; as a Cherokee visitor to London noted recently, 'Who isn't a full blood?' – that is we all have our regulation ten pints. In Canada *Métis* is used to describe people of mixed ancestry, whether Native and French, or Native and British. American English has neither a similarly elegant borrowing from the Canadian French, nor an equivalent to the Spanish *mestizo*. Similarly difficult are the new designations, ethnonyms and orthographies for specific peoples. These are employed here where there is consensus on spelling and application, but otherwise more traditional English usage is retained.

ACKNOWLEDGEMENTS

This text was prepared with the help of very many people, to whom I am most grateful. John Mack, Keeper of the Department of Ethnography, was encouraging at every stage of the project. Henrietta Lidchi provided critical assistance in both senses of the word as well as effortlessly organizing photography and photographic research. William C. Sturtevant, with most generous use of his time, commented on the text. Arni Brownstone, Hugh Dempsey, Sally McLendon, Scott Stephenson, Colin Taylor and Alika Webber kindly read chapters of the book. Joanna Champness and Colin Grant patiently edited the text and illustrations.

Many people helped with enquiries, logistical support and research. I would like to thank particularly: Lydia Black, Nancy Blomberg, Kathryn Bridge, Jim Burant, David Burgevin, Sarah Carter, Jill Cook, Nina Cumings, Paula Fleming, Rayna Green, Susan Herter, Dale Idiens, John Johnson, David Mattison, Colin McEwan, Doyce B. Nunis Jnr, Laura Peers, Karen Perkins, Nancy Marie Robertson, Morton I. Sosland, Dennis Stanford, Donny White and Robin Wright. The National Anthropological Archives and Smithsonian Institution, the National Archives of Canada, the Department of Prints and Drawings (British Museum), the Canadian Pacific Archives, the Henry Moore Foundation and the British Library provided archival and institutional support.

The financial arrangements for the Chase Manhattan Gallery of North America were organized by the British Museum Development Trust and the American Friends of the British Museum. The innovative and unstinting help of Elizabeth Duggal and Mollie Norwich ensured the smooth running of the whole project.

Phillip Taylor quietly and effectively supervised the organization of the collections, and their conservation and photography, over a period of several years. Dave Agar, Saul Peckham and Michael Row undertook most of the excellent photography, assisted by Alison Deeprose. Harry Persaud, Renée Evans, Carmen Grannum-Symister, Anne Alexander and Lucia Navascues helped with a wide variety of archive and library tasks. The maps were created by Sam Kirby, and the line drawings by David Williams. Dean Baylis paid the bills.

1 ANCIENT NORTH AMERICA

In many ways the question of when North America came to be inhabited by *Homo sapiens* is as much one of belief as of scientific proof, both for Natives and for archaeologists. Origin myths, in North America as elsewhere, often posit an origin in current place of habitation. Archaeologists have concluded, however, that during the Pleistocene or last Ice Age, when sea levels

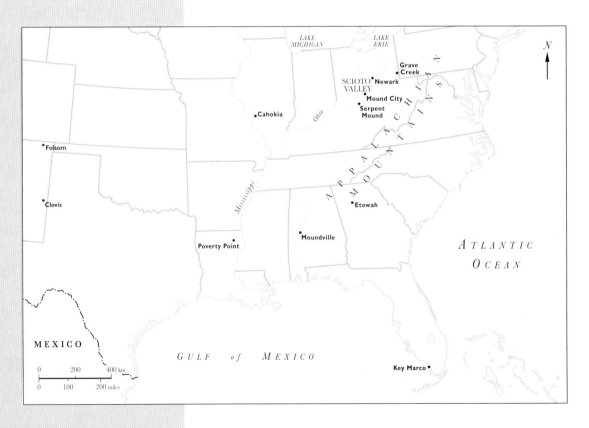

were much lower, and sometime before 12,000 years ago but probably not more than 40,000 years ago, people moved from Siberia to Alaska across what is called the Bering Land Bridge, or Beringia. They brought with them what is in Old World terms a stone 'tool kit' related to that of the Upper Palaeolithic, the Eurasian Levallois-Mousterian tradition. A drop of 45 m (150 ft) in the present sea level would have created dry land between Siberia and Alaska across Bering Strait. This land bridge may have been at its greatest extent 18,000 years ago, measuring more than 1600 km (1000 miles) east to west, and 960 km (600 miles) north to south, the sea level being then 60 m (200 ft) lower. At that time Beringia would have been a cold desert, with trees along river bottoms and plentiful horse, mammoth, caribou and bison.

No one is sure when people moved across the land bridge, or whether people came in a series of separate waves or in a series of continuous small-scale migrations at different times, although the latter now seems more likely. The land bridge existed 60,000 years ago, but there are few satisfactorily dated skeletal materials from North America before 10,000 years ago. This means that claims for earlier dates often depend on controversial ideas, dating what may or may not be cultural remains – particularly of course tools. An example of this is provided by a bone scraper from Old Crow River in the Canadian Yukon; associated with extinct Pleistocene fauna, it was dated to 27,000 years ago after its discovery in 1966. For a while this was perhaps the oldest North American tool, but in 1986 a more accurate, but less spectacular date of around 1350 years ago was obtained. Nevertheless, it is likely that ever-earlier dates for the peopling of the Americas will become accepted. Elsewhere – in the Calizo Hills, southern California, for instance – stone tools have turned out to have been created by natural action.

The first identified human populations in North America are the Big-Game Hunters, from the Paleoindian Tradition, *c.*12,000–8,000 years ago, although it is probable that people arrived in North America from Asia many thousands of years earlier. Paleoindian peoples hunted mammoth and other now extinct game, such as long horn bison, with spears tipped with long fluted, lanceolate, narrow, concave-based chert points. These were made by both pressure and percussion flaking. The points are named after kill sites such as Folsom and Clovis, New

Archaeological sites in the central and eastern United States.

1. Fluted bifacial Clovis point of chert, Arizona, *c.*8,000 BC. L 8.4 cm (3.3 in).

2. Fluted chert Folsom point in matrix, with rib bones of the long-extinct bison *Bison antiquus*, New Mexico, *c.* 8,000 BC. The first such point to have been found *in situ* at a kill site, it was discovered in 1927 during fieldwork by the then Colorado Museum of Natural History, which established the great antiquity of the Paleoindian tradition.

Mexico, at which examples of these flint tools were first found in the 1920s in association with butchered bison (fig. 2). The beasts may have been driven into swampy ground or water to tire them out, a technique which, of course, remains available to hunters today. Other animals included sheep, bear, musk ox and caribou. The megafauna disappeared in the following millennia in large part because of changing ecology, although perhaps with a little help from man. Conclusive evidence of an earlier human occupation of North America, analogous to the findings at Monte Verde in South America, may come to light. This Chilean site, dating to 12,500 years ago and later, has yielded bifacial stone tools and projectiles, and people lived in mastodon skin-covered huts. Big-game hunting was not the only hunting strategy in Pleistocene America. In some parts of eastern North America Paleoindians depended, at least seasonally,

on fishing and on gathering mussels, roots and nuts, and hunting small mammals. Linguistic evidence provided most recently by Johanna Nichols suggests an early date for first entry, most likely 40,000 years ago.

The Archaic Period

Whereas in the desert west, the Arctic and elsewhere, separate traditions evolved early on, in the east the Paleoindian tradition developed into a long Archaic Period from *c.*8000 to 1000 BC.

During this time gradual adaptations were made to create specialized technologies for the exploitation of ecological niches appearing in the post-glacial environment. But many Archaic traits, for instance in lithic technologies, survived into the period of European contact, indicating the extraordinary cultural time depth of Native North America. Apart from big game, fish and marine and riverine molluscs remained important foodstuffs, as did waterfowl and plant foods. After 5,000 BC pecked and ground stone objects came to join flaked flint implements in assemblages from archaeological sites. The new Archaic tool kit included mortars and pestles for grinding plant materials, and other pecked and ground stone tools, such as axes and adzes, for woodworking.

The Archaic Period is normally divided into three periods: the last of these, the Late Archaic (3000–1000 BC), was one of rapid change with increasing specialization and the development of riverine trade networks. From the Archaic Period onwards copper circulated in the Great Lakes and St Lawrence drainage; marine shell from the Gulf of Mexico began to appear *c.*1500 BC in the Great Lakes and continued to be used until the nineteenth century. Obsidian, a volcanic glass used for tools and prestige blades, was traded widely in the west. Archaic people in a riverine area might follow very deliberate patterns of collecting shell fish and gathering fresh summer vegetation, fishing, moving away from the rivers for autumnal nut-gathering and then winter hunting in the uplands. Concepts of nomadism imply a lack of intention in seemingly aimless movements. In reality, the reverse – focused intention – is actually required to ensure the seasonal availability of food sources through the year, and this too remains the norm for contempo-

3. Archaic Period tools, *c.*8000–1000 BC, including four bifacially flaked projectile points of quartz and other minerals, and a pecked and ground stone axe. Mostly collected in Virginia, they entered the collection of Hans Sloane, founder of the British Museum, in about 1730, making them possibly the earliest assemblage of North American archaeological materials. L of axe head: 23 cm (9.1 in).

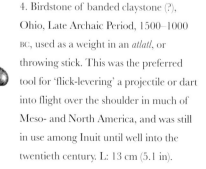

4. Birdstone of banded claystone (?), Ohio, Late Archaic Period, 1500–1000 BC, used as a weight in an *atlatl*, or throwing stick. This was the preferred tool for 'flick-levering' a projectile or dart into flight over the shoulder in much of Meso- and North America, and was still in use among Inuit until well into the twentieth century. L: 13 cm (5.1 in).

rary hunting people. In the Late Archaic, as in historic California, the exploitation of neighbouring but differing ecological zones enabled the development of a substantial population. At this time large settlements, such as Poverty Point, Louisiana, arose with a population of 5000 at 1000 BC, living around a vast series of embankments and mounds.

The Woodland Period

The Archaic Period is followed seamlessly by the Woodland, which is characterized by the intensified use of plants, leading by AD 700 to extensive agriculture, the development of elaborate burial mound complexes, and the expansion of the earlier Archaic trade networks. The Early Woodland Period also saw the beginning of elaborate mortuary rituals, which survived into the European period in Virginia and Louisiana. The Adena complex, in the middle and upper Ohio valley, is the most significant manifestation of an Early Woodland society in the last millennium BC. The economy was based on hunting and fishing, and from 100 BC apparently also on the growing of squash, pumpkin, sunflowers, goosefoot and marsh elder. Circular earthworks were created, both round banks and conical burial mounds such as those at Miamisburg and Grave Creek (fig. 6), West Virginia. The burial mounds were constructed in several stages, with log-lined pits containing burials with fine grave goods, including, for instance, smoking pipes. The Middle Woodland Period, from 200 BC, saw an intensification of social stratification, best indicated perhaps by the extraordinary development of spectacular earthworks, some of whose enclosures encompass more than 400 hectares (1000 acres). One important development was the creation of a new pottery type, with incised and rocker-stamped designs enclosing figurative forms.

The Ohio Hopewell of the Scioto Valley, from c.100 BC to AD 600, represents perhaps the most developed culture of the Woodland Period. While houses were relatively straightforward structures of thatch and pole, earthworks were often complex. They survive in numerous geometric forms, particularly squares,

5. Tubular smoking pipe of banded claystone with triangular flanged mouthpiece, Late Archaic or Early Woodland Period, 1500–500 BC. L: 33 cm (13 in).

6. Engraving of 1848 showing Grave Creek Mound, West Virginia. This burial mound, 21.6 m (71 ft) high, was the first from which Adena log-lined tombs, dating to the Early Woodland Period, were reported in the 1830s.

7. Sandstone tablets carved with rattlesnakes, usually identified as from the Adena culture, Middle Woodland Period, 400 BC–AD 1. Recovered by Squier and Davis from a Hopewell site in Ohio in the 1840s, they were probably used as pigment stamps for body, clothing or building decoration. 10 x 4 cm, 5.5 x 4 cm (3.9 x 1.6 in, 2.2 x 1.6 in).

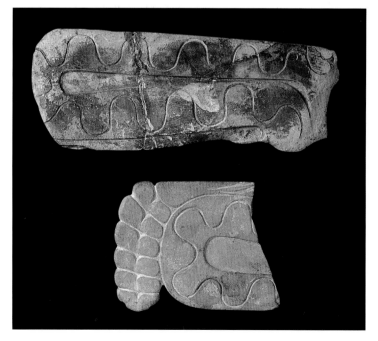

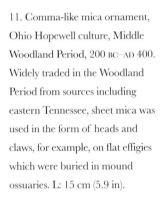

8–9. Zoomorphic effigy pipes from Mound City, Ohio Hopewell culture, Middle Woodland Period, 200 BC–AD 100. Excavated by Squier and Davis in 1846, these were probably carved with flint tools from claystone or pipestone and smoothed over with abrasives. The animals' eyes were originally inlaid, perhaps with freshwater pearls. L: 10 cm, 10 cm (3.9 in, 3.9 in).

10. Hopewell pipe in the form of an otter from Mound City, originally with a fish in the mouth. Initially identified as representing manatees which lived in Florida 1600 km (1,000 miles) away, such pipes fuelled a mid-nineteenth-century debate as to whether the mound builders were of external origin and unrelated to the present-day Native population. L: 11 cm (4.3 in).

11. Comma-like mica ornament, Ohio Hopewell culture, Middle Woodland Period, 200 BC–AD 400. Widely traded in the Woodland Period from sources including eastern Tennessee, sheet mica was used in the form of heads and claws, for example, on flat effigies which were buried in mound ossuaries. L: 15 cm (5.9 in).

12. Deer head effigy of boatstone, Ohio Hopewell culture, Middle Woodland Period, 200 BC–AD 400, possibly used as a ceremonial throwing-stick weight. Such superbly carved stone effigies, although of unknown purpose, may have been associated with the personal spirits of high-ranking chiefs and used in rituals. L: 11 cm (4.3 in).

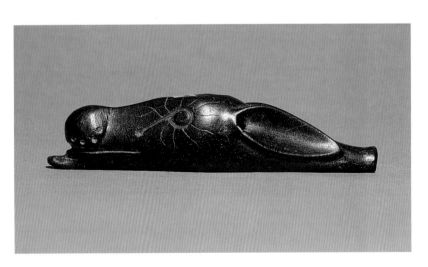

13. Hopewell Zoned pottery vessel, 200–100 BC. One or two double pots of this type have been recovered from mound sites, decorated with figurative designs which represent aquatic and/or raptorial birds, suggesting the ancient Woodlands dichotomy between creatures of the upper and lower worlds. H: 25 cm (9.9 in).

14. Stone plummet shaped as an aquatic bird's head and perhaps used as an amulet or a net weight. This was excavated before 1903 from a mound near Killarney, Orange County, on the Gulf Coast of Florida, where in a phase of the Middle Woodland Period (400 BC–AD 1) familial burial mounds with elaborate assemblages of grave goods were created.
L: 11 cm (4.3 in).

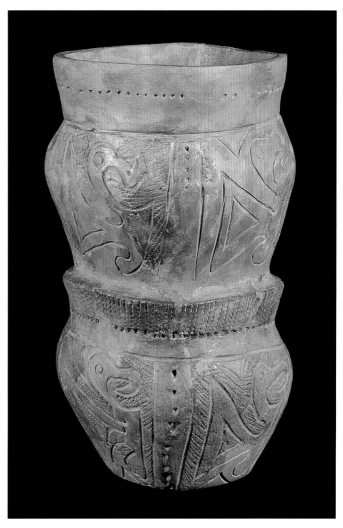

15. Copena culture steatite pipe in the form of a wolf, from Ross County, Ohio, AD 100–600. These big, boldly executed pipes, often shaped as birds or wolves and mostly found on the surface, seem to derive from the Copena complex of the Middle Woodland Period, in part in the Tennessee valley close to sources of steatite. L: 30 cm (11.8 in).

16. Engraving of 1848 showing the Hopewell culture Mound City, Ohio, which dates from the Middle Woodland Period, 200 BC–AD 100, and probably had a primarily ceremonial rather than defensive function. This was one of the sites in the Scioto Valley, Ohio, that the pioneering archaeologists E.G. Squier and E.H. Davis investigated and classified by perceived function during the 1840s. Their report *Ancient Monuments of the Mississippi Valley* (1848) was the first publication of the newly founded Smithsonian Institution.

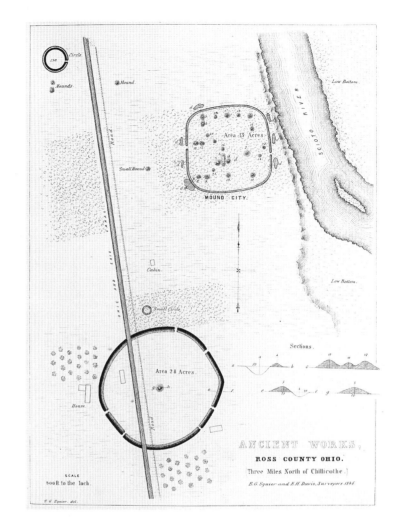

17. Aerial view of Mound City, Ohio. When first investigated in the nineteenth century, the earthwork, 0.6–0.9 m (3–4 ft) high, enclosed twenty-three mounds.

18. (opposite) Hopewell mounds at Newark, Ohio, including the Observatory, Circle and Octagon, which may have been used for observing the moon. The Circle is 320 m (1050 ft) in diameter, and the walls of the Octagon 186 m (610 ft) long and 1.5 m (5 ft) high.

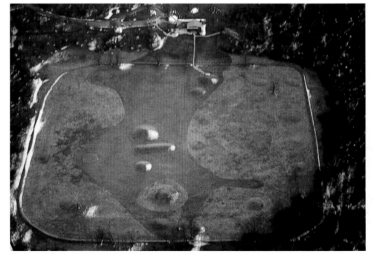

circles and octagons, with straight and parallel lines suggesting
stellar and lunar alignments, whose significance will, no doubt,
one day be more fully appreciated. Many of the larger earthworks contain burial mounds, up to twenty or more, and these in
turn were filled with sumptuous goods. At Mound City, north of
Chillicothe, Ohio, a spectacularly rich mortuary house was found
in Mound 8 with ninety-five or more carved zoomorphic monitor pipes. The name 'monitor' arose because, when discussed by
nineteenth-century archaeologists, they reminded antiquarians

19. Aerial view of the 400-metre (quarter-of-a-mile) long Serpent Mound, Ohio, usually assumed to date from the Adena culture (1000–100 BC) but recently found to have a radio carbon date of around AD 1070, suggesting that it was built by Mississippian people. Instead of a snake, perhaps eating an egg, it might represent some celestial phenomenon such as a comet.

of the flat-bottomed riverine Civil War battleship, the *Monitor*. In general terms wood-post buildings were created by the Hopewell for burials, cremations and the deposition of grave goods. They may have taken the form of palisaded enclosures, with smaller roofed chambers arranged around the main enclosure. The rich burial goods included, apart from monitor or platform pipes, copper and mica cut-outs, stone ear spools and decorative ornaments as well as throwing-stick weights and what seem to be resist-dyed fabrics of unknown vegetal materials. These burials were eventually almost all burned, and buried by mounds. Many of the objects may have been damaged during the burning or broken deliberately beforehand in order to avoid theft or ritual use or abuse by inappropriate people.

The Mississippian Period

In much of southern and southeastern United States the Woodland Period was followed by the Mississippian, which flourished from AD 1000 into the post-European contact period of the seventeenth and eighteenth centuries. While this period is characterized by the introduction of crops and cultural features from Mexico, it also included Woodland traits, such as the continued veneration of ancestors in shrines. This long stable period was built on floodplain agriculture in river bottoms in the American heartland. Maize, beans and squash were supplemented by fish and by hunting, although crops were less important on the periphery in Oklahoma and the Florida peninsula. Stockaded towns, such as Moundville, Alabama, and Etowah, Georgia, appeared. The greatest settlement is known as Cahokia (fig. 20), near the contemporary metropolis of East St Louis, Illinois, on the Mississippi. In a rectangle measuring 5.2 x 3.6 km (3.25 x 2.25 miles) there are more than 600 hectares (1500 acres) of monuments, particularly flat-topped pyramids arranged around plazas. These included mounds or flat-topped earthworks with shrines, designed for

20. Aerial view of Cahokia, Illinois, *c.* AD 900–1200. Cahokia was the greatest Native polity north of Mexico in this period, with a population of probably many thousands and the largest pre-contact structure, Monks Mound, 30 m (100 ft) high and now known to contain a large stone platform (?).

veneration of the ancestors, and residences for people of high status. A centre of this kind would have possessed political, ceremonial and economic importance over a wide area encompassing complex trading and economic patterns. Monks Mound at Cahokia is the largest mound north of Middle America, 30 m (100 ft) high and 5.25 hectares (13 acres) at the base.

While burial mounds remained important, with very significant grave goods, they are less important than in the Woodland Period. Contact with Mexico was probably intermittent, perhaps maintained through patterns of long distance trade; there were certainly no large transfers of population from what is now Mexico to what is now the United States. Linguistic evidence also suggests that the main language families of the area, particularly Muskogean, had been in the Southeast since remote antiquity. Particularly noteworthy is the association of art and decorative motifs from the latter stages of the Mississippian with elements recorded in the early European contact period from the sixteenth to the eighteenth and nineteenth centuries. Perhaps

21. Mississippian pottery vessel,
Deer Creek, Mississippi,
1200–1500 (?), modelled like
a human face with forked eye
motifs and a spiral design behind.
H: 9.5 cm (3.7 in).

most interesting is the use of motifs associated with raptorial birds, possibly falcons, in the creation of winged figures with forked or weeping eye designs, which have been speculatively associated with historic period depictions of thunderbirds. Other significant elements include the depiction of what may be trophy heads, the disarticulated bones of ancestors, and large stone monolithic axes and maces. The Mississippian collections in the British Museum do not include representative examples of the engraved shell work, stone sculpture, repoussé copper plaques or ceramics of this period. On the other hand, many of the pertinent early historic drawings of Southeastern life are in the Museum's Department of Prints and Drawings (see Ch. 3).

European contact

Europeans often consider North America *New Yorker*-style, as an East and a West Coast with little in between. Far from this misconception, before European contact the great rivers, particu-

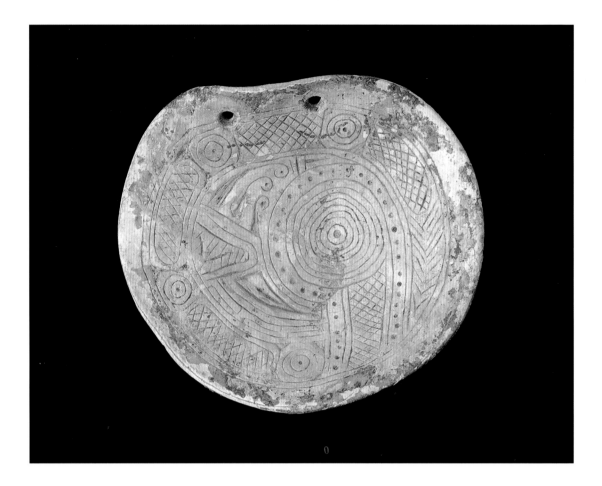

22. Shell gorget engraved with abstract curvilinear designs possibly representing a rattlesnake, Mississippian Period, 1200–1400, collected on the Tennessee River. Marine shells from the Gulf of Mexico remained important trade items into the eighteenth century and as far north as the Great Lakes. Diam.: 11.5 cm (4.5 in).

larly those of the Mississippi and Ohio drainages, were at the centre of civilization. And, as far as antiquity is concerned, Alaska, which became a state only in 1959, was the ancient point of entry for early Native Americans. Conversely, it was the other side of the continent from Alaska – Greenland and New-foundland – that was first visited by Europeans, the Vikings, a mere thousand years ago. Finally, it was Mesoamerican civiliza-tion which contributed much of the agriculture – maize and beans – that came to feed North America.

The European view of Indians, which is well known because it is well recorded, developed from medieval ideas of wildmen and woodsmen, the 'salvages', or 'sauvages', later altered to savages, innocent and free from the vices of civilization. In medieval and contemporary parlance Indians and their equivalents were green men. In the sixteenth century these won-drous people were initially conceived of as wearing feather skirts

23. Unfinished pipe in the form of a squatting figure with a rattlesnake around the neck and the possibly falcon-related forked eye motifs, from near Paint Creek, Ross County, Ohio, 1200–1500 (?). Large stone pipes of this kind are a feature of the Mississippian Period and were no doubt maintained in temples on mound tops for ceremonial use. H: 16 cm (6.3 in).

24. Stone human-headed bird pipe from Ohio, eighteenth century or earlier, probably representing a clan, lineage or societal spirit. The wings are engraved with meandering lines, possibly indicating the lightning (and thunder) sometimes thought by prehistoric peoples to be created by flight. Unusually the stem is set transversely to the pipe. L: 12 cm (4.7 in).

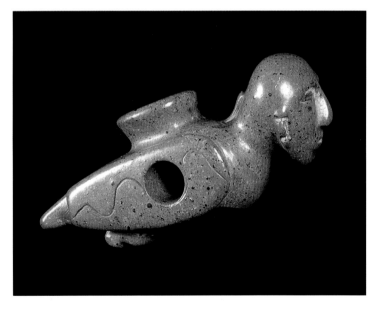

and straight-up headdresses in the Brazilian – specifically Tupinamba – fashion. But from the late sixteenth century images from Virginia and Florida of roach-headed, painted and tattooed people were much copied and came to represent the continent (fig. 73). Only in the late nineteenth century was this replaced by a new vision of America, the Plains Indian in an often long, swept-back, Sioux-style eagle-feather bonnet. Best known of European epithets is that of the 'Noble Savage', associated in principle with the eighteenth-century Enlightenment but traced back to these seventeenth-century lines of John Dryden:

> I am as free as Nature first made man,
> Ere the base laws of servitude began,
> When wild in woods the Noble Savage ran.
> (*The Conquest of Granada*, 1672)

Less well known is, of course, what Indians, and later Arctic peoples, thought of these strange people from overseas. Native views of Europeans were naturally rather diverse, divided by culture, circumstances and time. Contact was not a single event, but a many centuries-long process in which trade goods and diseases preceded the often sporadic first encounters with strangers. And ship-borne European traders arriving on the Northwest Coast would, of course, be perceived differently to canoe-borne traders on the Plains or in the Subarctic. A 1633 story, from a Montagnais girl in Québec, told of her grandmother seeing a ship as an island, the people from which offered the Indians ships' biscuits and wine, which they saw as wood and blood. The Mi'kmaq in Nova Scotia also noted the way the French drank wine or blood. Arrivals of strangers might become the subject of prediction, merging with new or traditional myths in the minds of shamans. The physical appearance of Europeans, hirsute and with white skin, was noted, as was particularly the technical excellence of cloth, glass beads, ornaments and metal tools – the latter ascribed to the spiritual qualities of the newcomers rather than anything more mundane. The Ojibwa, of the Great Lakes region, treated cloth like scalps, tying little pieces to poles to be passed around as trophy messages. When the Delaware on the New York and New Jersey coast first saw a Dutch ship, it was conceived of as a house for the *manitou*, or supreme being, a view confirmed when the human messengers distributed alcohol, cloth and metal goods.

25. John White, [*Woman*]
Of Florida, watercolour
after a sketch by Jacques
Le Moyne (*c.*1533–88)
showing an eastern
Timucua woman with
elaborate tattoos and a
garment of Spanish moss.
Offering maize and a
bowl containing (cactus?)
fruit, she epitomizes the
assistance given by
Natives to early European
explorers.

Later, a terrible reputation, as a people who brought devastating diseases and who might attack or kidnap without warning, was added to the initial view of Europeans. On the Northwest Coast similar stories were told of the arrival of foreigners. The Alaskan Tlingits saw the French ships of Jean-François de la Pérouse (1741–88) in 1786 as appearing like great black birds with white wings, as the Raven or trickster, who brought light and whose crow assistants on the boats furled the sail wings, and then came ashore as messengers. One old chief said he would go out to the strange vessels – his life was behind him – in fear because it was believed that anyone who saw Raven would turn to stone. He was offered rice to eat, which he took to be worms and would not touch. Meanings, however, never remain constant. On the Plains the Lakota call white people *wasichu*, which in the nineteenth century suggested that white people were seen as spirits sprung from the earth or water. Then, because white people were always talking and because they ate salt meat, this came to be translated as 'big talkers' and 'fat takers', with the more contemporary inferences, perhaps, that white people take all that is good and, in always talking, they are portrayed as untrustworthy.

European exploration

From classical antiquity Europeans sailed out of the Mediterranean, through the straits of Gibraltar, west and north. Most famous of these ancient voyages is that of the Greek Pytheas from Marseilles who reached the Arctic circle and a place he named Thule, possibly in Norway. Real voyages, and their mythic re-interpretations, fed the imaginations of later voyagers. These include, for instance, the Irish St Brendan in the sixth century, who is sometimes believed to have reached America, and also the entirely mythical medieval Welsh Prince, Madoc. The earliest Europeans known to have reached America were Norsemen, sailing in the tenth century from Iceland to Greenland and then Newfoundland. Their exploits are recorded in two sagas: 'The Saga of Eric the Red' and 'The Greenlanders' Saga'. Eric the Red named Greenland in the early 980s after the grassy fjords of southern Greenland, rather than the seemingly green glacier ice. He returned in 985 to create a permanent settlement. Later Eric's son Leif the Lucky (Leif Ericsson) is believed to have wintered in Vinland in *c.*1001, perhaps at a Norse site discovered by Helge Ingstad at L'Anse aux Meadows, Newfoundland, in 1960. The Norse settlements in Greenland survived until the fifteenth century, when they disappeared, probably because of intersecting factors, including the plague, a decline in the Arctic ivory trade as a result of competition from Portuguese elephant ivory and the cooling of the climate after 1200. Climatic change destroyed Norse agriculture, and so devastated the population. Inuit hostility, recorded in myths in the nineteenth century, may also have played a part in this first, failed colonization of America from Europe.

It is quite possible that, when Columbus reached the Americas in 1492, fishermen from northwestern Europe were already exploiting cod off Newfoundland. This would have been some years before the Genoan or Venetian John Cabot, at the behest of Henry VII, reached that great island in 1497, sailing along the western and northern shores without making contact with Natives. For the next century a series of voyages sponsored by European monarchs, like those of Columbus and Cabot, both travelled the coasts of North America and settled Europeans in what were for the most part unsuccessful colonies. During the 1520s the Tuscan Giovanni da Verrazzano was sponsored by François 1 of France to explore much of the coasts of the mid-Atlantic states and New England. In April 1524 he encountered Natives at the entrance to New York harbour: 'The people', he said, 'are almost like unto the others, and clad with feathers of fowls of diverse colours. They came towards us very cheerfully, making great shouts of admiration.' In what is now Newport Harbor, Rhode Island, named after the Island of Rhodes, he encountered Wampanoags: 'They are all naked, except their privy parts, which they cover with a deer's skin, branched or embroidered.' These encounters, both ephemeral and permanent, were dynamic cultural exchanges, rather than scenes of unremitting domination and conquest in which the Indians were passive recipients of European influences.

In two voyages in 1534 and 1535–6 the Breton Jacques Cartier, again for François I, explored the Gulf of St Lawrence. He entered the St Lawrence, the great waterway leading into the centre of North America to the Great Lakes, visiting, for instance, Hochelaga, now Montréal, where the Huron gave them maize bread: 'They threw so much into the boats that it seemed to fall from the air.' Henry Hudson, once credited as founder of both New York and Canada, was left to enter the other two main routes into northeastern North America. In 1609 he sailed through the Verrazzano Narrows at the entrance of New York and up the now-named Hudson River, thus identifying for the Dutch, and then the English, access to the fur-bearing heartland of upstate New York dominated by the Iroquois. Later, in 1610–11 Hudson sailed through what is now Hudson Strait, noted by Martin Frobisher and John Davis in the 1570s and 1580s, and into Hudson Bay as far south as James Bay, creating a route to the Cree and their sources of fur in the Canadian Subarctic. While many colonial enterprises of the late sixteenth century failed – for instance, the French in Florida and the British in North Carolina – others, particularly the Spanish in Florida and New Mexico, were successful. They were followed in the early seventeenth century by the establishment of John Smith in Virginia from 1607, and Samuel de Champlain in the St Lawrence valley a year or so later. As well as wonderful technology – in metallurgy, marine equipment and textiles – the Europeans brought disease, alcohol and, ultimately with superior numbers, an irresistible demand for land.

Disease

Of all the European imports to America, the most devastating was that of disease – waves of smallpox, and respiratory and other infections caused rapid, wholesale declines in populations, particularly perhaps in southeastern America in the sixteenth century, but eventually with the same devastating consequences across the whole continent. There are no generally accepted figures for the number of Natives in North America before contact or at around 1500; estimates vary between perhaps two and eighteen million, which declined to perhaps 200,000 people early in the twentieth century. When agriculture began in the Old World 6,000–8,000 years ago, sedentary populations emerged which were large enough to support micro-organisms dependent on human hosts: epidemics arose as diseases developed. Epidemiologists believe that many, if not most, of these originate in domestic and other animal populations close to humans. The proximity of animals to humans ensures the eventual transfer of infection from the former to the latter. In the Old World, as animals were domesticated, new diseases were introduced to humans by farm animals, both causing death and eventually creating immunities. In the New World, with rather few domesticated animals, principally the dog in North America, there was much less immunity. The way disease works can be illustrated by a relatively recent case, the flu epidemic of 1918–19. Although called Spanish flu, this virus is now believed, in one theory, to have originated with the pig population on the American Plains before jumping to humans. Between 20 and 50 million people died worldwide. Yet, inevitably, Native North Americans suffered particularly. In the Labrador Inuit village of Okak, for instance, almost the entire population died, leaving the dead to the dogs.

Epidemic diseases continued to affect Native populations at least into the 1960s, when Arctic people were perhaps particularly susceptible to tuberculosis and were sent to sanatoria in the south. To add to the effects of disease was the belief, seemingly correct of course until the early twentieth century, that the Indian was disappearing. Unofficial and official policies of dispossession and assimilation could be justified by the reality that in the nineteenth century Indian populations were declining in an apparently unstoppable fashion. Liberal opinion required that Indians be assimilated, ironically but tragically, to avoid their complete disappearance. This process was only gradually reversed by a combination of diverse factors including Native leadership, the acquisition of immunities and, in the United States under John Collier during the 1930s, New Deal policies.

2 THE NORTHEASTERN WOODLANDS

The Iroquois believe that the world is a great island floating in space. One day the Ruler, Great Mind, also known as the Great Creative Being, decided to create humans. He sent Sky Woman down into the cloud sea, and eventually earth was created on the back of the Turtle, who became the Earth Bearer. Sky Woman was pregnant, and gave birth to a daughter, from whom came Twin Brothers, spirits of good and evil who dominate much of Iroquois philosophy. To the northeast the Algonquian-speaking Mi'kmaq, from Nova Scotia, believed that the world was divided into several areas, in each of which the Sun, referred to as Grandfather and considered the original ancestor, created a man and a woman. Other Algonquian-speaking peoples, and also the Beothuk, believed that humans came from an arrow stuck in the ground. When Europeans arrived in northeastern North America 500 years ago, it was inhabited by peoples of these two great language families, the Algonquian and the Iroquoian, the former almost everywhere except for upper New York, Lake Ontario and the St Lawrence River. The numerous peoples into which these two groups were divided each possessed their own diverse traditions and languages.

In the Maritime Provinces of Canada and in northern

26. Pair of Mi'kmaq moccasins of commercial leather with a quilted interior, made by Jane Nevin, Whycocomaugh, Cape Breton Island, Nova Scotia, for Queen Victoria's 1897 Jubilee.
The decoration includes both the double-curve motif and crowns.
L: 26 cm (10.2 in).

New England the main Algonquian-speaking peoples were the Mi'kmaq, the Maliseet-Passamaquoddy and, in the south and west, the Abenaki. For subsistence they depended almost entirely on hunting, although tubers, nuts and ferns were collected, as was maple syrup in the spring. Some horticulture was practised, the cultigens including particularly tobacco. The annual cycle was dominated by hunting, and by fishing in the seventeenth century. For the southern Mi'kmaq the year began with seal hunting, followed by moose, caribou and bear hunting in the early spring, fishing for sturgeon and salmon, and collection of geese and other eggs seasonally through the year. Large mammals were hunted with bows and harpoons, while fish were trapped and speared with Y-headed leisters during their annual

The Northeast showing the approximate historic location of peoples.

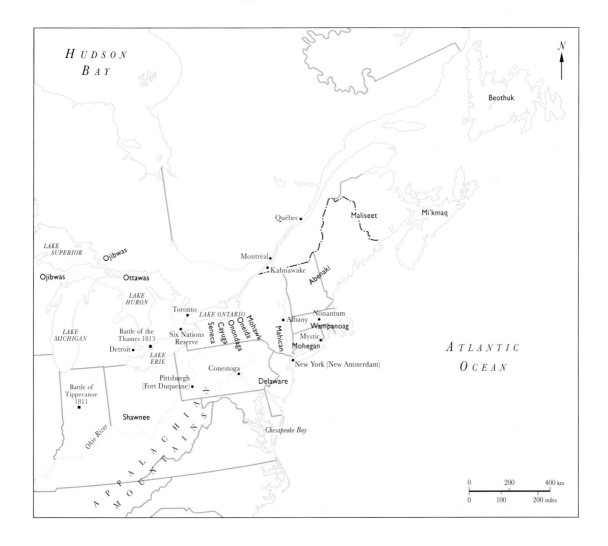

27. Nineteenth-century Mi'kmaq woman's cap of blue wool, decorated with ribbonwork and appliqué beadwork in traditional double-curve motifs, no doubt of protective significance. H: 40 cm (15.8 in).

28. Mi'kmaq or Maliseet shale pipe from Nova Scotia or New Brunswick, with a pierced keel for attachment to the stem, carved with four animals, including weasel, beaver and muskrat. Perhaps a few dozen pipes of this type from c.1830–70 are known. H: 6 cm (2.4 in).

29. Romantic nineteenth-century oil painting illustrating Mi'kmaq life. Inside the tent is a woman and her child with two quilled birchbark boxes in front of her. The men with guns in bark canoes are hunting geese and are also accompanied by wives (?), indicating the prominent role accorded to women.

runs. Religious beliefs followed hunting practices, as might be expected, given a strong emphasis on the sacred nature of the hunt and the importance of respecting all food sources and their spiritual persona. When the beaver, which was given a tail by Gluskap, the Mi'kmaq cultural hero and trickster, was eaten, its bones were carefully treated and were neither given to dogs nor thrown in the river.

European contact

Sporadic contacts between coastal Algonquian-speaking peoples and Europeans began from the sixteenth century onwards. In the seventeenth century the French came to dominate the area of the Canadian Maritimes known as Acadia, where fur trading was introduced, complementing already existing contacts in fishing and whaling. With the defeat of the French by the British in the 1760s, and then the British by the Americans in the 1780s, an influx of Loyalists (or refugees) from the United States affected the Mi'kmaq and Maliseet, marginalizing their position both on the land and in trade. In northern New England over the same period the Abenaki were able to maintain a certain distance between the competing colonial forces until the first half of the nineteenth century. Further to the south, in coastal New England, where cultural traditions were similar but with the substantial addition of horticulture and an emphasis on deer rather than moose hunting, European colonies made permanent settlements from the seventeenth century onwards.

It was therefore through the Algonquians that the coastal colonists first came to see Native America. Many Native-derived terms used in English come from the Algonquian: *wigwam*, *toboggan* (that used for dragging), *moccasin*, the now unacceptable *squaw*, *tomahawk* (hatchet), *pow-wow* (shaman or dreamer), *sachem* (chief) and *wampum* (white strings of beads). Similarly, the French often saw America through Iroquoian eyes, because of the fur trade in the Iroquoian St Lawrence Valley and because of the great series of records compiled by the Jesuits in the seventeenth century. All Europeans learnt particularly from Natives kidnapped or otherwise induced to visit Europe. Most often these visitors were turned into spectacles before dying of disease. Little survives of Native reaction to these visits. One Native story, recorded by Silas Rand in 1870, tells of the visit of a Mi'kmaq, Silmoodawa, to France, presumably in the eighteenth century or earlier. He was required to hunt a deer with a bow in front of a large audience. The animal was butchered, dressed, cooked and eaten. Then, to poke fun at the assembled worthies, the Indian relieved himself – just to complete the process.

The Beothuk

The tragic history of the Beothuk in Newfoundland encapsulates and in certain respects symbolizes that of Native North America as a whole. Originally caribou and seal hunters, and salmon and cod fishermen, who moved between the coast and

30. Drawing by Shanawdithit, 1828, of a Beothuk dancer and birchbark vessels similar to that below.

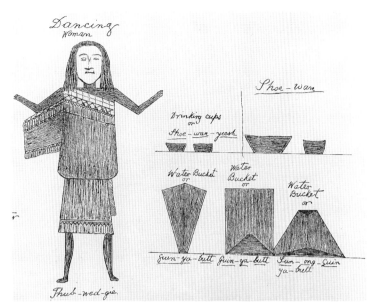

31. Nineteenth-century Beothuk water container of heavy birchbark, sewn with double lines of spruce root and decorated with red ochre. H: 17 cm (6.75 in).

32. 'Mary March a Female Native Indian of the Red Indians who inhabit Newfound land painted by Lady Hamilton 18[19]', miniature portrait of Mary March, or Demasduit. Captured in 1818 in an ill-conceived attempt to befriend the Beothuks, she was taken to St John's but tragically died in 1820.

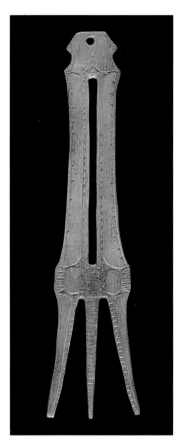

33. Engraved Beothuk caribou-bone (?) pendant, late pre-contact period, 1500–1800, of the kind that may have been attached to a shaman's necklace or to clothing associating the wearer with animal spirits, perhaps specifically including the bear. L: 4 cm (1.6 in).

the interior, the Beothuk were perhaps first encountered in 1497 by John Cabot from Bristol. They are often said to be the original Red Indians, so named not for reasons of race but because, along with other neighbouring peoples, they used copious red ochre paint. Available knowledge of these people mostly derives from accounts of the small number of people, less than one hundred out of an original population of perhaps 2,000, who lived along the Exploits River and Red Indian Lake in central Newfoundland during the late eighteenth and early nineteenth centuries. At this time the fishing and fur enterprises of Europeans, furnished with firearms, ensured regular and intense persecution. On the other hand, the Beothuk, provided with metal from seasonally abandoned fish camps, were, unlike the Mi'kmaq, never obliged to enter the fur trade to obtain European metal.

European contact, and particularly ever-present epidemics, brought about the disappearance of the Beothuk in the early nineteenth century. At that time Newfoundland colonial authorities, specifically Governors such as Sir John Duckworth, determined to establish friendly relations with the remaining Beothuk who had been driven into the interior by their murderous treatment on the coast. That this did not happen was due to entirely justified fears on the part of the remaining population that they would be killed. More important were continued complaints from British settlers of Beothuk thieving, and consequent demands for the recovery of stolen property. This confusion – official benevolence and private intolerance – gave rise to a number of incidents in which attempts to make contact with the Beothuk resulted in tragedy. Most notorious was the expedition of the fur-trading family called Peyton in the spring of 1819. This was intended to recover stolen traps, to establish trading relations with the Beothuk and to attempt to bring an individual back to the capital, St John's. The Peytons with their men travelled upriver to Red Indian Lake, where they encountered seven or eight individuals and took one, Demasduit, captive, killing her husband Nonosabasut when he tried to come to her rescue. Demasduit, or Mary March as she became known (fig. 32), was taken to St John's where she much impressed the English who determined to use her as an intermediary; she died of consumption in early 1820, however, before this could happen.

34. This bowl of a spoon, whose handle is now lost, was probably made from the breast plate of a great auk. Acquired by John Winthrop (1681–1747), the botanist and correspondent of Hans Sloane, it was made by Papenau in 1702 and is thus one of the earliest Native articles created by a named person. L: 10 cm (3.9 in).

Indians and colonies in seventeenth-century New England

In the early seventeenth century the first permanent colonies were set up, usually with the positive assistance of local Natives on the Atlantic coast and the St Lawrence. In the previous century Europeans, including Basques, British, French and Portuguese, had developed a significant fishing industry off Newfoundland and Nova Scotia, but there were no permanent settlements. North America was first brought into the world economy through this trade in cod. In 1607 Captain John Smith (1580–1631) established himself in Chesapeake Bay with 144 colonists; in 1608 Samuel de Champlain founded Québec. After Hudson's 1609 voyage the Dutch established themselves in the Hudson Valley from 1614, founding New Amsterdam on Manhattan Island in 1624 at the entrance to the river that provided the route for the Dutch, and after 1664, British fur trade. In 1620 the Pilgrims arrived in Massachusetts and established themselves with the help of Tisquantum, or Squanto, and Massasoit of the Wampanoag. Tisquantum is credited with assisting

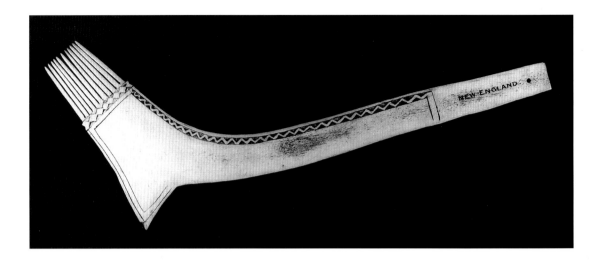

35. Moose-antler comb acquired by Sloane before 1730. His description suggests an Algonquian provenance, although a similar comb was excavated at Conestoga Town, Pennsylvania, the home of the Susquehannocks, *c.*1697–1738. The surface is carved with a zigzag line reminiscent of lightning, and adorned with red ochre. L: 40 cm (15.8 in).

the Europeans to grow corn successfully by telling the Pilgrims to fertilize maize with the ample fish available. From Indians the British learnt to plant maize in mounds, instead of using European broadcast sowing. William Wood in the 1630s provided fulsome acknowledgement of Native assistance:

Many wayes hath their advice and endeavour been advantagious unto us; they being our first instructers for the planting of their Indian Corne, by teaching us to cull out the finest seede, to observe the fittest season, to keep distance for holes, and fit measure for hills, to worme it, and weede it; to prune it, and dress it as occasion shall require.

However, Native reaction to European arrival was very mixed. Often Indians were hospitable, teaching the British how to survive: Indians were amazed by the lack of European skill in hunting. They taught the newcomers about country trails, fishing and hunting locales, and useful flora and fauna, the last reflected in Algonquian names: squash, possum and racoon, for instance. Desired above all else by Natives were the cloth and metal tools which appeared largely without precedent, although Indians possessed knowledge of Native copper traded from the Great Lakes. But at the same time the Europeans had a propensity to plunder Native supplies of food and fur. This, combined with the slaughter of villagers and an inability to distinguish friendly Indians from foes, meant that Indians were perpetually divided, within and between themselves, as to the best approach to these difficult and often treacherous strangers. Overriding

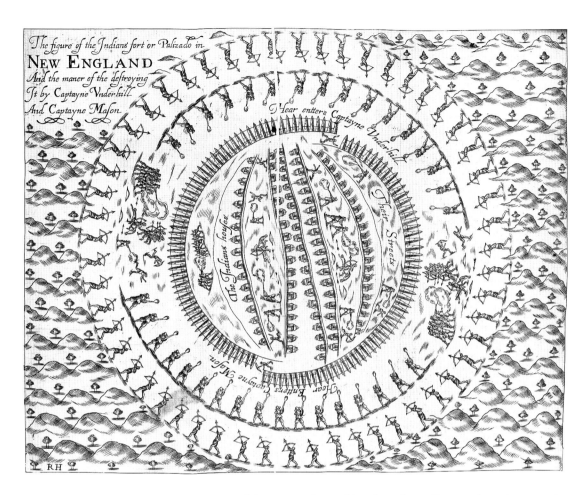

The figure of the Indians fort or Palizado in NEW ENGLAND And the maner of the destroying It by Captayne Vnderhill And Captayne Mason

Hear entters Captayne Vnderhill

The Indians houses

Their Streets

Hear Enters Captayne Mason

RH

36. Diagrammatic engraving of the English attack on the Pequot fort at Mystic in 1637, from John Underhill's account, *News from America…* (1638). Underhill (1597–1672) can be seen either as a founding father of Connecticut, trying to counter a savage threat, or as a pathological killer engaged in exterminating Indians.

everything were the epidemics of smallpox, whooping cough, the plague and other diseases, which more than anything else brought by Europeans decimated Native populations, in New England particularly in 1616–19 and 1633. But of course many diseases, such as tuberculosis and influenza, were endemic in North America, and though Europeans often commented on the normally excellent health of Indians, archaeologists in New England have often noted malnutrition in the osteological record. The colonists also brought Christianity: conversion in New England was originally only significant from 1646 with the founding of the first of the 'Praying' Indian towns, Nonantum near Boston. These communities provided servants and labourers to the English for about thirty years.

In New England two major wars occurred in the seventeenth century. The first arose out of what were seen as the significant infringements of the rights of the English colonists –

July 14th. 1703.
Prices of Goods

Supplyed to the

Eastern Indians,

By the several Truckmasters ; and of the Peltry received
by the Truckmasters of the said *Indians.*

One yard Broad Cloth, *three* Beaver skins, *in season.*
One yard & half Gingerline, one Beaver skin, *in season*
One yard Red or Blew Kersey, *two* Beaver skins, *in season.*
One yard good Duffels, *one* Beaver skin, *in season.*
One yard & half broad fine Cotton, one Beaver skin, *in season*
Two yards of Cotton, one Beaver skin, *in season.*
One yard & half of half thicks, one Beaver skin, *in season.*
Five Pecks Indian Corn, one Beaver skin, *in season*
Five Pecks Indian Meal, one Beaver skin, *in season.*
Four Pecks Pease, one Beaver skin, *in season.*
Two Pints of Powder, one Beaver skin, *in season.*
One Pint of Shot, one Beaver skin, *in season.*
Six Fathom of Tobacco, one Beaver skin, *in season.*
Forty Biskets, one Beaver skin, *in season.*
Ten Pound of Pork, one Beaver skin, *in season.*
Six Knives, one Beaver skin, *in season.*
Six Combes, one Beaver skin, *in season.*
Twenty Scaines Thread, one Beaver skin, *in season.*
One Hat, *two* Beaver skins, *in season.*
One Hat with Hatband, *three* Beaver skins, *in season.*
Two Pound of large Kettles, one Beaver skin, *in season.*
One Pound & half of small Kettles, one Beaver skin, *in season*
One Shirt, one Beaver skin, *in season.*
One Shirt with Ruffels, *two* Beaver skins, *in season.*
Two Small Axes, one Beaver skin, *in season.*
Two Small Hoes, one Beaver skin, *in season.*
Three Dozen middling Hooks, one Beaver skin, *in season.*
One Sword Blade, one & *half* Beaver skin, *in season.*

What shall be accounted in Value equal
One Beaver in season : Viz.

One Otter skin in season, is one Beaver
One Bear skin in season, is one Beaver,
Two Half skins in season, is one Beaver
Four Pappcote skins in season, is one Beaver
Two Foxes in season, is one Beaver.
Two Woodchocks in season, is one Beaver.
Four Martins in season, is one Beaver.
Eight Muncks in season, is one Beaver.
Five Pounds of Feathers, is one Beaver.
Four Raccoones in season, is one Beaver.
Four Seil skins large, is one Beaver.
One Moose Hide, is two Beavers.
One Pound of Castorum, is one Beaver.

37. American broadside of 1704
listing prices of trade goods
denominated in fur.

the theft of livestock or the killing of marginal colonials who
had abused their position *vis-à-vis* Indians. The Pequot war of
1637 occurred because of minor incidents of this type combining with a more general fear of Indians by the new colony of
Connecticut. The neighbouring Narragansetts allied with the
British and together they surrounded the Pequot fort near
Mystic in eastern Connecticut (fig. 36). During capture the village and its inhabitants were burnt, the few survivors being sent
into West Indian slavery. The Narragansetts regretted the
killing, including so many women and children, and found their
position, and those of other Algonquian-speaking neighbours,
particularly the Wampanoags, constantly eroded over the next
forty years. Until the 1660s Native groups were able to maintain
their status, and traditional reciprocity, through trade in fur and
with wampum, which was used as currency until there was sufficient European money in circulation. With population growth
and changes to trade, pressure on Natives to sell land increased,

giving rise to what was a loose-knit rebellion in 1675–6. This, the War of King Philip, or Metacom (1640–76), a Wampanoag sachem or chief previously friendly to the Pilgrims, seems to have arisen out of the competitive expansion of the colonies of Massachusetts Bay and Connecticut. While there were sporadic hostilities elsewhere, the colonists took action first against potential allies of the Wampanoags, destroying a Narragansett fort near West Kingston, Rhode Island, before killing King Philip the next year near his home at Mount Hope. Fifty years later Hans Sloane possessed in his London cabinet a 'piece of some *instrument of musick* found… in some plowed land on a spott where King Philip lived & undoubtedly was made before any tools were invented', probably attesting to Metacom's continued fame rather than a historic Wampanoag artefact – presently unlocated.

Wampum

With the defeat of the Pequots, and other Algonquians, tribute in wampum was demanded. Wampum consists of small cylindrical

38. Purple wampum belt strung on wool, with a design of three white rectangles suggesting an alliance of three groups in war. The belt was originally associated with an eighteenth-century Maliseet costume from Maine or New Brunswick decorated with glass wampum. L: 110 cm (43.3 in).

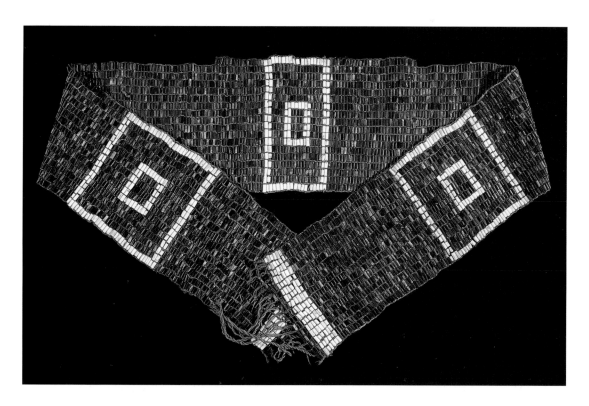

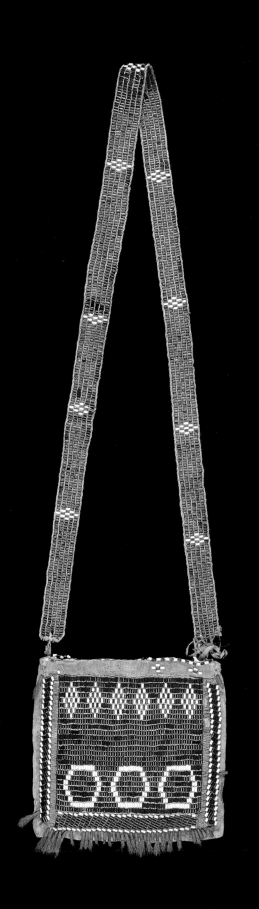

39. Eighteenth-century glass-bead wampum pouch decorated with white hexagonal designs suggesting an alliance between three peoples or polities in war, from the collection of Samuel Rush Meyrick (1783–1848), the antiquary who initiated the scholarly study of arms and armour in England. 20 x 18 cm (7.9 x 7.1 in) without strap.

beads, often about 5–7 mm (0.20–0.28 in) long and 1.5 mm (0.06 in) wide. Historically these were constructed with metal tools from purple and white shells, the purple coming from the edge of the quahog clam (*Mercenaria mercenaria*), and the white from the columns of univalve whelks (*Busycon* sp.). The beads were manufactured by Algonquian-speaking peoples along the coast of New England, by Iroquois women and by white – Dutch, for instance – manufacturers, and later in specific factories in New Jersey and elsewhere, until the nineteenth century. It was the Dutch in the early seventeenth century who realized the marine shell wampum could be used as a currency in the inland fur trade; in the 1620s they introduced the idea to the Pilgrims in Massachusetts. The beads had value as currency because of shortages of coins, and the wampum in the original foundation collection of the British Museum was acquired with specific denominations or values; in trade the beads were used loose or else strung. After the 1637 Pequot defeat, as the currency inflated and coastal fur sources disappeared, wampum was traded away from the coast to the inland Iroquois from the mid-seventeenth century. There, in Seneca territory, for instance, hundreds of thousands of beads have been excavated on single archaeological sites.

For the Iroquoian- and Algonquian-speaking peoples wampum had special decorative value, as adornment and later as a material from which to construct woven belts containing, in the two colours, mnemonic devices commemorating agreements and events important in politics, history and religion. The decorative use is reflected in the older term for a wampum belt, *collier*, or 'necklace', adopted by the French. In the seventeenth and eighteenth centuries large numbers of belts were presented or exchanged, particularly by the Iroquois Confederacy and their European allies – colonial authorities also possessing the ability to construct these document-like artefacts for use in diplomacy, such as in formal treaty negotiations and for ratifications. In Iroquois lore the origin of wampum is rather different. The beads appeared to Hiawatha when crossing a lake, Oneida in New York state. A flock of duck flew away magically taking the water with them and revealing wampum beads on the bottom of the lake. These were linked to create a belt showing five people with joined hands, who represented the coming together of the five Iroquois peoples in a confederacy (see below), thus symbolizing the creation of the Hodenosaunee.

The Iroquois

Of all Northeastern peoples the best known are the Iroquois. This northern, Iroquoian-speaking people dominated upper New York state, the Lake Ontario region and St Lawrence through much of the seventeenth and eighteenth centuries. Separated from the Cherokee, the other main Iroquoian nation, for perhaps 3500–4000 years, Iroquoian culture can be traced back more than 2000 years in New York and Ontario. Horticul-turists and hunters, of deer particularly, they emphasized respect for the animals they killed by not feeding bones to dogs, by placing carcasses in trees away from predators and by sacri-ficing the first deer of the year to eagles. Iroquois also hunted the now extinct eastern woods buffalo. The growing of crops can be dated to a thousand years ago or more. The main veg-etables, maize, beans and squash, are regarded as three sisters in Iroquoian thought. Shifting agriculture was conducted jointly by men, who cleared the fields, and women, who planted, tended and harvested crops. Every twenty years or so, as land became exhausted, new fields were cleared. A minimum period of 120 frost free days is required for agriculture. The annual cycle was significantly different among the agricultural Iroquois: notable is the June Strawberry Festival, celebrating the ripening and preservation of wild fruit, followed by the Green Corn and Harvest Festival celebrating maize. Communities consisted of a number of elm bark-covered longhouses, with perhaps three to six families or hearths in a dwelling perhaps 25 m (80 ft) in length, although these ranged up to 60 m (200 ft) long. Iroquois, a word of unknown, probably Algonquian derivation, call themselves Hodenosaunee, 'People of the Longhouse'.

The League of the Iroquois was founded sometime between the beginning of the fifteenth and the beginning of the seventeenth centuries at a time of war. The Great Peace was initiated by Dekanahwideh with Hiawatha (to whom Henry Wadsworth Longfellow's tale, *Hiawatha*, 1855, bears no relation) as messenger; he persuaded the five peoples – Mohawk, Oneida, Onondaga, Cayuga and Seneca – to meet annually, with the Onondaga as the central people and 'Fire Keepers',

40. A twined pouch of basswood or hemp (?) fibre, perhaps seventeenth century, decorated with moose hair and false embroidery, and described in the Sloane collection as an 'Indian *purse* made by the Huron Savages of Canada with the crin or hair of the *Orignac* wch they dye with roots'. 12 x 12.5 cm (4.7 x 4.9 in).

namely the Keepers of the Council Fires, through which disputes were settled by fifty hereditary sachems. In 1722–3 the Five Nations became Six, with the addition of the Tuscaroras, refugees from the southern colonies. Among the peace-keeping arrangements was the organization of compensation payments for the relatives of those who had been killed: ten strings of wampum for a dead man and twenty, appropriately in a matrilineal society, for a dead woman.

The Mohawk, at the eastern of end of Iroquois territory, were closest to Europeans active in the fur trade and to the Lake Champlain route to the St Lawrence. From the second quarter of the seventeenth century the Iroquois competed with neighbouring Algonquian and Iroquoian peoples for fur, as New York itself became devoid of beaver. Many peoples were defeated, and in a time of catastrophic epidemics women and children were absorbed into the victorious group or, as in the

41. Iroquoian (?) stone and metal pipe, *c.*1625–75, in the form of a wolf clasping the bowl, perhaps suggesting a clan usage and also possibly acknowledging the wolf's role in creation. L: 14 cm (5.5 in).

42. Iroquois pipe of fine-grained wood from New York, *c.*1700–1725, the front figure with a metal bracelet and pierced geometric designs, originally hung with feather pendants and relating to painted body and clothing decoration. L: 37 cm (14.6 in).

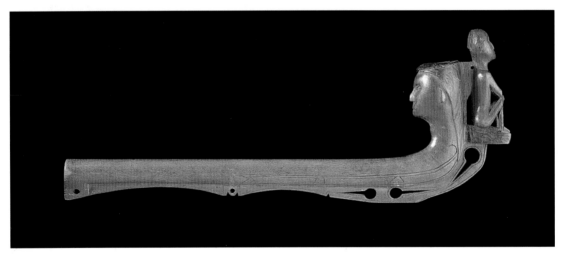

43. *The Flying Head Put to Flight by a Woman Parching Acorns*, 1820s, engraving after David Cusick, a Tuscarora. In Cusick's account of the origins of the Five Iroquois Nations an Onondaga woman frightens away the cannibal monsters Ko-nea-rau-neh-neh, or Flying Heads, because she seems to be eating red hot coals.

44. A nineteenth-century Mohawk lacrosse team from St Regis on the borders of the US and Canada. Of Native origin, lacrosse, or the stick ball game (*tewaarathon* in Mohawk), is played throughout much of eastern North America, with two male teams, two goals and netted rackets in a variety of forms.

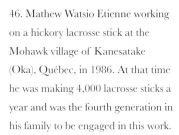

45. Ric Glazer Danay (b. 1942), *Mohawk Lunch Pail*, *c.*1983, a conceptual sculpture in which the pink buffalo on the exterior of the box indicate animals seen in a stupor. It is constructed out of a lunch pail, the ubiquitous box used by Mohawk construction workers. L: 34 cm (13.4 in).

46. Mathew Watsio Etienne working on a hickory lacrosse stick at the Mohawk village of Kanesatake (Oka), Québec, in 1986. At that time he was making 4,000 lacrosse sticks a year and was the fourth generation in his family to be engaged in this work.

47. Native 'Unloading construction steel', 1970s. As early as 1709 a British surveyor, John Lawson, noted the Iroquois ability to work at great heights.

case of the Christianized Huron in 1648–9, expelled from their traditional territories. Situated at the watersheds of the Delaware, Ohio and Susquehanna Rivers, the Iroquois came to dominate the fur trade, not merely in New York and Ontario but through Pennsylvania into Ohio country. The Mohawk were also closest to the colonists in time of war. From the seventeenth century onwards the League strove to maintain both a degree of control over the fur trade and a balance between European powers, particularly from 1664, with the British defeat of the Dutch, until 1763, with the British defeat of the French. From the early eighteenth century, while trying to maintain territorial integrity, the Iroquois – and particularly the Mohawk – took the British side but were divided during the American Revolution. The British were aided particularly by the Mohawk leader Thayendanegea, Joseph Brant (*c.*1742–1807), whose friendship with the then recently deceased Superintendent of Indian Affairs, Sir William Johnson, ensured their loyalty. While initial British setbacks in the American Revolution were partially reversed in the early 1780s, the British to all intents and purposes abandoned their New York Iroquois allies to the Americans at the 1783 Treaty of Paris, just as they did their Creek and Cherokee allies to the south. Joseph Brant and many Iroquois, particularly Mohawk, moved to Ontario, where they were granted a large reserve, now Six Nations on Grand River running into Lake Erie, traditional Mississauga territory. This was soon depleted by the sale of leases to non-Indians, Brant's idea being that the whites would teach Indians European farming techniques.

But, of all the contemporary issues in Native–white historiography, none is more contentious and more interesting than the extent to which the concept of the Iroquois confederacy influenced the US constitution – and particularly the association of the thirteen original colonies in a union. On the one side are Oren Lyons (the Onondaga leader), John F. Kennedy and Congress, who have maintained that the US Constitution is Indian influenced. On the other side are historians, most of whom argue that the details of Iroquois influence on the founding fathers are rather slight. Most famous of the evidence for Iroquois influence is a 1744 speech by Canasatego telling the squabbling British colonies to combine in a union against the French.

The Middle Ground: the Ohio drainage

Until the early nineteenth century much of eastern North America was dominated by the fur trade. As already mentioned, Indian New Englanders nearly exterminated the beaver, as did the Iroquois in New York state. In the seventeenth century the Iroquois dispersed their rivals, the Huron, and came to dominate the St Lawrence Valley. In the eighteenth century the trans-Appalachian country running down to the Mississippi stood at the centre of diplomatic relations – for Natives, for (French) Canada,

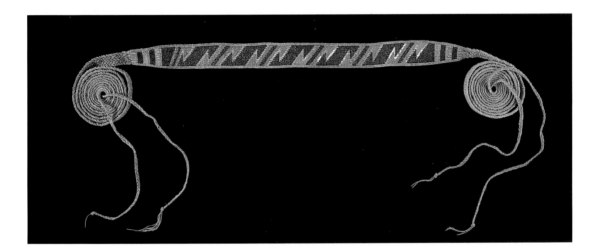

48. Tumpline (*gushaa*) of twined bast and hemp (?) with false embroidered decoration in dyed moose hair, brought to London by the 'Four Indian Kings' in 1710. The broad decorated section was held by women against the forehead, the long ties being attached to the load carried on the back. L of central section: 50 cm (19.7 in).

for Britain and for the US. In the middle of the eighteenth century French influence extended from Montréal westwards through the Great Lakes, and from New Orleans north up the Mississippi. So before French defeat this vast area was to a large extent under the influence of the Montréal-based fur trade, competing with the expanding Iroquois.

In simple matters of transportation the Iroquois were at a disadvantage to the Algonquians, using relatively crude elm-bark canoes rather than the lighter birchbark canoe employed by Algonquians and Subarctic peoples. However, more importantly this vast area south of the Great Lakes was already regarded by the covetous eyes of the soon-to-be American colonists. Virginia gentlemen, led by George Washington, launched an attack as early as 1754 against Fort Duquesne (Pittsburgh) as part of a scheme for a speculative land company. After the French defeat the whole vast area became a major

49. *Tee Yee Neen Ho Ga Row, Emperour of the Six Nations*, mezzotint of Theyanoguin after a portrait executed in London in 1710. Born a Mohegan but adopted into the Mohawk wolf clan, Theyanoguin (*c.*1680–1755) was a prominent Native leader and British ally who visited London in 1710 with three colleagues – together the Four Indian Kings.

50. One of a number of Native artefacts left in London in 1710 by Theyanoguin and his associates, this snake- or lightning-shaped stick of hickory was described as an '*instrument* for cleaning the *stomach*' and may have been used as an aid to achieve ritual purification. L: 82 cm (32.3 in).

bone of contention between the Atlantic colonies and the Montrealers, newly dominated by British entrepreneurs. Initially, this territory was taken away from Canada, but then returned by the Quebec Act of 1774. This had the unfortunate consequence of indicating to the Americans that the Crown was determined to prevent the westward expansion of the frontier across the Appalachians.

Central to this whole question, and to US and Canadian

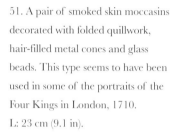

51. A pair of smoked skin moccasins decorated with folded quillwork, hair-filled metal cones and glass beads. This type seems to have been used in some of the portraits of the Four Kings in London, 1710. L: 23 cm (9.1 in).

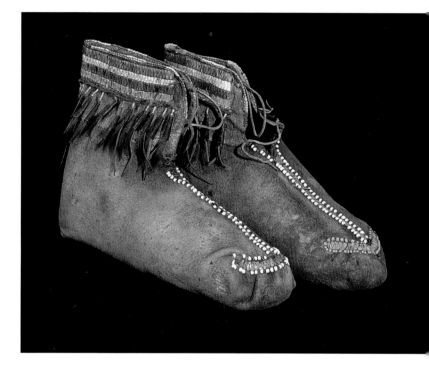

law as it relates to Indians even now, was the Royal Proclamation of 1763. This reserved the trans-Appalachian West as Indian country, with full hunting and fishing rights for Natives, and forbade the private purchase or occupation of territory by non-Indians. The reasoning behind the Proclamation may have been multi-purpose: it was no doubt designed to protect the rights of Indians, particularly in the aftermath of their assistance during the French and Indian War; it may also have been intended to avoid further disturbances such as Pontiac's Revolt in the same year. Either way, it served to infuriate the American colonists and to keep the control of the area as a peripheral issue during the American Revolution. At the end of the war in

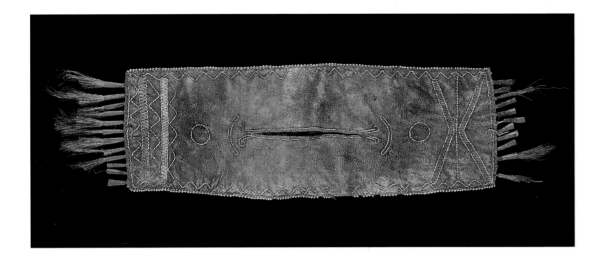

52. Rectangular, black-dyed skin slit pouch worn at the belt, before 1830 and of a type used in the eighteenth century, Algonquian or Iroquoian from the Great Lakes. Before metal tools were commonly available, clothing and pouches would often be left untailored in the original shape of the animal skin.

L. without fringe: 38 cm (15 in).

1783 this area, traditionally part of Canadian influence, was transferred to American colonists. But it was not of course vacated by the Indians who continued to trade with Canada. Additionally, the British did not leave the main forts in American territory – Oswego, Detroit and Michilimackinac – until after Jay's Treaty of 1794. This guaranteed Montréal access to the fur country, although this privilege was whittled away by fiscal measures and by the great influx of American settlers. The latter group in the late eighteenth and early nineteenth century maintained a definite view that the British were stirring up Indian hostilities, which was not necessarily the case. Nevertheless, it provided an excuse for American retribution and provoked the rebellion of the Shawnee leader Tecumseh (*c.*1768–1813), who in conjunction with his brother, the prophet Tenskwatawa, led the last pan-Indian military campaign at the time of the War of 1812.

This last war, fought between Britain and the USA apparently about British attitudes to neutral American shipping during the Napoleonic War, decided the fate of both Canada and Indian country. While Canada was invaded and Toronto (York) devastated, for which in retaliation the Washington Capitol and the White House were burnt, the United States did not take Montréal and could not hold the conquered parts of Ontario or Upper Canada. On the other hand, British determination to restore satisfactory trading rights with America left Indian country to the Americans. A little later Canadian fur-trading rights in the US were extinguished by the conventions of 1817 and 1818 which followed the 1814 Treaty of Ghent. Nevertheless, Native leaders from the old American North West – the Great Lakes – continued to visit British posts in Canada for annual payments from the Crown until the 1840s. In all during this century of wars (until 1814) the Native population played a vital but subsidiary role, in which their interests were always made subservient to those of the metropolitan powers.

Population movement

Settlement is usually viewed as a static factor, particularly in Native North America. The reality was and is that populations move, and were moved, across the continent. Unlike the French, the English colonists in New England, and then New York, craved rich agricultural land. Much of the acquisition of land occurred under doubtful circumstances: Indians sold land under pressure, and sometimes the vendors had no right to sell land, particularly when held communally; the English required title to satisfy colonial authorities and, when necessary, acquired land titles fraudulently. The purchase of land from Indians, their rapid population decrease and the wars arising from fur and other economic factors saw the disappearance of populations of dwindling Native peoples or their rapid integration with those, like the Iroquois, who survived. Coastal peoples, even more than the interior-dwelling Iroquois, bore the brunt of the European onslaught. In many areas coastal populations moved west, such as the Delaware of the New York and New Jersey coast, who now in part live in Oklahoma, and the Oneida nation of Iroquois, who are now largely in Wisconsin. The Iroquois from New York came to dominate the eastern Great Lakes, St Lawrence and the Ohio valley, and with the fur trade moved west and entered Oregon territory. Their abandonment by their British allies after the American Revolution left the Iroquois open to both unequal treaty-making and American settlement.

After the colonial wars finished in 1814 there came improved communications to the west and an unlimited stream of Americans, whom the Federal government favoured dealing with over Indians. In the United States, as in Europe, transport for the products of the early Industrial Revolution centred on

53. Native buckskin map, which was brought to
England in 1825 from St Louis and may date from
1774 or 1775. Perhaps relating to a land grant, this
illustrates a vast drainage basin from Cairo, at the
confluence of the Ohio and
Mississippi rivers, northwest to
St Louis, north nearly to Lake
Michigan and northeast to Cincinnati.
L: 125 cm (49.2 in).

54. Wooden gunstock club, before 1821, with a blade
pierced by a heart, reminiscent of Montréal-made
silver brooches used in the Indian trade. The shaft is
engraved with an image of the owner and user, and
a series of rectangles represents his achievements,
probably war parties in which he participated.
L: 60 cm (23.6 in).

55. Nineteenth-century ball-headed
wooden club, with engraved face and
scalp-lock. Its small size suggests it
was originally used in a medicine
bundle or for other ritual purposes.
The carved human face may relate to
a mythic or historic hero and was no
doubt intended to assist in war.
L: 45 cm (17.7 in).

56. Eighteenth-century scalp,
stretched on a wood hoop and
painted red with a face perhaps
representing the person from whom
it came, possibly from Sloane's
collection and described as 'Indian
scalp from Hudsons Bay'. Scalping
was much encouraged by colonial
authorities as a means of reducing
Indian foes. Diam.: 20 cm (7.9 in).

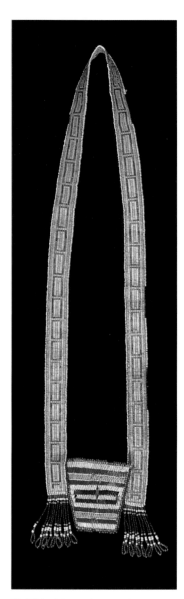

57. Skin sword belt or sash decorated in loom-woven and folded-line technique quillwork. One or two eighteenth-century examples of such articles, made for Natives or whites active in frontier wars, are recorded. L: 68 cm (26.8 in).

58. Late eighteenth-century pipe-tomahawk with turned stem and shaft, engraved on one side with the US arms. Such instruments, designed for use in both war and peace-making, were traded in large numbers to Indians, as well as being created for presentation to allied chiefs, as here. L: 31 cm (12.2 in).

59. This eighteenth- or early nineteenth-century 'roach' – named after the arched back of the fish – is constructed from U-shaped animal skin and decorated with quillwork enclosing red-dyed animal hair. When folded as a crest, it would be attached to a scalp-lock on the head, the rest of which was probably shaven. L of skin: 8 cm (3.2 in).

the creation of canals connecting natural waterways. The first major canal to contribute to western expansion was the Erie canal. Built *c.*1817–25 at a cost of $7 million, this enabled New York City to trade from the Hudson River through the western Iroquoian territory in the state to the Great Lakes. In opening up the continent across Indian country, this highly profitable 584-km (363-mile) canal (financed by the Manhattan Company, one of the predecessors of the Chase Manhattan Bank) acted much like the railroads half a century later.

Prophetic movements

Messianic or prophetic movements characterize Indian resistance to European invasion in the eighteenth and nineteenth centuries. Religion was, as elsewhere, associated with war. In many cases religious prophets worked closely with military leaders in actions against Europeans and Americans. Pontiac (*c.*1712–69), already mentioned, was the most famous of these military men. He was a charismatic leader, as a Lieutenant Alexander Fraser noted: 'He is in a manner Ador'd by all the Nations hereabouts, and He is more remarkable for his integrity & humanity than either French Man or Indian.' An Ottawa, Pontiac was brought up in a village near Detroit as an ally of the French. The Seven Years War (1756–63) saw the gradual erosion of French power, culminating after 1760 in the loss of Montréal and Detroit. British forces were lead by Geoffrey Amherst, a leader without substantial knowledge of Indian affairs. He was advised by Sir William Johnson, Superintendent of northern Indians from 1755, to continue French payments of supplies and ammunition to Native leaders. He refused to do this, also suppressing the rum trade, causing widespread suffering and indignation. Pontiac came under the influence of Neolin, a Delaware prophet, who told a French official that God had appeared to him and said: 'I warn you that if you allow the English among you, you are dead, maladies, smallpox, and their poison will destroy you totally, you must pray to me and do only my will.' Neolin advocated the cessation of trade – hunting was to provide food not fur – and banishment of the trade in alcohol; British soldiers were 'dogs in red coats'. In the late spring of 1763 a general Native uprising under Pontiac occurred, many forts fell to Indians, while Pittsburgh and Detroit were besieged. It was now that Amherst made his notorious suggestion that smallpox should be sent among the rebels. Eventually, however, news of European peace, the failure to take Detroit and Montréal, and the refusal of the Canadians and French to join the revolt gradually created dissension among Pontiac's supporters and dissipated his power. In 1769 he was murdered by a Peoria enemy in East St Louis.

Neolin and Pontiac, however, inspired Tenkswatawa and Tecumseh, respectively Shawnee prophet and leader in the War of 1812, and at that time allies of the British. In 1805 Tenkswatawa had a vision in which he saw a paradise – with abundant game and fish – for those who remained pure, avoiding alcohol and eschewing all aspects of white civilization. As war between America and Britain became inevitable, the prophet came to accept Europeans into his vision. Tenkswatawa lost his prestige after the Battle of Tippecanoe in 1811, when he forecast a great rain that would spoil American powder. Tecumseh assumed Native leadership until his death in 1813 at the Battle of the Thames in Ontario, which saw the end of general Native resistance to American westward migration. A similar, and entirely religious movement arose earlier among the Iroquois. Led by Handsome Lake who began recounting his visions from 1799, the Good Message, or *Gaiwiyo*, forecast a hunting paradise and advocated a return to certain ancient Iroquois ways, including the Strawberry Festival and White Dog Sacrifice. These were combined with selective adaptations of European ways, such as nuclear or single family residence. The Way or Code of Handsome Lake – the Iroquois Longhouse reformed religion – remains fundamental to the lives of many Iroquois.

While the earliest of these movements occurred in northeastern North America, similar leaders arose elsewhere. Among the Creeks the prophet Josiah

60. Engraved designs from two shamanistic Mide scrolls collected by Episcopalian/Anglican missionaries before 1858 from Bad Boy, a Chippewa/Ojibwa, in Minnesota Territory. Some of the designs are conventional, for instance representing Thunderbirds and Underwater Lynx or Panther, while others require the esoteric spiritual knowledge of the ritual practitioner to understand them. L: 68 cm (26.8 in), 46 cm (18.1 in).

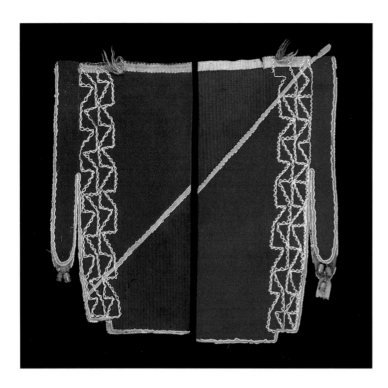

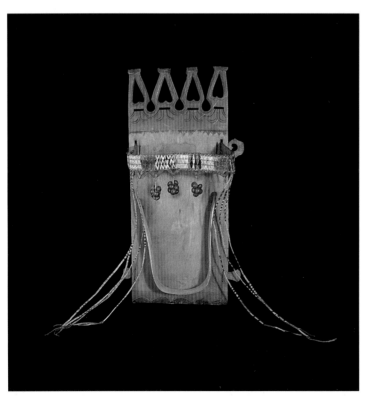

61. Pair of wool leggings, mid-nineteenth century, decorated with glass beads and thimbles, and with sides suggesting the buckskin prototype for this item of costume. L: 60 cm (23.6 in).

62. Cradle with wood board, foot rest and hoop, the latter decorated with porcupine quillwork and clusters of bells. While this is said to have been collected on the Upper Missouri before 1825, it is of Algonquian and possibly Ojibwa form. H: 63 cm (24.8 in).

63. Wood calumet, or pipe, carved of ash (?). The bowl is shaped as a human head facing the smoker; perhaps a guardian spirit, it wears a circular gorget marked with the four cardinal points, suggesting use in the propitiation of the seasons. L: 51 cm (20.1 in).

64. (left) Black-dyed deerskin pouch made perhaps between 1790 and 1830 by Algonquian-speaking peoples in the eastern Great Lakes and decorated with quillwork, beadwork, ribbonwork and hair-filled metal cones. This side may show a beaver contributing mud from the bottom of the sea for the creation of the world. L: 45 cm (17.7 in).

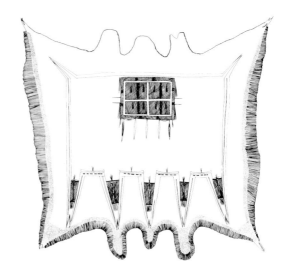

65. Drawing of a nineteenth-century or earlier smoked skin robe with an impressed and painted abstract zoomorphic design, apparently representing a four-legged mammal such as a deer or buffalo, from the Great Lakes. 180 x 150 cm (70.9 x 59.1 in) .

66. 'Harvesting wild rice', 1970s. Wild rice, unrelated to domesticated rice, is a staple amongst the Ojibwa and other peoples in the western Great Lakes. Collected communally in the autumn from canoes, it is dried and parched for long-term storage, and then a 'first fruits' ritual is celebrated to give thanks for its availability.

67. A military drum painted with Mide dream symbols, probably collected by Henry Christy perhaps on Manitoulin Island, Ontario, in the 1850s. The paintings include Thunderbirds and, in the bottom half, horned cows, spiritually powerful creatures analogous to buffalo and underwater panther, and to be treated with respect. Diam.: 45 cm (17.7 in).

Francis (see pp. 82–6) was associated with the Red Sticks Revolt during the War of 1812. In the Far West and the Plains, the Ghost Dance movement arose in the 1880s. Intended to sweep away America, it instead aroused gross misunderstanding and fear which ended in the 1890 massacre at Wounded Knee. Even the North-West Rebellion, 1885, in Canada (see pp. 238–9) can be considered as having been lead by the mystic Louis Riel with the military leader Gabriel Dumont.

The Museum record

Little remains of the material culture and art of Northeast North America. In the seventeenth and most of the eighteenth-century collectors systematically acquired for collections neither costume nor religious paraphernalia. Instead, trophies or weapons of Native North America were incorporated in European cabinets of curiosities, particularly moccasins, wampum, model snow shoes and canoes, and calumets, or pipes. The little that survives offers tantalizing glimpses of a world in which material things were, in many ways, only a minor aspect of cultures. Oratory, for instance, was a prime cultural expression, both in a religious and a political context, since leadership was dependent on charismatic qualities as well as on hereditary (both patrilineal and matrilineal) principles. Mnemonic devices, whether religious or primarily political like wampum belts or Mide scrolls, may mean little without the words spoken with them on the relevant occasions, such as treaties between separate entities or Iroquois songs and prayers of condolence during the mourning of old chiefs and the appointment of new ones. However, all material things are invested with ideas of spirits or spiritual beings: their breath or soul control and form the real world, and they are considered to have as concrete a significance as straightforward technical matters. Natural phenomena in particular are thought to be imbued with a separable life-principle, in the sense of their being divine and worthy of worship. In the seventeenth and eighteenth century explorers frequently commented on the manner in which Natives, when on a journey, might continually make offerings of tobacco to rivers, mountains, winds or other features of the given world. Little of this spirituality was recorded with articles collected and brought to Europe in the colonial period. Allied with this animistic view of the world was the primacy of dreams, as an unrecordable mechanism for divining the future, for determining hunting strategies and for explaining – in a functional manner – the way the world works. Similarly, no thought was given to the ethnicity of the objects collected. Virtually no early object in the British Museum's collection is assigned to a tribe or people, let alone furnished with the name of the owner. Indeed, most Northeastern artefacts were until very recently assigned to origins on the Great Plains.

On the other hand, by the nineteenth century most Northeastern peoples had developed a significant trade in articles made for sale, which, with superbly beaded military-style costumes, are the most frequent components of museum collections. Of particular note are birchbark boxes and other articles such as canoes, cradles and panels for European-style furniture, decorated with porcupine quillwork. Beadwork pouches, moccasins and caps with abstract curvilinear designs, including the double-curve motif, were also created in large numbers. The resultant complex designs are perhaps related to dreams and to the protective and curative qualities of the plants and animals so symbolized.

68. Benjamin West (1738–1820), detail from *The Death of General Wolfe* (1770) showing an Indian with a pouch (fig. 70), and an earring and tattoo drawn from a pipe (fig. 69). In a series of images of North America, West portrayed Natives realistically, employing as studio props artefacts which have survived.

69. Soapstone pipe bowl, mid-eighteenth century, from the southern Great Lakes. The bowl and the now missing stem were used by West in both *William Penn's Treaty with the Indians* (1771) and *The Death of General Wolfe* (above), in the latter to provide the facial decoration and metal ear ornament for the grieving Indian. L: 10 cm (3.9 in).

70. Finger-woven or plaited yarn pouch incorporating glass beads and hair-filled metal cones, with resist-dyed decoration. Such pouches, of which a few dozen survive, may originally have been woven from buffalo wool, although most are likely to have been made from unravelled manufactured wool textiles. Pouch: 20 x 16 cm (7.9 x 6.3 in).

71. Sheffield steel (?) knife, and skin sheath decorated with quillwork and metal cones. Such multi-purpose tools, mainstays of the fur trade, were worn around the neck, and are depicted in several of West's paintings, including *The Death of General Wolfe*. L of knife: 27 cm (10.6 in).

3 THE SOUTHEASTERN WOODLANDS

The greatest political entities in North America, large chiefdoms, arose during the Mississippian Period in the Southeast. Towns grew up in riverine areas close to flood plains suitable for agriculture. Major Mesoamerican-style mounds were used as temple platforms for the practice of cults relating

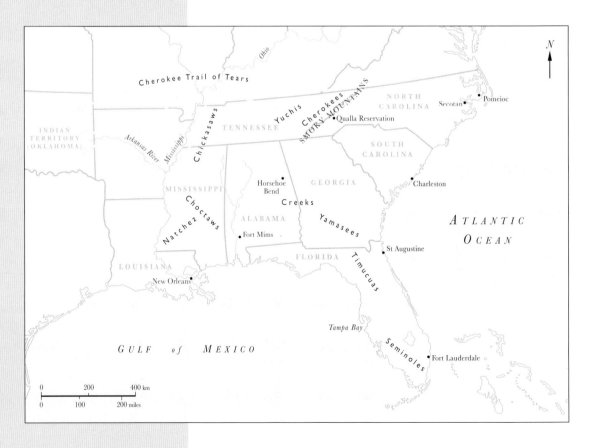

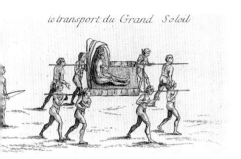

72. Eighteenth-century engraving of the Natchez chief, called Great Sun, on a Mississippian-style litter at the time of the Green Corn Ceremony, celebrating the first maize of the year.

73. John White, *The flyer*, 1585–6, watercolour of an Algonquian shaman in a stylized pose, but with realistic detail including a bird headdress and animal skin pouches on a belt around his middle. The headdress may have been both a badge and an indication of the personal spirit employed in curing practices.

The Southeast showing the approximate historic location of peoples.

to the sun and also, probably continuing on from the Woodland Period, to ancestors. The largest of these settlements was Cahokia (see pp. 25–6), now in East St Louis, Illinois, where mounds were constructed in stages over a period of centuries. Their use continued into the historic period, amongst the Natchez, for instance, in the Lower Mississippi Valley. The head of the community derived his position by inheritance through association with descent from the solar deity. Ancestor shrines were important for legitimizing inherited social control by chiefs

72

The Tombe of their Cherounes or cheife personages, their flesh clene taken of from the bones saue
the skynn and heare of theire heads, wth flesh is dried and enfolded in matts laide at theire
feete. their bones also being made dry ar couered wth deare skynns not altering
their forme or proportion. With theire Kywash, which is an
Image of woode keeping the deade. ✕ ✕ ✕ ✕ ✕

9

74. This watercolour and description of an Indian tomb by John White provides important evidence of the interment of high-ranking individuals and the maintenance of sculptures such as the 'Kywash' on the right, the 'keper of the kings dead corpses', suggesting elaborate ancestor worship above ground followed by secondary burial.

over populations. Mortuaries contained sacred objects of spiritual power, just as had Hopewell mortuaries a thousand years before (see pp. 18–25). Also, as earlier, it is likely that political and economic power were intertwined so that spiritual function and ceremonial activity, for instance surrounding the use of smoking pipes, could not be entirely separated from the kind of rituals that are likely to have preceded economic transactions. These chiefdoms were at the centre of powerful trading networks, which stretched through to Mexico and north to the Great Lakes. While Mesoamerican agriculture and architectural influences were strong in the Southeast, no Mexican artefacts have been found there, so it is not likely that there was direct contact between the Mississippi Valley and, for instance, the Aztec Empire, which flourished for nearly two centuries from 1325. Whereas the Aztec Empire was destroyed by a combination of political and military factors, the Southeastern chiefdoms suffered first devastating epidemics and then, in contrast, gradual colonization from Europe.

While anthropologists know of Mexican influence in the Southeast and can trace the cultural sequence, the Native view is different and depends on stories identifying separate cultural origins. Most Creeks and Choctaws believe that they come from the west, having originated in the navel of the world or the backbone of the earth when the ground opened up. They travelled towards the east, crossing rivers towards the rising sun, guided by a stick, perhaps a pole, painted red, which they set up each day and watched to see where it bent, so as to obtain directions. The earth itself was created in a manner similar to that elsewhere on the continent, at a period when there was only water. The beasts of the upper world met to decide on whether to have some land, but the pigeons could not find any. So a crawfish dived down and came up with mud in its claw, and eagle, who had been elected chief, created an island, which he enlarged as the waters receded. The Yuchis tell a similar story about the creation of the earth by a crawfish called Lock-chew. Another aspect of Southeastern mythology, important in colonial times, relates to the Great Spirit creating people of different colour: in some versions man is washed too much, or too little, after creation and is black or white, Indians being in the middle and just right; in another version man is made of clay or dough, and baked too little or too much, Indians again being made just right. The Creeks also had stories about the arrival of Europeans which parallel those from other parts of North America. They stood in Georgia and Alabama at the gateway of the continent and saw a great duck floating on the ocean; this turned into a ship, and everyone ran away, only to be seduced into friendship with barrels of sweet-smelling alcohol. Flour was also brought by the white people, and treated as body paint.

European exploration

The first major accounts of the Southeast – before epidemics devastated Native polities – are provided by the exploits of the Spanish explorer Hernando de Soto and his colleagues in 1539–43 and by the part-Quechua chronicler, Inca Garcilaso. As a young man de Soto accompanied Francisco Pizarro to Peru and, thus fortuitously enriched by Inca gold, sought a Spanish grant of further territory. Instead of lands in Ecuador or Guatemala, he was granted rights in the 'flowered' country, Florida, where he landed with 600 soldiers, near Tampa Bay on the west coast of what is the now much reduced state. From there de Soto travelled inland and north, then west reaching the Mississippi, which he may or may not have been the first European to see but which was definitely to provide his final resting place in 1542. De Soto's expedition recorded large rich towns, with major flat-topped pyramids adorned with buildings, storehouses filled with food, excellent agriculture and matrilineal societies – exemplified by the princess of Talomeco in Georgia, who gave de Soto pearls and escaped his tender mercies before worse could befall her. Perhaps the largest town that may have been visited by de Soto was Etowah, near Atlanta, a sometime Cherokee community which may have had a population of a few tens of thousands of people. The interior of the continent was not to be explored further for nearly a century and a half, and then particularly by the French Louis Jolliet and Jacques Marquette, being the first Europeans to reach the upper Mississippi in 1673, the country claimed by René-Robert, Sieur de La Salle. In 1682 he was to be the first recorded person, and possibly the first ever, to sail down that vast river to the Gulf of Mexico.

More successful, eventually, were coastal settlements,

contested particularly by the Spanish and French, and also by the British. The first of these incursions to succeed were those made by the French and Spanish into the territory of the Timucuas in Florida. The French efforts reached a climax with the expedition of René de Laudonnière, who built a colony in northeast Florida on the St Johns River in 1564, only for it to be destroyed the following year by the Spanish, who created a fort, St Augustine, from which the colonization of Florida proceeded. The best documented, visually, is the failed colony of Roanoke, in what was then conceived of as Virginia but is now North Carolina. It was promoted by Sir Walter Raleigh in the 1580s, and in 1585–6 Governor John White created a series of drawings of Algonquians, which were prepared for publication by the Flemish engraver and publisher Theodor de Bry in *A briefe and true report of the new found land of Virginia* (Frankfurt 1590). That particular attempt at colonization was destroyed by a hurricane, and the colonists returned to England with Sir Francis Drake.

75. Engraving of Pocahontas, the daughter of the Virginia leader Powhatan. Most famous for saving the life of John Smith, the founder of Jamestown, in 1607, she allied her people to the European strangers through her marriage to John Rolfe and in 1616 visited London.

The colonial process

In the seventeenth century the British founded colonies at Jamestown in Virginia from 1607 and at Charleston in Carolina Territory in 1670. Unlike the French and Spanish, British settlement was associated with agricultural development. Slightly later, the French established colonies on the Mississippi River and the neighbouring Gulf coast. The Native peoples first encountering Europeans were devastated by a combination of disease, extermination of game resources and a flourishing trade in slaves. Most pernicious of all, perhaps, was the manipulation – for purposes of war – of internal divisions in individual peoples to the advantage of the outsiders. Through these means nations such as the Timucuas in Florida, the Yamasees in Georgia and the Waxhaws in the Carolinas disappeared. The

76. Panoramic or composite watercolour by John White of the Algonquian town of Secotan, first visited by the British on 15 July 1585. The scenes depicted include praying, a ceremonial performance round a series of posts carved with faces, different stages in the growing of maize, and a temple, or *machicomuck*.

few remaining individuals joined other peoples. Another tribe, the Tuscaroras, left Virginia after being defeated and in *c.*1722 joined the Iroquois Confederacy as the Sixth Nation in what is now upper New York state. As in northern Canada, where the primary trade item was beaver, so in the Southeast the Europeans desired deerskin. This, like the beaver skin, was required in Europe because populations of local animals had effectively disappeared. In the early eighteenth century around 100,000 deerskins were exported from Charleston each year, so that people in London, for instance, could wear skin breeches and gloves. For the Native peoples of this area deer, of course, were not just practical items of trade: white deerskins were important articles in rituals. The origin stories of deer were regularly recorded: the first fawn grew into a beast of monstrous size and was killed by wolves, wildcats and, for the Alabamas, by human prophets; when this happened each hair turned into a separate animal and ran off into the woods. The trade in skins radically affected Indian societies: in particular women tanned skins instead of farming, tying peoples into trading systems, particularly for guns. Deerskin was not the only important article of trade. In the eighteenth century Indian slaves were sent perhaps to Bermuda, the Bahamas and the Caribbean, where, although they were generally no more able to withstand Old World diseases than at home, descendants may survive.

77. John White, *A cheife Herowans wyfe of Pomeoc and her daughter of the age of 8 or 10 yeares*, watercolour. The child is holding a European doll, probably exchanged by the British for food, while her mother, with tattooed arm bands, necklace (?) and face, is wearing a skin apron and copious shell beads.

The dilemma of relations between Indians, minorities in their own homelands, and colonial settlers was quite straightforward. The metropolitan authorities, in England as in Spain, recognized that Native polities possessed rights. However, colonial officials often found it impossible to defend those rights, because in so doing they were required to attack – militarily – their own kith and kin. This dilemma is best illustrated by an exception, the unsuccessful rebellion of 1675, in Virginia, of Nathaniel Bacon (1647–76). Bacon believed that Indians had no rights; the Governor, Sir William Berkeley, attempted to eradicate unprovoked attacks on Indians. Bacon rebelled and burnt Jamestown before being defeated and killed by Berkeley's forces. More usually, officials acquiesced in lawless frontier behaviour. During the eighteenth century Indian rights were sometimes viewed as the tyranny of a minority over the growing majority of European frontiersmen; the 1763 Royal Proclamation, prohibiting trans-Appalachian settlement, was seen by rebellious Americans as a curtailment of

The manner of their fishing.

78. John White, *The manner of their fishing*, watercolour composite showing a weir with a fish trap and a dug-out canoe with a fire, perhaps indicating a method of construction or a lure for night fishing. Fish are shown being speared and netted, and other animals include a hammerhead shark.

79. Asante-style African-American drum of wood, vegetable fibre and deerskin, collected by Sloane 'from Virginia' before 1730. It is a poignant symbol of the slave era but also refers to the history of Native Americans in the coastal regions. The slave trade arose because Europeans tried and failed to enslave Native Americans; escaped slaves intermarried with Indians particularly along the Atlantic coast. H: 40 cm (15.8 in).

their rights to migrate and settle where they wished. Today the same problem remains; the federal governments in Canada and the US act as arbiters in often bitter disputes between tribes, on the one hand, and provinces and states on the other. And in issues put to the vote, Natives, except where in a majority, as in parts of the Arctic today, may be overwhelmed by the democratic process.

Southeastern Indians from 1750

In the eighteenth and nineteenth centuries most Natives in the Southeast were of three main language groups: the Algonquian-speaking peoples of the Atlantic coast, Iroquoian-speaking Cherokees in the Appalachian interior, and the Muskogean-speaking Creeks, Chickasaws and Choctaws. At the margins of the area lived peoples of other language groups, such as the Timucuas in the northern half of the Florida peninsula and the

Siouan-speaking Catawbas near the Atlantic coast. While cultural patterns were not uniform, a degree of similarity may allow one people, the Cherokees, to provide an example.

Perhaps the central feature of Cherokee life was, and is, the clan system, a series of seven matrilineal groups, bound by ties of descent in the female line. Each requires exogamous marriage – that is union with a partner from another clan. Clan names include Wolf, Deer, Bird and Red Paint. Each clan, bound by ideas of blood relationship, is defined by totemic association with the clan name. So, traditionally, people of the Deer Clan were thought to be both swift at running like deer, and good hunters. Wolf Clan members associated themselves with wolves: killing wolves brought bad luck, while raising wolf cubs was an appropriate activity. During the twentieth century each of the half a dozen or so North Carolina Cherokee communities has been predominantly of one clan, but in the eighteenth century the spatial arrangement of the village reflected the clan organization. With both winter and summer dwellings for nuclear and extended families, the centre of the village contained a plaza for communal celebrations and activities as well as a seven-sided council house chamber for use particularly in winter. Dances, for the Cherokees as for other Southeastern peoples, remain important. Many, if not most, are associated with animals – partridge, pheasant, pigeon, racoon, bear and beaver. Others such as the Green Corn dance celebrate seasonal activities, while the Bugah or Booger Dance is a winter event in which masked dancers, in a boisterous and bawdy ritual, celebrate gender and other role reversals. The Green Corn celebration is a two-part event, recorded from the eighteenth century onwards, and important not only elsewhere in the Southeast but also among the Iroquois. In August the first ripening of green maize is celebrated; then in September the second part of the festival, the Ripe Green Corn feast, is performed. In the eighteenth century this was conducted over four days by men but including female participation in the social dances. Men lead the dances, sing and provide the music with drums and gourd rattles, whereas women, as elsewhere, perform with turtle rattles attached to the legs.

During the middle of the eighteenth century there may have been eighty Cherokee villages in the southern Appalachians, in the states of North Carolina, Tennessee and Georgia. During the period 1756–94 a series of conflicts arose with the English and Americans, in part because of blood revenge required for the deaths of Cherokees killed by colonists. During the American Revolution loyalty to Britain brought further destruction, but between 1794 and the removal to Oklahoma in 1837–8 successful communities were re-established in Georgia under the leadership of people of mixed descent. The Cherokees, unlike the Iroquois, were never conclusively unified, each principal town coming under the leadership of the *uku*, or white chief, a position entailing responsibility for civil affairs inherited from a maternal uncle.

80. Watercolour by Alexandre de Batz, 1732, showing an Acolapissa temple, surmounted by three wood birds, and chief's cabin, as rebuilt after 1722 in their new village on the Mississippi near New Orleans. Both structures were made using the wattle and daub technique widespread throughout the Southeast.

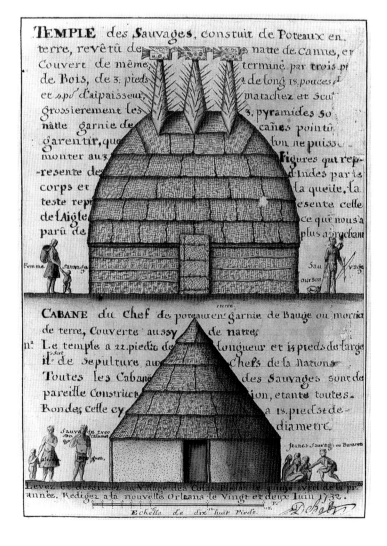

81. Watercolour by Alexandre de Batz, 1730s, showing two Choctaw warriors, allies of the French, painted for war and holding trophy scalps. It includes at the top right a Natchez chief, and at the bottom right an early depiction of an African American, a child perhaps playing with the tonsured Indian.

82. A rattle, described by Sloane on acquisition in c.1730 as a 'Maracca or rattle of a gourd made use of by the Indians of Carolina in their triumphs'. John Smith had noted the range of rattle sounds more than a century previously: 'they have Base, Tenor, Countertenor, Meane and Trible'. L: 24 cm (9.5 in).

The Creek War, 1813–14

Whereas the Cherokees held the balance of power in the southern Appalachians, the Creeks, to the southwest in Alabama and Georgia, lived on rich agricultural lands, coveted eventually for the growing of cotton for the Liverpool market. The dissolution of Creek power at the beginning of the nineteenth century can be told through the story of one of the religious leaders or prophets of that nation during the period of the War of 1812 between the United States and Britain. Hilis Hadjo, or Josiah Francis, was the child of a white blacksmith trader father, David Francis, perhaps of French descent, and a Creek mother from Autaga, Alabama. He was brought up traditionally as a Creek. In 1811 Tecumseh, the Shawnee leader, came south to persuade Native groups to join him in the fight against the Americans, the so-called Long Knives. The Choctaws and Chickasaws were not receptive to his message, but the Creeks listened with some interest. Two developments seem to have stirred up their feelings. The first was the appointment of Benjamin Hawkins (1754–1816) as Creek agent. Sometime Senator, he was made superintendent of Indians south of the Ohio from 1796. In this post he successfully pursued assimilationist, but fair policies, which nevertheless divided communities – between traditionalists and non-traditionalists. Perhaps more importantly, as new roads were built through Georgia and Alabama, American settlers appeared in increasing numbers, indicating forcefully that Creek land was under threat.

Tenskwatawa, the prophet and the brother of Tecumseh, did not come south but was replaced by Sikaboo (of either Algo-

83. Seven Cherokees in London, 1730, dressed in presentation clothes, apart from their moccasins. One is holding a European-style bow, two have gourd rattles, and most are tattooed or painted. On this visit organized by Sir Alexander Cuming as part of a plan to obtain land, Attakullakulla (*c.*1700–1780), the figure second from the right, met George II.

nquian or Muskogean origins), who seems to have much influenced Hilis Hadjo, the components of whose name originally meant 'medicine' and 'crazy'. Tecumseh and Sikaboo's message is said to have been reinforced by a number of predictions of a comet and of an earthquake which partially destroyed the settlement of Tukabatchee. Hilis Hadjo, as a disciple of Sikaboo, was strengthened by these events. He was given to flamboyant gestures, in particular communicating with river spirits by spending spectacular periods of time underwater. His movement needed both military leaders and arms. After an unsuccessful attack on peaceful Creeks, a small American force was routed at the Battle of Burnt Corn Creek in 1813. Emboldened by this, the Creeks attacked Fort Mims, Alabama, killing many hundreds of people, including 200 Creeks of the peace party. American forces under General Francis Claibourne then moved against the hostile Creeks, attacking Ecunchattee, or Red (Holy) Ground. This settlement, or rather two settlements, was built for Creeks only and was protected, according to Hilis Hadjo, by invisible

The Three Cherokees, come over from the head of the River Savanna to London 1762.
& Their Interpreter that was Poisoned.

2 Ostaite or Man-killer; who Sets up the War-Whoop, as, (Woach Woach ha ha hoch Waoch) with his Wampum.

3 Austenaco or King a great Warrior who has his Calumet or Pipe, by taking a Whiff of which, is their most sacred emblem of Peace.

4 Uschesees or Great Hunter, or Scalper; as the Character of a Warrior depends on the Number of Scalps, he has them without Number.

Sold in Mays Buildings Covent Garden, according to Act by G. Bickham

84. Engraving of three Cherokee leaders, who visited England with Lieutenant Henry Timberlake of Virginia in 1762; Thomas Jefferson listened to their farewell speeches before departure. This visit arose just after the disastrous Cherokee War of 1759–61, which was ended by the Treaty of Charleston negotiated by Attakullakulla, 'Little Carpenter'. The British as always sought land sales.

fortifications: the Great Spirit would, it was said, kill Americans as they crossed the barrier. This was not to be the case. The then major-general in the Tennessee militia, Andrew Jackson (1767–1845), waged a decisive campaign against the Creeks in 1813–14. With his victory at the Battle of Horseshoe Bend he was able to force the Treaty of Fort Jackson on thirty-four Creek allies and one hostile prisoner, ceding the United States some 8.9 million hectares (22 million acres) of land. In the same year, 1814, the British prepared set-piece battles – attacks on Mobile and New Orleans – against the Americans, with Indians as allies and also witnesses, as it turned out, of their own conclusive defeat. The United States was never again seriously threatened, militarily, by Europeans or by Indians.

After the end of the war the British agent Edward Nicolls settled the Creeks with supplies at Prospect Bluff, and signed a

85. Watercolour self-portrait by Hilis Hadjo, or Josiah Francis (*c.*1770–1818), the non-literate prophet who led the hostile Creek faction against the US in the Red Stick War of 1813–15, so called because of the red paint on Indian clubs. While in London in 1815–16, he unusually donned this European military outfit.

86. Finger-woven pouch edged with white beads, made of wool probably unravelled from European cloth, and taken to London by Hilis Hadjo in 1815. This type of envelope-shaped pouch or bandoleer was made in the Southeast from *c.*1810 to 1860 and may derive from Great Lakes costume. H of pouch: 27 cm (10.6 in).

treaty with them guaranteeing their independent position. Hilis Hadjo was then despatched to London, so that this treaty could be witnessed and also to enable him to express his loyalty to the Prince Regent. He arrived in London on 14 August 1815. Earl Bathurst, Secretary of War, was unaware of Nicolls's treaty, and in any case British policy had altered. Britain now wished for good relations with the United States, in part so that the Canadian fur trade on the Great Lakes could be salvaged. The United States was therefore able to allow the harsh terms of the Treaty of Fort Jackson to supersede those of the more favourable international Treaty of Ghent. Bathurst avoided seeing Hilis Hadjo for

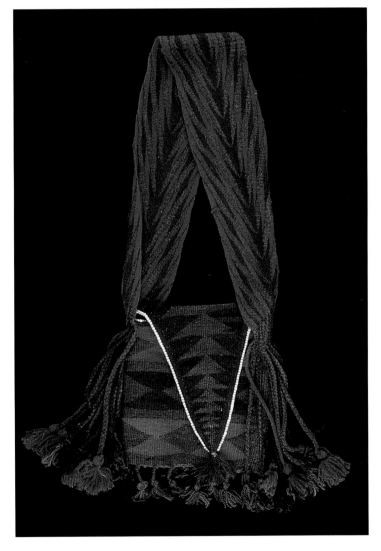

as long as possible, and then kept him from leaving the country. In compensation the prophet received gifts worth many hundreds of pounds. Eventually, Hilis Hadjo was allowed to go home at the end of 1816, although he left his son in England to be educated. On his return to America he established himself at St Marks and made contact with his former Creek enemies, such as Old Warrior, who had become alienated from America through the actions of Jackson. After the killing of a Lieutenant R.W. Scott and more than forty other Americans by other Natives, Jackson invaded Florida, forcing Hilis Hadjo to flee. He was lured on to an American ship flying the British flag, in part, it seems through the treachery of one Duncan McKrimmon, a young man whose life may have been saved at the suggestion of Hilis Hadjo's

87. Smoked skin moccasins from Hilis Hadjo's costume brought to London in 1815. All the articles of clothing seem small and may never have been worn, suggesting that they were intended as models rather than for wearing.
L of moccasins: 23 cm (9.1 in).

daughter Minny. In captivity Hilis Hadjo demanded to see Jackson: when his hands were tied a scalping knife fell out of a sleeve. Just before the hanging on 18 April 1818, he boasted that he had planned to kill Jackson before dying.

The Trail of Tears

In 1803 President Thomas Jefferson acquired the central wedge of riverine America, the 'Louisiana Purchase', from Napoleon, with funds borrowed from British and Dutch bankers, the Barings and Hopes. Jefferson realized that space was now theoretically available for the resettling of Indians west of the Mississippi River. Indians were already being pushed westwards by settlers, particularly from the old North West, the trans-Appalachian areas of conflict during the War of 1812. But this process was ruthlessly formalized and legalized after Congress passed the Indian Removal Act of 1830 under President Andrew Jackson. Particularly at issue was the land of the so-called Five Civilized tribes: the Creeks, Choctaws, Chickasaws, Cherokees and Seminoles. The US military subsequently oversaw the apparent clearing of Indians from the Southeast, leaving small remote communities, including the Cherokees in the Smoky Mountains of North Carolina, a few Choctaws in Louisiana and Mississippi, and Seminoles in south Florida.

88. 'Tony B.M. Tommy at Musa Island', Miami, working in the tourist industry, *c.*1917. Not all Southeastern peoples were removed to Oklahoma, and some Creek-speakers, the Seminoles, survived on their own terms in southern Florida. Sumptuous patchwork clothing, as in this costume, evolved from Creek traditions.

89. Ingram Billie carving a knife of ash at the Seminole Ah-Tah-Thi-ki Museum, Big Cypress, Florida, 1998.

90. Mikasuki red-maple (?) spoon carved by Takosímáthlî, Old Tommy, from New River near Fort Lauderdale, Florida, in the late nineteenth century and used for eating *sofki*, a soup or drink made from boiled maize. Many Southeastern stories refer to the creation of maize from the body of Corn-woman. L: 54 cm (21.3 in).

Land could then be made available to Americans, particularly for cotton plantations. By the 1840s the United States was growing 75 per cent of the world's cotton, much of it sold to the British textile industry. In this sense the removal of Natives from the Southeast and the expansion of African-American slavery was driven by the Industrial Revolution. The Seminoles were the only people to effectively resist America militarily, which resulted in sporadic war from 1835. While this continued until 1842, Osceola (*c.*1804–38), their most famous leader, had been captured by trickery with 2,900 other Seminoles, and removed by 1838. In that same year Congress established an Indian Territory, mostly in what is now Oklahoma (meaning literally in Choctaw 'red earth country'), for Indians from effectively throughout the United States.

Best known of the battles between Congress, the military and an Indian nation is that which settled the fate of the Cherokees. The language employed by the Removal Act, and by the legislators, was far removed from the European, metropolitan idealization of the noble savage. Rather it was the murderous savage that was emphasized along with denial of Indian sovereignty either in person or in land. Yet the Cherokees of all people had achieved most, not so much to assimilate with European America but to develop their own institutions. In 1808 they created their first written law. In 1821 George Guess, or Sequoya, invented a syllabary with eighty-five symbols so that Cherokees could write in their own language and, for instance, create a newspaper, the *Cherokee Phoenix*, in 1828. Additionally, in the 1820s one estimate suggests that a third of Cherokees could read and write in English. Then in 1827 the Cherokees adopted a constitution, modelled on that of the United States. In 1830 they also presented Congress with a plea for justice, the 'Memorials of the Cherokee Indians', which employed similar language to that of the Declaration of Independence, implicitly paralleling the injustices meted out by the Crown with those instituted by the Congress and the President. The major difference between the two documents is that, while the United States declared independence in 1776, the Cherokees were in 1830 simply affirming their existing sovereignty.

Perhaps most interestingly, the Cherokees took a legal challenge against their removal up to the US Supreme Court by successfully claiming, in 1832, that they were a sovereign nation to which the laws of Georgia did not apply. The ruling was, however, ignored by the President, Andrew Jackson, who challenged the Supreme Court to enforce it. Inevitably perhaps, the Cherokees were forced to negotiate a treaty, divided in two factions: pro-removal led by Major Ridge and anti-removal by John Ross, both leaders having been loyal to Andrew Jackson in the Creek War. In 1835–6, after negotiations with Major Ridge and only a few hundred supporters, the Treaty of New Echota was signed and ratified by the Senate. Under this treaty some 18,000 Cherokees were required to move to Oklahoma and accept $5 million and 2.8 million hectares (7 million acres). While the Treaty Party left in 1837, most of the remaining Cherokees were rounded up by General Winfield Scott and removed westwards on the Trail of Tears, so called because of the suffering and death that resulted in the following year. More than 1,000 Cherokees remained behind, however, in the mountains of western North Carolina, where their descendants live today. In 1839 Major Ridge and his son were assassinated. Within seventy years, however, the pressure of white newcomers resulted in the conversion of Indian Territory into the state of Oklahoma.

One of the most succinct and famous comments on the removal was provided by Alexis de Tocqueville (1805–59), the French social philosopher and traveller. In general terms he believed, with other Europeans and Americans, that Indians occupied the country without possessing it, noting that 'It is by agricultural labour that man appropriates the soil...' But he also, with what is generally considered biting sarcasm, emphasized that 'the Americans have accomplished this... purpose [the destruction of the Indian people] with singular felicity, tranquilly, legally, philanthropically, without shedding blood, and without violating a single great principle of morality in the eyes of the world. It is impossible to destroy men with more respect for humanity.' Not all American frontiersmen wished for Indian removal. David Crockett (1786–1836), who had fought with Jackson in the Creek War and was to die defending Texas at the Alamo, campaigned unsuccessfully against the Removal Act in Congress.

91. Cherokee 'Pre-ball game dance, Qualla Reservation, NC', 1888. A row of women dancers stands behind the dance leader with a drum; on the left the men's dance leader and medicine man is shaking a gourd rattle. The ball-players stand round the fire, the ballsticks hanging on racks.

92. Creek players watching the ball after one has thrown it with a racket, Oklahoma, *c.*1938. In the late eighteenth century John Pope noted that 'On this Game Property to a very considerable Amount is generally risqued… A dislocated Joint or Fractured Bone is not uncommon…'

93. Pair of wood and skin Creek ballsticks, made by Jo Sulphur, Oklahoma, *c.*1977. In the eighteenth and nineteenth centuries the Creek stick ball game was played between two towns, each side with sixty-two players and goals 400 metres (a quarter of a mile) apart. It was considered a substitute for war and played vigorously. L: 83 cm (32.7 in).

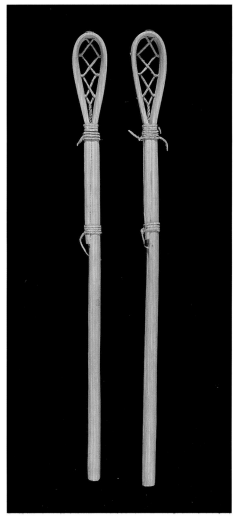

94. Sequoya (*c.*1770–1843) from Tennessee, who, although non-literate, adapted symbols from European books for his syllabary, creating a unique eighty-six-character Native writing system that spread rapidly among the Cherokees.

Eighteenth-century ethnographic collections

Virtually no material evidence survives from the extinct peoples of the Atlantic Coast, apart from archaeological materials. In being avaricious in trade, the colonial traders were insufficiently curious about the people they were destroying. They did not acquire and preserve, for instance, a single Yamasee artefact. Instead, Sir Hans Sloane obtained a small number of objects for scientific purposes from inland peoples, particularly the Cherokees in the Great Smoky Mountains of North Carolina and Tennessee. In the Southeast Sloane's greatest memorial lies in the extraordinary series of natural history watercolours, executed by Mark Catesby (1682–1749) during the 1720s. Catesby undertook expeditions supported by Sloane and other patrons. Sloane also possessed albums of drawings of seventeenth-century Virginia plants and copies of the John White drawings of sixteenth-century North Carolina Algonquians. He obtained wide-ranging scientific materials and information about, for instance, 'the charming & poison of rattlesnakes'. Quite incidentally, he also acquired a few ethnographic items, some of which have survived.

The process of collecting was neither simple nor straightforward. In November 1723, for instance, Catesby wrote to apologize that the previous collection of botanical specimens had become disordered when it was seized by pirates. The following 12 March he wrote again from Charleston announcing his plan: 'I am now Setting out for the Cherickees a Nation of Indians 300 miles from this place & who have lately declared War with another Nation which diverts them from injuring us and gives me an opertunity of going with more safety.' Catesby then goes on to say that Sloane's collecting requests 'shall be faithfully observed to ye best of my capacity'. We do not know what Sloane asked him to collect. On 27 November that year, however, Catesby again wrote to Sloane: 'I now send ye capt. Easton in ye Neptune a Box of Dryed plants with an indian Apron made of the Bark of the Wild Mulberry this kind of Cloath with a kind of Basket they make with Split cane are the only Mechanick Arts worth Notice.'

The apron no longer exists. Indeed, there are no mulberry bark cloth articles, and only a very few objects from the Cherokees preserved from before removal to Oklahoma in 1837–8.

Best known is perhaps a double-weave basket (fig. 95), which came to Sloane's collection in the 1720s from Sir Francis Nicholson, founder of the College of William and Mary, Virginia. Other items which have not survived include a '*nutt cracker* for walnutts made of cedar wood', 'A Cherokee Indians *garter*', arrows with different points and 'A *stick* made of the *sorrell* tree in Carolina painted wt. brown lines'. Superficially, these things seem to be mere curiosities, added by Sloane into his catalogue of *Miscellanies* entirely coincidentally. Yet, while cultural bias is everywhere indicated, for instance in the description of what may be the earliest published Cherokee(?) pipe as 'The head of a *tobacco pipe*… belonged to the King of Carolina' – because every Native was considered a chief and every chief a king – the reality was more complex. In the description of these things, the emphasis on 'Mechanick Arts' indicates an equation of beauty with morality, usefulness and goodness, with the implied creation of moral judgements, couched in terms of aesthetics. A little later James Adair (*c*.1709–*c*.1783), a trader, described the high esteem in which Cherokee baskets were held:

They make the handsomest clothes baskets I ever saw, considering their materials. They divide large swamp canes into long, thin narrow splinters, which they dye of several colours, and manage the workmanship so well, that both the inside and outside are covered with a beautiful variety of pleasing figures; and though for the space of two inches below the upper edge of each basket, it is worked into one, through the other parts they are worked asunder, as if they were two joined atop by some strong cement. A large nest consists of eight or ten baskets, contained within each other. Their dimensions are different, but they usually make the outside basket about a foot deep, a foot and a half broad, and almost a yard long… Formerly, those baskets which the Cheerake made, were so highly esteemed even in South Carolina, the politest of our colonies, for domestic usefulness, beauty, and skiful variety, that a large nest of them cost upwards of a moidore.

It is possible to speculate as to how baskets such as Sloane's were collected. The Governor, in Charleston, would have been in contact through a network of intermediaries with people inland. These may have been traders, who, in selling cloth, metal tools and tobacco to prominent Native leaders, would have received copious deerskins in exchange, and per-

95. Lidded basket (or possibly two basketry trays), the historic earliest example of Cherokee basketry brought to London in the 1720s: 'A large Carolina *basket* made by the Indians of splitt canes some parts of them being dyed red... & black They will keep any thing in them from being wetted by rain.' Lottie Stamper (see opposite) named the top design 'The Casket', i.e. coffin, and the bottom, 'The Pine Tree'. L: 50 cm (19.7 in).

haps also a basket or two given as a gesture by a wife or other woman related to the prominent Cherokee trader, and then passed on, to be received as a gift outside the normal spheres of utilitarian exchange. In this it may have possessed no high monetary value, yet it would also have been a symbol of cultural and economic allegiance, possibly destined to grace a colonial dwelling before being sent to Europe.

The twentieth-century Cherokee view of basketry is rather different. In the words of Aggie Ross Lossiah (1880–1966), 'When my grandma was making baskets she showed me how to make them – and when she got her a load of baskets made we went to peddle... I took my few baskets that I had made and I had enough to buy me a cotton dress...'

Associated with basketry are stories of the origin of this vital art form. Cherokee say that a basket was created by Kanane-ski Amai-yehi, or Spider-Dwelling-in-the-Water, a real water-boatman-like creature, so that she could capture the first fire. She, like the water-spider, crossed boundaries between land and water and wove the material that Cherokee women associated with water carrying and used for many other of their daily tasks. Baskets feature in much of Cherokee mythology. Whilst leaning over a basket, Selu, the first woman, seemingly gives birth to maize by rubbing her belly, and to beans by rubbing her sides.

Eighteenth-century commentators universally noted the excellence of basket work, which was and remains a primary trade item for women in North Carolina. The material used is

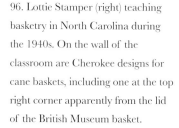

96. Lottie Stamper (right) teaching basketry in North Carolina during the 1940s. On the wall of the classroom are Cherokee designs for cane baskets, including one at the top right corner apparently from the lid of the British Museum basket.

river cane, a bamboo-like grass that used to be found in abundance in stands 2.4–12.2 m (8–40 ft) high. River-cane baskets (*talu-tsa*) are constructed from striped splints of the hard glossy exterior of the cane woven in a variety of plaited and twilled weaves, the patterns developing both from the weave and from the use of dye – black walnut and pokeweed berries in the example shown here (fig. 95). Most spectacular are those (like this one) of double weave, that is to say a double basket. In this technique the weaver begins in the middle of the base of the inner basket, weaves up to the edge and then, bending the splints, continues down the outside with a second layer, meeting at the bottom. According to the historian Sarah Hill, Lottie Stamper (b. 1906) was one of the pre-eminent weavers of the mid-twentieth century, teaching basketry, and selling and displaying her work throughout the country. During the late 1930s she was sent photographs of this basket in the Sloane collection and copied the designs so that she could reproduce them.

4

CALIFORNIA

In southern California Natives say that the people were born of sky and earth deities. The Luiseño, for instance, believe that the Heavens, Tuupash, and the Earth, Tamayowut, became the parents of the universe. Tuupash heard Earth speak

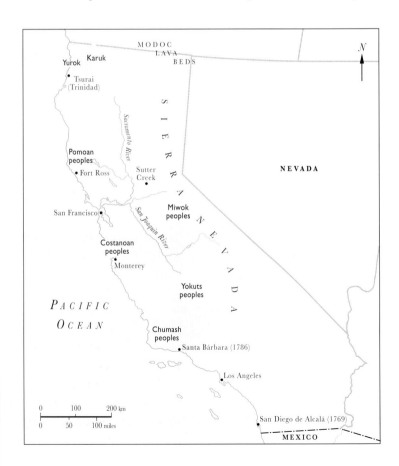

and asked who it was; they came together and Tamayowut became pregnant, defending herself with light against Heavens' attempt to kill her. She gave birth leaning against two stakes, onto which she held, as was the practice. For the Kashaya Pomo, as recorded by Herman James in 1957, Coyote created the ocean by digging, made the waves and tides with a stick, and then filled sea and land with animals created from different-sized logs and twigs. Elsewhere, earth was thought to be created during the flood by a diver, such as Water Bird, who brought up dirt underneath its finger nails from which to make land. Chumash peoples, of the south central coast, say that humans were created after a great flood. When it came to make man, Coyote-of-the-Sky kept arguing with Great Eagle about the shape of the hands. It was agreed eventually that Coyote would provide a paw impression, but just before the impression was made, Lizard ran forward and put his foot down. That is why people have fingers and not claws. Coyote also thought that when humans became old they should be rejuvenated in a lake, but he lost that argument too, and so people die, even today.

Aboriginally, California was inhabited by a thousand distinct peoples, speaking sixty different languages, an apparently extraordinary linguistic mosaic. There may have been 300,000 Natives at the time of European contact in the third quarter of the eighteenth century. Each of the languages was spoken by perhaps dozens of tribes in small autonomous towns or villages. Every one of these peoples had its own name and territory, with boundaries delineated, as elsewhere on the continent, by drainage or watershed ridges. As in the rest of North America human occupation is believed by archaeologists to have begun more than 10,000 years ago. California is a state of wide ecological variation, largely of Mediterranean and desert climates. Running north–south, the Central Valley of the Sacramento and San Joaquin rivers, which exit to San Francisco Bay, is the main geographic feature of the state. Around the valleys are the foothills rich in species of oak and other vegetation, and further away still, beyond the foothills, are the mountains of the Coast Range and, inland, the Sierra Nevada. While in the south and east the state is fringed with desert, in the north forested mountain ranges, pierced by rivers, continue into the states of Oregon and Washington. California was once hugely rich in natural resources. The area of land used by Native peoples always

The State of California showing the location of peoples mentioned in the chapter.

crossed several ecological zones, so that while one food source might predominate, this would always be complemented by a wide range of alternative foods. Apart from providing a varied diet, this option was particularly significant on the rare occasions that a main food source, a species of oak or fish, failed.

Acorns, from more than half-a-dozen preferred species of oak, were the principal food throughout much of California. Although oaks do not grow everywhere – neither in the desert areas, for instance, nor on the immediate coast – they are important in the valleys, foothills and low mountains which edge the coast and the desert. In 1877 it was estimated by Stephen Powers, the journalist responsible for the first account of California Indians, that 56 per cent of their diet came from acorns, 28 per cent from fish and 14 per cent from game. The superabundance of acorns is indicated by the vast quantities

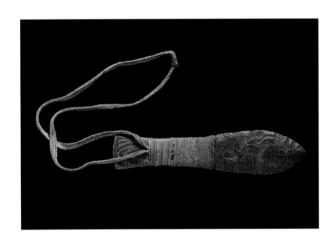

97. Bifacially flaked chert knife, lashed to a wood handle, probably collected on George Vancouver's voyage in 1792–4, perhaps from the Yurok of northern California, where it would have been used especially in preparing salmon, both for broiling and for preservation by smoking. L: 25 cm (9.9 in).

which were collected: the anthropologist Robert Heizer suggested that a family of five might gather 15 tons, working eight hours a day during a two-week harvest. Religious observances were vital, to give thanks for the harvest and to ensure, for instance, that the crop was not spoilt by rain. Acorns were harvested in a hierarchy of preferred species, the least bitter naturally being collected first.

Europeans in eighteenth-century California noted the spectacular beauty of much of the country, an endless game-filled parkland dotted with oaks. While it seemed natural, California Indians created and managed their environment. Burning of the undergrowth, for instance, was regularly undertaken. This facilitated the gathering of acorns in the autumn and encouraged the growth of wild grain-bearing annuals, as well as the new shoots required for basketry materials. Game, also, was attracted by the fresh growth of plants sprouting in burnt-over land. Acorns would be collected in autumn camps and carried back home. There they would be dried, cracked, hulled and soaked to remove the skin. They would then be dried again and ground to fine powder on a bedrock or movable mortar. In northern California the tannic acid was removed by leaching or

98. 'Yokuts cooking mush [acorn porridge] with hot rocks in basket', 1938–9.

soaking in a sand pit, while in southern California this was accomplished in baskets. The Cahuilla, in whose territory the desert resort city of Palm Springs now sits, have a myth in which acorns were made bitter by the Creator, Mukat, in anger. Some peoples simply buried acorns in swamps or near rivers for up to a year to remove the acid. Acorn flour could be made into a highly nourishing meal, which would then be boiled in large baskets with heated stones to make porridge. Or bread could be baked in earth ovens, or even dry-baked on hot rocks.

Fish was and is in almost all areas the complementary food resource. In most coastal areas, and also the Sacramento River, anadromous species of salmon are caught during their runs upriver to spawn; further south significant species include steelhead trout. In northwest California salmon was synonymous with food, the Yurok name *nepa* also meaning 'that which is eaten'. More significant than the reliance on a single food source, acorns, was the extraordinary diversity of food resources. The sea provided an unlimited abundance of clams and mussels, for instance, in San Francisco Bay, as well as tuna, sea lions and seals for Chumash peoples around Santa Barbara. Game included particularly deer, antelope and elk. Inland, too, different grain, greens, tubers, pine nuts and small animals were collected to supplement a diet which might be seasonally affected by very occasional adverse climatic conditions.

Basketry was the vital art and technology which made the processing of acorns possible. Its importance is indicated in oral literatures, where culture-heroes or creators occasionally explain, early in the narrative, the origins of this all-important technology. So for the Yuki, Taikomol created the earth out of a pitch-covered coiled basket, according to Ralph Moore. In a Yana story, told by Sam Bat'wi, Lizard, Gray Squirrel and Coyote created people by breaking up a stick and making different California peoples, which involved boiling the sticks up with stones in a cooking basket. Baskets and the women who made them were universally respected. In a Yokuts story Coyote ridiculed an old basketry winnowing tray with a hole in the middle that he found lying around. He said that it was good for nothing and put it round his neck to make fun of it; so the basket strangled Coyote.

In California Native basketry was more highly developed than elsewhere on the continent, in both twining and coiling techniques. Coiled baskets predominated in northern and central California, while Pomoan peoples north of San Francisco used both techniques equally, and in northern California twining was used exclusively. It is probable that basketry has been known in California for more than 5,000 years in connection with seed preparation; the first baskets are more likely to have been twined and to have been followed by coiled baskets perhaps around 3,000 years ago. The great variety of basketry types include carrying and seed-gathering baskets, winnowing trays, basketry hoppers used with grinding stones, scoops, and storage and cooking vessels. Basketry was also used to make cradles, hats and ceremonial items, such as the Jump Dance baskets employed on the Klamath River (fig. 105), perhaps in imitation of the elk-antler purses that held dentalium-shell currency. Pomo coiled baskets, sometimes entirely woven with feathers on the exterior, were used as gifts and destroyed in mourning for the dead. A variety of baskets were employed in hunting and fishing – conical-shaped traps for fish, and for quail and woodpeckers, and also basketry cages for eaglets.

Almost everywhere basketry was mostly the work of women, although men often co-operated in the collection of materials, an activity whose importance is usually underestimated. Men did, however, construct traps and other large twined utilitarian articles, and could make some other types of basket. The largest baskets were granaries, made of willow by Chumash peoples, for instance, to hold up to 450 kg (1,000 lb) of acorns. The Europeans early on recognized the beauty of Native basketry. Francis Drake, for instance, was eloquent, and accurate, in his description. Baskets, he said 'were so well wrought as to hold Water. They hang pieces of Pearl shells, and sometimes Links of these Chains on the Brims, to signify they were only used in the Worship of their Gods; they are wrought with matted down of red Feathers in various Forms.' Superb examples were produced by Mission Indians for European use. Little of this survives, but there are a few notable presentation pieces which incorporate, for instance, Spanish coats of arms taken from coins.

European and American contact from 1769

Although governed by Spain and then Mexico for less than eighty years, California had been visited by Spanish explorers, and other Europeans, on several notable occasions in the sixteenth century. Juan Rodríguez Cabrillo was probably the first European to land and explore the coast of Alta, or Upper California, the present state of California, in 1542–3. He followed the coast to somewhere north of present Monterey, and died on one of the Channel Islands occupied by Chumash. The surviving summary of the log noted of Chumash-speaking peoples that 'They have houses, well covered down to the ground. They wear skins of many differnt kinds of animals, eat acorns… They live well…' Cabrillo's aim was to find the Strait of Anian, the mythic way through to the Northwest Passage and Europe. Cabrillo was followed by Francis Drake in 1579, who probably landed amongst the Coast Miwok in northern California, where he spent a month.

Colonization only began much later in 1769 with an expedition lead by the soldier Gaspar de Portolá, Governor of Baja California, with Franciscan missionaries led by Junípero Serra. The first mission was founded at that time, San Diego de Alcalá. Another twenty were set up along the coast, as far north

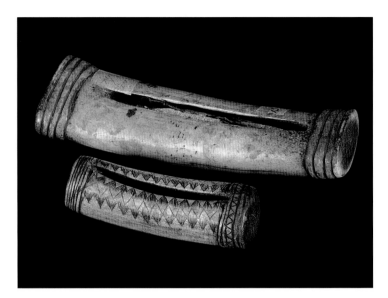

99. Elk-antler spoon, collected at Tsurai (Trinidad), 1793. These were used by men for eating acorn porridge, while women employed mussel shells, pieces of deer skull or scoop-shaped antlers. L: 17 cm (6.75 in).

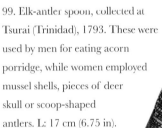

100. Two elk-antler and dentalium-shell purses, perhaps the first to be collected by Europeans, at Tsurai on Vancouver's voyage in 1793. In northern California an important measure of wealth was the miniature tusk-shaped univalve shell, *Dentalium* sp. These were carefully graded and furnished with names reflecting their size. L: 17 cm (6.75 in), 10 cm (3.9 in).

101. (above right) Twined basketry Yurok woman's hat from Tsurai, 1793. Such dress caps, of which this is the earliest example, are the highest expression of Yurok and Karuk basketry. Hazel or willow shoots are used for the foundation, the twined elements being made of split roots of, for instance, spruce or pine. Diam.: 18 cm (7.1 in).

102. (left) Bertha Peters, noted northern California basket-weaver, wearing a twined cap and dentalium-shell currency necklace, 1993.

103. Joseph Goldsborough Bruff
(1804–89), 'Ind. Village Trinidad.
Cabins constructed of drift slabs of
pine', 1851. Possibly the earliest
depiction of a Yurok community,
this drawing of Tsurai shows in the
foreground a woman wearing a
twined hat and vegetal fibre skirt,
with perhaps a child on her back.

104. White Deerskin Dance, or Summer Dance, Hupa Valley, before 1897.
This annual World Renewal ceremony was performed at the end of the summer
by men of the Klamath River peoples, who danced on ten successive afternoons
and evenings in mythologically significant locations, after a recital describing
the origins of the ceremony.

105. Hupa
participants in the
Jump Dance
(a World Renewal
ceremony) at
Pekwon, a Yurok
town on the
Klamath River, in
1893. The men are
wearing buckskin,
headdresses and
deerskin blankets
around their hips.
Around their necks
are dentalium
shells, indicating
wealth, and in their
hands Jump Dance
baskets.

as Sonoma, in the years to 1823. The purpose of the missions was to Christianize and civilize Indians through voluntary baptism and the learning of doctrine. Most missionaries were genuinely good people who thought that they would assist Indian people by conversion. Under sixteenth-century Spanish laws, the Laws of Burgos of 1512 and the New Laws of the Indies of 1542, the right of Indians to full citizenship was recognized after, that is, they had received instruction in Christianity and the ways of Spanish civilization. It is difficult to imagine what this meant to the individuals involved. What happened is that Indian people – with entirely different languages, ethnicity and life styles to those of the intruders – were assisted into Christianity. Priests, good-hearted and well intentioned, felt obliged to help, out of a sense of generosity and humanitarianism, in providing the overwhelming, self-evident benefits of conversion. While conversion was a personal initiative, priests were quite unforgiving, if after baptism Indian people wished to revert to their own beliefs. Those who ran away were brought back, beaten and coerced into remaining Christian. Indians, in any case religious to ensure their own well-being and the appropriate functioning of the world, were impressed by the superior technical abilities of Europeans, while their own beliefs were undermined by epidemics. Furthermore, after 1800 soldiers led expeditions to capture new Indian people for conversion. From 1803 Chumash converts were no longer allowed to live in their own villages, but moved to the missions. Initially, the neophytes in one mission might sometimes be of the same tribe or town. Later, as the missionary net spread wider, a mission sometimes came to hold peoples of a number of different Native nations. A Native view of the missionary process was recorded by Pablo Tac (1822–41), a Luiseño trained as a missionary, who wrote an autobiography in Rome in about 1835. As he succinctly put it, 'we lived among the woods until merciful God freed us of these miseries through Father Antonio Peyri, a Catalan, who arrived in our country in the afternoon with seven Spanish soldiers'.

Since the missions had to be self-supporting, labour, of unfamiliar kinds, was introduced. This was especially so with the introduction of agriculture and the foreign architectural styles of the Franciscans. Since many articles, both of ritual and everyday use, were imported from Mexico, a surplus of agricultural and other products had to be created for export. Among the numerous features of mission life was the segregation of the sexes, quite contrary to usual practice. Some 80–90,000 Indians were converted before 1834. This was the year in which Mexico, independent of Spain from 1821, abolished the mission system. The 15,000 or so then remaining mission Indians were seemingly absorbed into the population, although this was not always the case. Some practised trades, such as leather-working, already learnt, others remained or became *vaqueros*, 'cowboys'. A few returned to the areas of the country from which they had come. But as elsewhere in North America, after establishment, and the first wave of proselytization, the church came to retain the loyalty and affection of converted Natives and their descendants. Most missions were returned to the Roman Catholic Church in 1862.

Death from epidemics was a central feature of early European settlement. During the Spanish period, before 1821, only the coastal peoples from San Francisco south were affected by European settlement, although epidemics spread inland. The 1824 republican constitution of Mexico recognized all people as equal. From the 1830s the development of Mexican ranches began to affect northern Indians away from the coast. During this period Americans and Europeans sought land grants: Indians became free to sell their labour, and to exploit and be exploited by the newcomers. Before the Mexican War and the 1848 Treaty of Guadalupe Hidalgo, by which the United States annexed the Southwest and California, there may have been 2–4,000 Spaniards and Mexicans in California, living in settlements on or near to the coast. In the 1830s the arriving Europeans and Americans turned inland, to seize land and to ranch. One such person was the Swiss immigrant, John Sutter, who, arriving in San Francisco in 1839, acquired a Mexican land grant in the Sacramento valley north-east of San Francisco. There he built a fort, mill and station. After the discovery of gold on Sutter's property by James Marshall in 1848, mining was added to Euro-American accomplishments in California. The population of newcomers grew so quickly that statehood was achieved in 1850.

In the middle of the nineteenth century it is estimated that the Native population of California collapsed from 150,000 to 50,000 people. Most of this, as elsewhere, was due to disease; for instance, 50,000 people in 1830–33 alone may have died in

106. Ferdinand Deppe, *Mission San Gabriel*, 1832, oil painting depicting a Corpus Christi procession. The Gabrielino, aboriginal inhabitants of Los Angeles and Orange Counties, reluctantly suffered early colonization after the establishment of the mission in 1771. A major revolt was lead by Toypurina, a chief's daughter, in 1785.

107. Chumash paddle blade collected in 1793 by G.G. Hewett on Vancouver's voyage. Vancouver commented specifically on Chumash 'paddles... about ten feet long, with a blade at each end; these they handled with much dexterity, either intirely, or alternately on each side of their canoe'. L: 29 cm (11.4 in).

108. Replica of a Chumash plank canoe, the *Helek*, at sea in 1976 with double-ended paddles in use. L: 7.6 m (25 ft).

109. *Bateau du port de Sn. Francisco*, 1816, lithograph after Louis Choris. In much of California tule reeds were employed for a wide variety of constructions, including bound tule balsas or boats, such as here, where Costanoans, like the Chumash, are using double-bladed paddles in the San Francisco Bay area.

110. Two Chumash cane hairpins, decorated with various materials, including feathers, shell beads and cloth, and collected in 1793 by Archibald Menzies, who noted: 'They [the men] wear their hair gathered up in a bunch on the crown of their head and fastened there by running a skewer of wood or bone through it.' L: 21 cm (8.3 in), 11 cm (4.3 in).

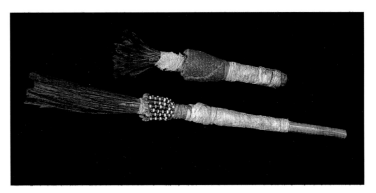

a malaria epidemic along the Sacramento River, and 10,000 in a smallpox epidemic that started in Fort Ross in 1837. However, the influx of Americans had other, far wider-reaching and more culturally destructive effects than those of the Spanish who preceded them. Additional factors at work included the state subsidization of private militias set up to 'end' Indian hostilities. This often meant expeditions setting out simply to murder Indians going about their own business on Indian land that was now desired for white ranching. By 1860 more than 4,000 people were killed in these hostilities. California was admitted to the Union as a state without slavery; however, Indians were denied legal rights, so that various forms of near-slavery existed until after the Civil War. No Indian, for instance, could testify against a white man in court. Women and children were also widely kidnapped for purposes of 'labor and lust'. Yet Natives were not passive victims: some sought out sympathetic ranchers and obtained indenture papers from them to ensure their own protection. Chiefs favoured the marriage of daughters to Americans, who then protected Native interests. In a sense the tragic contact history of Native California is similar to that of Newfoundland, and of Tasmania, during the same period, with the important difference that in California Native peoples survived.

The last military action in California was fought in the 1870s by an overwhelming US force against the Modoc in northeastern California on the Oregon border. In 1864 the Modoc had agreed to relinquish their traditional lands and move with other displaced tribes into a reservation in the Fort Klamath area of Oregon. This was not satisfactory, and they returned home to the discomfort of the colonizing Californians who, through the Indian Bureau, called in the US army for this, the last military action in the state. The Modoc leaders, Kintpuash, or Captain Jack, and Scarfaced Charley, moved into impenetrable lava beds on the northeastern state borders, where with sixty men and ten women they held at bay 1,000 soldiers for five months in 1872–3, until divisions in the leadership caused the group to scatter. Kintpuash had made Americans welcome: 'I have always told the white man heretofore to come and settle in my country; that it was his country and Captain Jack's country; that they could come and live there with me...' He was, however, to be betrayed by his erstwhile colleague Hooker Jim, captured, and with three others tried and hung,

Captain Jack's body subsequently being embalmed and exhibited in eastern sideshows. The Modoc War was the first to be attended by journalists interviewing both sides in the conflict. William Simpson of the *Illustrated London News* broke a round-the-world trip in San Francisco to spend a week reporting these events with California colleagues, including H. Wallace Atwell of the *Sacramento Record*, with whom he collected a bow and arrows now in the Museum. Modoc bows, recurved and sinew-backed, were used for hunting deer and duck. In the latter case arrows were furnished with a ring towards the tip to enable the projectile to skip along the surface rather than bury itself in the water.

The Chumash and George Vancouver, 1793

British interest in California arose as an aspect of the search for the Northwest Passage; in this endeavour George Vancouver mapped in 1792–4 the coast of North America between Santa Barbara (originally spelt Bárbara), California, and Anchorage, Alaska – an exceptional and unequalled achievement. Peoples speaking Chumash languages occupied part of the southern coast, and immediate interior, of California from Malibu north to San Luis Obispo. At the time of European settlement in 1769 there may have been between 10,000 and 20,000 people living in settlements along the coast and interior valleys. They lived in 150 autonomous permanent towns and spoke six different languages. The Spanish set up five missions at San Luis Obispo (1772), San Buenaventura (1782), Santa Bárbara (1786), La Purísima Concepción (1787) and Santa Ynez (1804). In 1804, thirty-two years after the founding of the first missions, all Chumash were forced into the missions against the better judgement of many Spanish.

Early commentators noted the extreme friendliness and good nature of the Chumash, which no doubt facilitated Franciscan proselytization. They lived in patrilineal descent groups in villages with streets and tall domed houses. These were up to 15 m (50 ft) in diameter, constructed from pliable poles bent towards the middle and tied in the centre, thatched with grass, and fitted in the interior with discrete apartments built of reeds. The high coastal mountains, and the islands and the channel between, provided access to varied ecological zones with a great wealth of resources, from mussels and clams to swordfish, tuna, barracuda, seals and sea lions. Sea hunting was achieved with harpoons, a technology shared with Northwest Coast and Arctic peoples. Acorns, from the live oak, were stored in the autumn for use through the year. Tubers were roasted and eaten, and wild grain, particularly chia, were collected. The Chumash were great carvers in wood and stone, but of the former very little survives. Of the latter, steatite was used particularly for bowls, for charmstones or amulets, and for tubular smoking pipes. An interesting and important aspect of Chumash technology was the use of asphaltum, which rises along the coast at points of natural oil seepage. This tar was used as a setting for shell beads on stone objects, to set arrow heads and to caulk their plank canoes. Shell was widely used for decorative purposes and for money, employed, for instance, in gambling.

111. Hat, or *sumulelu* (from the Spanish *sombrero*), decorated with crosses as well as traditional geometric designs. Chumash women sometimes wore coiled brimless caps, but Pedro Font indicated in 1776 that basket-weavers were experimenting with new shapes; this unique hat may have been made for a favoured priest. Diam.: 36 cm (14.2 in).

Vancouver's first extended contact with Native Californians was in the spring of 1793 as he was travelling north to begin the surveying season in what is now British Columbia. He stopped at the Yurok village of Tsurai, where he took on board 22 tons of water, and mentions acquiring bows, arrows and other articles (fig. 99). He noted that the arrows and knives were fitted with flint blades; knives, two of which were collected (fig. 97), were used particularly in the preparation of salmon, the essential food source featured in the following story. Common in northern California are myths telling of mythological heroes who inhabited the earth before the arrival of human beings and created animals. An elder from the neighbouring Karuk people, Sweet William of Ishipishi, told the anthropologist Alfred Kroeber early in the twentieth century about one of the heroes, or *ikhareya*. This hero's name was Sugar Loaf Mountain, at Katimin. The mountain man created salmon and kept them in a pool; when they grew he allowed them to go down to the ocean, and then to return upriver. He created a net to catch the salmon and a club to kill them with. To begin with he had no knife and could only cook the salmon whole. Finally another creature, Fish Hawk or Chukchuk, decided to make a knife of stone, *yuhirim*. He created a flint flaker, *taharatar*, so that when people arrived on earth they would be able to make knives, keep them sharp, and prepare the fish properly. Other articles collected at this time by Vancouver included basketry, spoons and antler purses (fig. 100) for money.

Later in 1793, after the surveying season was over, Vancouver visited San Francisco and Monterey, where he and his expedition were not made to feel welcome, in part because the Spanish were, quite appropriately, unsure of British colonial intentions in California. On the other hand, at Santa Barbara, founded only seven years before, Vancouver was very cordially received. The collection made at this time, now in the British Museum, seems to be composed of two sections: materials collected from people who remained outside the mission system, and those collected from the mission neophytes at Santa Barbara. The first encounter with the Chumash occurred just before Vancouver arrived at Santa Barbara in November 1793. He described what happened:

112. Coiled rush (*Juncus*) basketry bowl, probably collected by Archibald Menzies at Santa Barbara in 1793. Such vessels were constructed from bundle coils, with split *Juncus* for the weaving material. After boiling acorn meal in a deeper basket with near vertical sides, porridge might be served from a flatter vessel of this type. Diam.: 45 cm (17.7 in).

The want of wind detaining us in this situation afforded an opportunity to several of the natives from the different villages, which were numerous in this neighbourhood, to pay us a visit. They all came in canoes made of wood, and decorated with shells… They brought with them some fish, and a few of their ornaments; these they disposed of in the most cheerful manner, principally for spoons, beads and scissars. They seemed to possess great sensibility, and much vivacity, yet conducted themselves with the most perfect decorum and good order…

This is perhaps the occasion on which the shell and feather ornaments were acquired (fig. 110), along with a bow, arrows, unique harpoon and the canoe paddle blade (fig. 107). The Cruzeño Chumash informant Fernando Librado, or Kitsepawit (d. 1915), described in *c.*1913 the use of the harpoon, *kalui*, in the nineteenth century: 'I prepare the harpoon for use. I begin by making a little coil of the line, and I grasp the coil and the harpoon in my right hand... The harpoon they use is an instrument of some weight so that they could throw it far... They usually stood in the middle of the boat when spearing a [sea] otter...' Fish such as barracuda were lured to the boat with bait and then harpooned. Both marine mammals and fish like the swordfish were celebrated in dances by Chumash peoples.

Shortly afterwards Vancouver anchored at Santa Barbara, where they were very affably greeted by the commandant of the garrison, or *presidio*, Felipe de Goycoechea, at the shore. Goycoechea, who had acted as godfather to the first three Chumash converts, invited the British to stay for a few days to replenish their supplies. They then went to the mission itself and met Father José de Miguel, who was also very friendly, and provided all assistance to the foreigners. The garrison offered the use of their cart, while the mission proffered Indians to help carry supplies to the ships. Vegetables and meat were purchased from individuals, and the mission gardens provided further vegetables. When the commandant realized that the English ships were short of soap and candles, these too were supplied. There was some difficulty in locating sweet water, but when a suitable supply had been found, the mission cart was used to transport a supply to the ships. On 14 November the commandant entertained the expedition, and the following day the priests provided the hospitality. In between time Archibald Menzies, the expedition botanist, and no doubt his deputy George Hewett, collected scientific specimens. They may also have acquired some of the cultural materials at that time, and especially of course the superb coiled baskets (fig. 112), which may have been made in the Chumash town on the shore. These were coiled from *Juncus*, gathered in June and July.

This idyllic scenario, of mission Indians living at ease with benign European soldiers and priests, was to change radically after 1800. One of the most unfortunate aspects of the mission system was that the Native population was eventually concentrated in specific places, which facilitated the spread of new Old World diseases. Once introduced, these moved through the missions very quickly. Soon after 1804 most Chumash had been attached to the missions; in 1824 a short-lived revolt at several missions, including Santa Barbara, was suppressed. By 1831 there were only 2,788 people living at the five missions, where there had been perhaps 20,000 people before. On the secularization of the mission system in 1834, the Chumash were left to their own devices. Several small land grants were made to leaders of separate groups, but much of this was alienated as people became *vaqueros* on Mexican ranches. Today there are perhaps several hundred people of Chumash descent with one federally recognized tribe of 350 people. The last speaker of a Chumash language, Mary Yee, who spoke Barbareño, died in 1965.

The Pomo

An illustration of the art created by Native Californians is provided by Mary and William Benson (1878–1930 and 1862–1937), two Pomoan artists whose life work, in creating basketry and regalia, is complemented by William Benson's publications of mythology and oral history. Pomoan peoples live along the coast, and through the neighbouring coastal range of redwood and winery country north of San Francisco. This area of California was north of the furthermost Spanish missions, yet was influenced by the Spanish in speech and no doubt in trade and technology. Pomoan peoples, perhaps numbering several thousand individuals at contact, and the same again today, would not therefore have been affected by European intrusion until the early nineteenth century, apart from the effects of disease. Pomoan peoples indicate the cultural and linguistic complexity of California, speaking seven distinct languages. All are as different from each other as English, Dutch and German. Politically and culturally, the Pomo divided into seventy-two autonomous towns, with shared marriage, religious participation and trade. There was no overall cultural identity, but merely a series of overlapping and partially shared traditions.

Like other California peoples, they depended on fish, hunting, gathering acorns and exploiting a variety of ecological niches. Dried fish and acorn porridge were constituents of a typical meal. Given this complexity, nomenclature for this people was initially uncertain. They shared no single name for themselves. An early designation was *Kulanapo*, or 'water lily people/place', from the Eastern Pomo name of one of the seventy-two towns or tribes. *Pomo* itself, the name of another town, comes from Northern Pomo and means 'at red earth hole'. The red earth refers to magnesite and to the red earth used as leavening in acorn bread.

From 1811 to 1841 the Russian-American Company maintained a southern post in Kashaya Pomo country at Fort Ross, some 145 km (90 miles) north of San Francisco Bay. This was employed as a base for the hunting of sea otter, as it happens, to extinction. It was also a means to lay claim to that coastal region and to provide, in a manner similar to the farms of the Hudson's Bay Company in Oregon Territory, agricultural produce for the northern, or Alaskan, coast. Some one hundred Kashaya people were employed as farm workers by the Russians. After California became a colony of Mexico in 1821–2, land grants, or ranchos, were established deep in the territory of peoples speaking Pomoan languages. Outsiders in the 1830s moved into the Sonoma and Napa Valleys. Further major depredations came before and during the Gold Rush as it developed to the northeast of the Sacramento River. One notorious 1849 incident, 'The Stone and Kelsey Massacre', was to become the subject of an innovatory ethnohistorical paper by William Benson. In this he described the starvation and mistreatment which brought about the killing of these two ranchers and the subsequent massacre of Pomoans by the US cavalry. After California statehood in 1850 and the arrival of Americans, Pomoan peoples were brought into ranchos, and the land deeded to the newcomers. Some people were forcibly removed to reservations in the north. When the reservations were discontinued in 1867, people found themselves homeless and landless. One strategy for coping with this situation was for families to establish themselves in rancherias on the now American-owned land, where in return for this privilege they worked harvesting crops. By the end of the 1870s several former Pomoan tribes had banded together and bought back their own land, where they formed communities that survive to the present. The Pomoan population declined rapidly due to the epidemics already mentioned. Disease, for the Pomo, was caused by poisons, so that the Native explanation for these catastrophes was compounded by the suspicion that each death was caused by a person. Pomo ritual included spring ceremonies, major events relating to thunder and to death; most significant for the Eastern Pomo was the Ghost Ceremony, in which members of the secret society impersonated the dead.

William and Mary Benson were born into two of the seven separate Pomo linguistic communities speaking different languages. William Benson, like others of the late nineteenth- and early twentieth-century Native commentators, was descended from a white settler father, Addison Benson, but was also raised in the culture of his Native mother. At the turn of the century California, like perhaps Florida in the 1920s, was a state dependent on vigorous promotion, marketing the healthy warm climate, agricultural opportunities and cheap real estate. As part of this process magazines, clubs and indeed architecture featured the unique qualities of California living. One aspect of this, relating to the arts and crafts movement, was the development of an interest in things Indian. Because of the pre-eminence of basketmakers, this emphasis, from the 1880s onwards, lead to a demand for baskets handmade by women brought up traditionally. Grace Nicholson was a scholarly and exceptional dealer in this ethnic art and later in Asian materials which decorated many Los Angeles houses, be they in modest real estate developments, such as Hollywood, or smarter areas, such as Pasadena, a winter resort for rich easterners, where Nicholson lived. But she was also interested in Native art, and spent much of the first thirty years of the twentieth century acquiring basketry for resale from the Makahs, for instance, to the north in Washington state, as well as from California Natives. She recorded her purchases in writing and photography, and educated her clients in a unique and unparalleled manner.

Nicholson met the Bensons in 1903 and became an important patron for nearly thirty years. It was in part through her that the Bensons encountered the wider world. Through her influence a wealth of superb baskets and exquisite ceremonial Pomo objects came to end up in private collections and eventually in museums. It might be assumed that this sort of

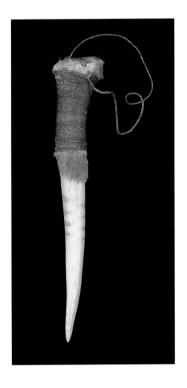

113. Polished elk-antler dagger made by William Benson. The hilt is wrapped in fibre cord and otter (?) fur, and the engraved designs include geometric forms and an arrow. Worn around the neck by Pomo bear doctors, such knives were employed to initiate male adolescents into the bear society and to kill. L: 35 cm (13.8 in).

114. William Benson photographed in 1906 posing with a bear doctor's costume he had made and holding an elk-antler dagger.

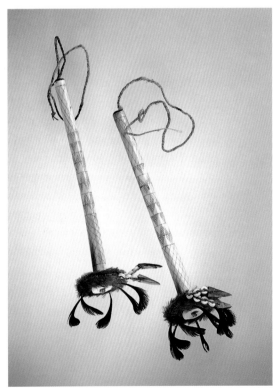

115. Pair of bone, shell and feather ear ornaments made by William Benson. Benson created several of these during the first two decades of the twentieth century, using heron leg bones (which he engraved), twined milkweed cord, coiled basketry discs, California woodpecker scalps and top knots from California quail. L: 12 cm (4.7 in).

116. Frances Joaquin Jack, 1923, posing with ear ornaments worn at the shoulder, probably made by Benson.

117. Mary Benson, 1905, wearing a great wealth of clam-shell necklaces and, atypically, a headdress including a flicker-feather headband.

118. Headdress of flicker feathers placed alternately quill to tip and strung with two shell discs at one end, collected by Edward Belcher during visits to San Francisco and Monterey in 1826 and 1827. This type of decoration, of which this may be the earliest example, was widely used in central California. L: 71 cm (28 in).

119. 'Pomo dancers led by Dave Smith', 1995. Posed in front of the roundhouse at Chaw'se, Indian Grinding Rock Park, they wear traditional feather headdresses. The dancers perform for the health and well-being of everyone.

relationship was one-sided, but according to the linguist Sally McLendon, this does not seem to have been the case. Nicholson treated the Bensons with warmth and friendship, which was reciprocated. Funds were made available to pay for an operation to save Mary Benson's sight and for an annual stipend, which enabled them to continue traditional artwork and to acquire a camera, and also a car in 1918 so as to be able to search for the finest materials for basketry. The Bensons, like a few other named artists such as Charles Edenshaw on the Northwest Coast, created art which expressed Native and non-Native social relations, thus enabling Americans and Europeans to understand something of Native aesthetics. William Benson also took up the more female task of basketmaking, in addition to creating bone and feather hairpins and ear plugs, and other feathered ceremonial regalia. During the 1920s and 1930s William Benson worked with anthropologists at Berkeley to record his Eastern Pomo and his wife's Central Pomo languages and cultural traditions. For instance, during the 1930s William Benson recounted in a creation myth the story of how basketry was invented: 'Then Marumda [or Coyote] said to the women: "Over there is *kuhum*." "What is *kuhum*?" they asked. Then Marumda went to dig some [roots] and brought it back. "This is weaving material for you." He [also] brought willow roots. "With these you will make baskets."'

California collections

Nothing survives from Cabrillo's or Drake's visits to California in the 1570s, and there are probably no collections of California artefacts from before the 1790s. In Madrid there is a grand accumulation probably from the voyage of exploration of Alejandro Malaspina in California in 1791, two years before Vancouver's extended stay. This includes numerous superb gold-coloured baskets collected from Chumash peoples. Various crew members acquired collections on Vancouver's voyage. Archibald Menzies, as official botanist and medical officer with Vancouver, dutifully listed his collection, which came to the British Museum through George III and Sir Joseph Banks in 1796. It then disappeared, probably because at that time a gallery of Pacific materials was already in existence, well endowed not only with Polynesian materials but also North

American items. The likely destination of Menzies' collection was one of the basements of the original museum, Montagu House. One of these surviving cellars was excavated in 1997, and found to be exceptionally damp, which might provide an explanation for the disappearance of most of that collection. Three large Chumash baskets survived, however, as did a couple of Yurok fish knives. The collection of Menzies' deputy, George Goodman Hewett, seemingly of minor items, remained in private hands for another century until presented to the Museum by A.W. Franks. Hewett's collection also contains Chumash baskets, which, unlike Menzies' examples and those in Madrid, are very small, but most significantly are associated with unique and what must have seemed then like trifling articles relating to hunting and to adornment.

A rather separate group of material was obtained by an uncharacteristic American collector, the Reverend Robert William Summers (1827–98). Born in Kentucky, he became a homesteader in Oregon in the 1850s before returning east and joining the clergy, perhaps after a sojourn in Europe, as an Episcopalian or Anglican minister. He returned to the west, where from 1871 to 1873 he served as first pastor in the new city of Seattle; his duties would not have been arduous – he baptised seven adults in three years – and seems otherwise to have developed a wide-ranging amateur interest in Native culture in the locality, and in natural history. He knew, for instance, Angeline, the daughter of the chief, Seattle (1800–1850), after whom the city was named, and from whom he recorded an account of how he lost land. From Seattle Summers returned to Oregon, where he established the first church in McMinnville, on the South Yamhill River in the drainage of the Willamette River, south of Portland. Living in Oregon from 1873 to 1881, he again established an Episcopal church, and devoted much of his time to a brief journal which accounts for his contacts with Indians, both at home and on expeditions made to various parts of the coast.

The Willamette Valley is the home of a number of related groups of Natives speaking different languages, named collectively the Kalapuyas by anthropologists. Originally these thirteen peoples were in some minor cultural respects similar to those of neighbouring California, the Yurok and Karuk, to the southwest. While they used acorns, other vegetable foods,

120. *Danse des habitans de Californie à la mission de St Francisco*, October 1816, lithograph after Louis Choris. Several missions affecting the Costanoans (from *costaños*, 'coast people' in Spanish) were created in the area between San Francisco and Carmel between 1770 and 1797, including San Francisco de Asís in 1776.

121. Costanoan (?) necklace, nineteenth century, composed of fourteen plaques of abalone shell attached to two rows of opaque white, blown (?) glass beads – substitutes for shell beads. Created with a stone, saw-like tool, such necklaces were worn by people of high status in ceremonials and were traded widely in California. L: 33 cm (13 in).

122. Ear ornament of engraved bone, basketry and feathers, collected from Costanoans at San José by Ferdinand Deppe in 1837. L: 40 cm (15.8 in).

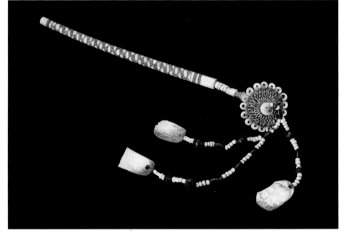

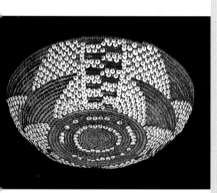

123. Coiled Costanoan
basket, nineteenth century,
decorated geometrically
with woodpecker feathers
and *Olivella* shell beads
woven into the exterior of
the coils. The hard enamel
of the central columns of
the *Olivella* mollusc was
used as currency, the value
depending on the labour
involved in manufacture
rather than on appearance.
Diam.: 24 cm (9.5 in).

particularly camas root, provided the main source of food, along with hazel nuts and varied seeds. Fish and game were abundant. Society as elsewhere on the Northwest Coast was differentiated, rank extending from chiefs to slaves, with dentalium shells acting as currency. Significant European contact came in 1812, with the arrival of fur traders, followed inevitably by epidemics, as happened to the south, particularly in the 1830s. American settlement was accompanied in 1855 by the ratification of treaties, and the following year the consolidation of the remaining Kalapuyas, and other peoples in western Oregon, on the Grande Ronde reservation. This survived until it was terminated by the Eisenhower administration a century later in 1956. While federal recognition of the Confederated Tribes of Grande Ronde was restored in 1983, reservation lands were not returned to the Indians.

A century earlier Summers devoted his time in McMinnville to collecting examples of basketry, smoking pipes and domestic implements from the Kalapuyas and others resident on the Grande Ronde Reservation. He was not a missionary, however, and his congregation would have been composed of Americans rather than Natives in an otherwise Evangelical community. While possessing prejudices characteristic of his age, Summers recorded sympathies towards Indians, noting that Americans 'take away even what they hold most dear: their Native homes, the graves of their ancestors, their own mode of life and the religion in which they were reared'. It is not likely, however, that Summers took a direct interest in assisting with Native welfare. It has been suggested by Father Martinus Cawley that Summers possessed elements of a medical education and that he practised without authority, as was often the case on the frontier, thus arousing the ire of professionals. This eventually resulted in Summer's removal with his collection to San Luis Obispo in northern Chumash territory, between San Francisco and Los Angeles. Here he served in the new Episcopal church, ending his life as first librarian of the town. Much of Summers's last years were devoted to excavating shell middens and other sites, acquiring particularly stone implements used in acorn and other food preparation. The collection eventually came to the British Museum in 1900, one of the Museum's largest North American collections, consisting of more than 500 relatively well-documented artefacts.

5

THE MOWACHAHT AND CAPTAIN COOK, 1778

On the west coast of Vancouver Island, in country which may once also have formed part of Drake's New Albion, live a series of autonomous peoples, known since 1980 collectively as the Nuu-Chah-Nulth ('those living at the foot of the mountains'). This name replaces Nootka, a mistaken epithet introduced by Captain James Cook. In the centre of Nuu-Chah-Nulth territory live the Mowachaht, or 'people of the deer', whom Cook encountered almost exactly 200 years after Drake visited California. Cook was instructed to explore the rivers and inlets of that coast, between latitudes 45° and 65° north to find a 'water passage' leading through the continent to Hudson Bay. In pursuit of this Northwest Passage, Cook was ordered to 'put into the first convenient Port to recruit your

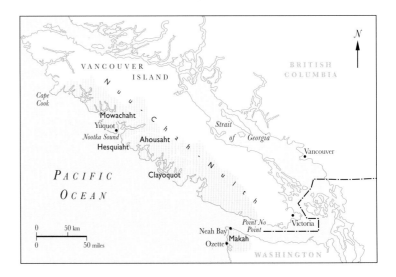

124. John Webber, *A View in King George's Sound*, 1778, watercolour showing Nuu-Chah-Nulth in Nootka Sound. The figures are wearing cedar-bark clothing, and the man standing holding a pike also has a fur cape of perhaps sea otter.

The Mowachaht and Nuu-Chah-Nulth in British Columbia.

Wood and Water and procure Refreshments'. So on 29 March 1778, after a seven-week voyage from the Hawaiian Islands, he sailed into an 'inlet', Nootka Sound, with difficulty in becalmed weather, having 'resolved to anchor to endeavour to get some Water, of which (we) were in great want'. The Mowachaht account of the occasion, as recorded by Winifred David during the 1970s, is rather different.

The Indians didn't know what on earth it was when his ship came into the Harbour… So the Chief, Chief Maquinna, he sent out his warriors…they went out to the ship and they thought it was a fish come alive into people. They were taking a good look at those white

125. Hupquatchew, or Ron Hamilton (b. 1948), *The Whaler's Dream*, 1977, silkscreen print. Dreaming was an important part of the preparation before the whale hunt, and this print, according to the artist, 'illustrates some of the images that might flow through a man's mind' in the days before a hunt. 93.5 x 62.5 cm (36.8 x 24.6 in)

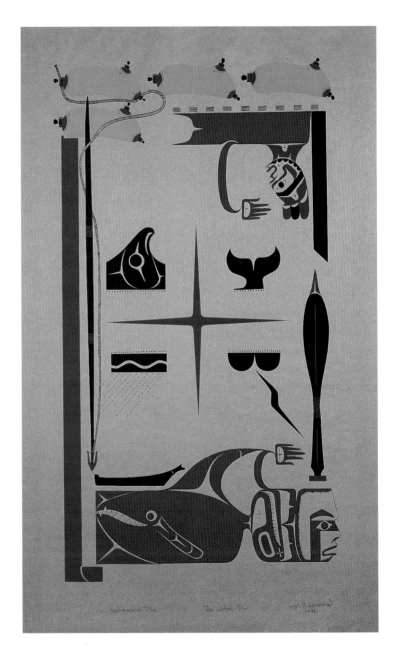

people on the deck there. One white man had a real hooked nose, you know. And one of the men was saying to this other guy, 'See, see…he must have been a dog salmon, that guy he's got a hooked nose.' The other guy was looking at him and a man came out of the galley and he was a hunchback, and the other one said, 'Yes! We're right, we're right. Those people, they must have been fish. They've come back alive… Look at that one, he's a humpback [salmon].

Peter Webster, from Ahousaht north of Nootka Sound, added to this account: 'We say they explored North America or Vancouver Island. But they didn't. They were led into a shelter, these ships. They got stuck… [the Indians] directed these ships that couldn't get in…' So Cook established a base at Resolution Cove on Bligh Island on 31 March, and set about his immediate concern: the repair of the ships, for which there was an abundant supply of timber. Rotten wood had to be removed and replaced, a foremast needed repairs, while a mizzenmast had to be entirely renewed from a tree selected from those growing nearby. This work took nearly a month, so that there was time for Cook to fulfil those parts of his instructions of 6 July 1776 which told him to record information about the Native peoples encountered.

Linguistically and culturally the Mowachaht belong, with the Makahs of Washington state, to part of the Wakashan language group. Cook used this last name, from the expression 'Wak'ash', an expression of friendship, as a term for the people and named the place Nootka after the advice proffered by the Natives when becalmed: 'Nootka-a' – 'Go round' the point, he was told, into the inlet itself. The Mowachaht, his hosts, were one of twenty-two distinct peoples recorded in the late nineteenth century on the 400 km (250 miles) of the west coast of Vancouver Island from Cape Cook to Point No Point. Each was a loose confederacy, formed through conquest and alliance, with ranked chiefs, the most senior of whom possessed distinct rights in land and resources, and in non-material property: songs, names, dances, and traditions, or *topati*. A general pattern of seasonal movements allowed for the fishing of, for instance, herring during the spawning season, which was graphically described by Cook and his men. In the summer the Mowachaht came together at Yuquot, the village visited by Cook, to participate in the fishing of the different salmon runs, at weirs whose excellent construction was also noted by the expedition.

Central to the religious beliefs and observances of the Mowachaht were ceremonies conciliating game for allowing themselves to be caught. The best known were those relating to the whale hunt, events accompanied by elaborate rituals by chiefs to ensure success. The Mowachaht Whaler's Shrine, whose constituent parts are now in the American Museum of

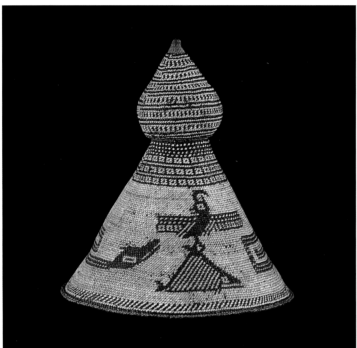

126. (left) Twined Nuu-Chah-Nulth whaling hat of bulb-topped cedar bark, spruce root and surf grass, eighteenth century. Such hats represent one of the few recorded basketry traditions with figurative designs from pre-contact North America. The story here concerns a Thunderbird, a transformational creature, catching a whale. Diam.: 24 cm (9.5 in).

127. Three eighteenth-century knives. The blade of the middle knife is of forged iron and steel, while that at the top is of steel. When European explorers reached the Northwest Coast, metal, particularly iron perhaps of Asian origin, was well known to Native peoples. L of longest knife: 33 cm (13 in).

128. (right) Twined red cedar bark whaler's hat, woven by Caroline Mickey from Hesquiaht in 1981. H: 29 cm (11.4 in).

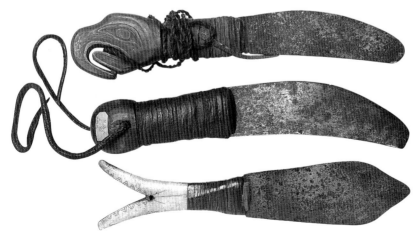

131. Eighteenth-century yew and whalebone lance or harpoon shaft carved with a series of Lightning Serpents and Owls, no doubt intended to assist with the killing of a wounded whale. L: 175 cm (69 in).

129. 'Lighthouse Joe [or Jim] with Whaling Outfit': Dúkbis poses with a yew harpoon, canoe and floats, 1909, probably on the occasion of the last successful whale hunt by the Makahs. Vigorous attempts are now being made to resume whaling.

130. Single-piece alderwood model canoe presented by Edward Belcher before 1842. Painted black with micaceous paint, it is engraved with a red-painted Lightning Serpent and inlaid with white glass beads. The sweeping form of the prow is sometimes said to have inspired that of the American clipper ship. L: 128 cm (50.4 in).

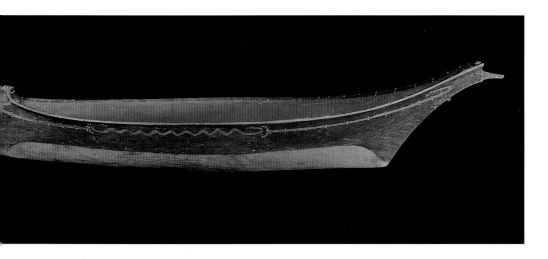

132. Hesquiaht woman packing rolled-up cedar bark, before 1915. She is holding a 'D' adze, which may have been used to cut the bark off the tree, but which in any case was a vitally important tool for carving.

Natural History, New York, is the most famous of these places. The Europeans were regaled with stories of this hunt:

They told us the method they made use of to manage these enormous Animals; which was by means of a Harpoon (some of which they sold us) composed of bone and shell, made exceeding sharp, and indeed a compleat Instrument for the purpose; this is firmly fix'd to a strong Cord, at the other end of which is [attached] fast either [to] a large Bladder, or something so compact as to answer the same purpose, by holding a quantity of Air, and by that means becoming very buoyant… into a Cavity of this Harpoon is stuck a very strong Spear, with which it is forced into the Whale; the Spear disengaging itself, the Harpoon is left in him & they pursue & worry him by means of the bladder.

No whales were seen migrating north to feed in the Arctic, but examples of the eighteenth-century chief's whaling hat were both collected and much commented on. These were twined in two layers, the inner lining of red cedar bark, and the exterior a mixture of materials including spruce root and various grasses. The surface design was achieved by wrapping the warps with grass, probably surf grass (*Phyllospadix torreyi*), to create a white ground. The expedition was favourably impressed with these hats, as well they might be since they are an almost unique example of a surviving pre-contact North American basketry artefact whose woven decoration incorporates figurative designs. The official account commented:

We have sometimes seen the whole process of their whale-fishery painted on the caps they wear. This, though rudely executed, serves, at least, to shew that though there be no appearance of the knowledge of letters amongst them, they have some notion of a method of comemorating and representing actions, in a lasting way, independently of what may be recorded in their songs and traditions.

In most of these hats the whaler is shown standing up in the prow, perhaps getting ready to despatch the whale by piercing a lung or attempting to cut the fluke sinew, thus imobilizing the creature. That the whales have already been harpooned can be seen by the lines attached to their backs, with seal floats attached (fig. 128). After the whale was brought in, a ceremony would be performed around the dorsal fin of a whale or its wood image. It was here that the person or soul of the whale was thought to reside; four nights would be spent singing ritual songs to the whale, after which the soul would depart and the feasting would begin. The words of a Makah song, sung by a chief at such a gathering and recorded by James Guy, are 'I come in, I am rolling (not walking) but I am a man', suggesting that the successful harpooner-chief had been long at sea pursuing the dying creature. During the festivities the fin would be extravagantly painted and decorated with sacred eagle down and cedar bark. Cook's artist recorded a wooden sculpture of a dorsal fin at Yuquot.

More interesting is the association, mentioned above by Winifred David, of the explorers with salmon and particularly dog salmon. The Mowachaht and their neighbours observed strict regulations in the treatment of fish, symbols, like the explorers, of wealth and plenty that required respect. The first dog salmon caught each year was, for instance, called *hita'utl*, an expression meaning 'bright fish' – that is one that has just passed from the sea to fresh water before ascending upriver to spawn. All the first catch of salmon 'were laid on new mats in the chief's house. The owner of the trap [i.e. the chief] sprinkled them with [bird] down, and "talked" to them, saying, "We are glad you have come to visit us; we have been saving these [feathers] for you for a long time, and hope you will return to visit us soon."' Of vital importance was the specific preparation of these fish for eating, and the maintenance of the head, bones, guts and tail, to be returned to the sea when a specific species of migratory duck, the butterball, returned. If the people failed to return the salmon parts to the sea, then the salmon would be born deformed, and deformed salmon – for instance with crooked jaws – could not be eaten. Numerous other taboos existed – for instance they could only be cut up with mussel shell knives, chinks in cracks in the house had to be filled in, and later the food of white men, *mumatline*, could not be eaten at the same time as salmon.

The explorers might have been perceived equally well as other respected animals such as bears or whales, but the connection of the Europeans with salmon provides an explanation of how the Mowachaht treated the intruders. They were to be exploited, like salmon, in trade, yet respected, confined to usage by the local group, and as far as possible insulated from neighbouring peoples. The Mowachaht showed a particular aptitude for commerce; they began to trade almost as soon as the ships entered the Sound, and continued until they departed. First the salmon-like explorers were treated to an appropriate welcome after momentary uncertainty, and then were invited to the shore:

The first men that came would not approach the Ship very near & seemed to eye us with Astonishment, till the second boat came that had two men in it; the figure & actions of one of these were truly frightful; he workd himself into the highest frenzy, uttering something between a howl & a song, holding a rattle in each hand, which at intervals he laid down, taking handfulls of red Ochre & birds feathers & strewing them in the Sea; this was follow'd by a Violent way of talking, seemingly with vast difficulty in uttering the Harshest, & rudest words, at the same time pointing to the Shore, yet we did not attribute this incantation to threatening or any ill intentions towards us; on the contrary they seem'd quite pleas'd with us.

The speech was probably part of a ritual attached to the welcoming of a visiting chief on arrival at a potlatch or feast. Later visitors, particularly traders, observed the same ceremony, frequently becoming irritated at the length of time that had to pass in this way before trading could begin. A minor but significant aspect of the welcome ceremonies was the interest by the British in the Indian music and vice versa. Although Cook, Lieutenant James King and others refer to the harshness of some of the songs, Cook also talks of songs sung as a 'peaceable amusement' having a very good effect. One evening King and others listened to a 'young man with a remarkable soft effeminate voice', who repeated his song several times because of the attention it received. In return a demonstration of European music was organized: 'As they were now very attentive & quiet in list'ning to their diversions, we judg'e they might like our musick, & we orderd the Fife & drum to play a tune... they Observd the Profundest silence, & we were sorry that the Dark hind'red our seeing the effect of this musick on their countenances'.

After a few days of contact, the Mowachaht lost their fear of the strangers and came on board to mix freely. Much trade, particularly in sea otter pelts, was relatively balanced – that is bargaining was conducted in a reasoned and affable

133. Eighteenth-century cedar-bark and nettle-fibre cloak, with wool and a large crest in the form of a long-billed bird painted in red ochre (?), with figures on either side that may represent helpers. W: 152 cm (59.9 in).

manner. But from a European point of view, the overwhelming power of Cook's expedition gave every advantage to the expedition should force be necessary. From a Native point of view, the loss of power in home territory was compensated for by the appropriation of European goods by what were seen by the expedition as trickery and theft. It was clear to Cook that trade relations between Native groups depended on questions of force and power. On one occasion they saw outside Native groups – who had come to trade – entirely stripped of their goods by the Mowachaht without compensation or complaint. It is often assumed that the explanation for Native theft of European goods relates to the communal ownership of property. Yet here everything was owned, and shared. The explanation of 'theft' is perhaps more to do with the absence of relationships of dependency and reciprocity between the Mowachaht and their neighbours. Non-Mowachaht people, whether European or Native, were there to be traded with and exploited, if and as the situation allowed.

From a Native point of view, one of the crucial aspects of relations with the Europeans was the control of their relations with the non-Mowachaht. At Resolution Cove Cook chose to anchor the ships away from Yuquot, so as not to impinge on Native affairs. This was on the borders of the territory of the Muchalaht, who occupied an area to the east and south. As Cook put it, 'It was evident they engrossed us intirely to themselves, or if at any time they allowed Strangers to trade with us it was...in such a manner that the price of their articles was always kept up while the Value of ours was lessening daily.' Furthermore, Cook noticed that the trade did not end with the Mowachaht, but spread out to include other neighbouring peoples.

The Native peoples of the west coast of Vancouver Island were intensely interested in the definition of property rights. However, these could not be exercised by the Natives except where their preponderance in numbers ensured compliance. This meant that for instance the wood and water, from apparently deserted places, seem not to have been paid for, although Cook would have accepted these demands:

134. Carved and engraved Nuu-Chah-Nulth or Makah amulet of bone or antler in the form of the head of a Lightning Serpent or Wolf, nineteenth century, acquired *c.*1868. L: 4 cm (1.6 in).

The very wood and water we took on board they at first wanted us to pay for, and we had certainly done it, had I been upon the spot when the demands were made; but as I never happened to be there the workmen took but little notice of their importunities and at last they ceased applying.

135. Mask of wood and human hair with eyes of mica set in spruce gum, and teeth of quills, collected in 1778 at Yuquot. H: 24 cm (9.5 in).

When Cook and the expedition artist John Webber visited Yuquot towards the end of their stay, they were both obliged to comply fully with the niceties of Native ideas of property. Cook decided to acquire fodder for the ships' animals:

Having a few Goats and two or three sheep left I went in a boat...the Moment we landed I sent some (men) to cut grass not thinking that the Natives could or would have the least objections, but it prooved otherways for the Moment our people began to cut they stoped them and told them they must *Makook* for it, that is first buy it... and there was not a blade of grass that had not a seperate owner, so that I very soon emptied my pockets with purchasing, and then they found I had nothing more to give they let us cut wherever we pleased.

More interesting still was the lesson learnt by Webber, probably on the same day, when inside a large communal house. Here, when of course he was entirely in Native territory, the painter found himself obliged to pay for the privilege of depicting the images at the end of the interior:

Afer having made a general view of their dwellings I sought for an inside which would furnish me with sufficient matter to convey a perfect Idea of the mode these people live in. Such was soon found; the people being employed in boiling their fish for a meal and seemingly appear'd without any displeasure at my being present… While I was employ'd a man approach'd me with a large knife in one hand seemingly displeas'd when he observ'd I notic'd two representations of human figures which were plac'd at one end… he soon provided himself with a Mat, and plac'd it in such a manner as to hinder my having any further a sight of them… I considered a little bribery might have some effect, and accordingly made an offer of a button from my coat, which when of metal they are much pleas'd with… but he return'd & renewd his former practice, till I had disposed of my buttons, after which time I found opposition in my further employment.

This excellence at negotiation survived well into the twentieth century. George Hunt (1854–1933), the Kwakwaka'wakw (but of English and Tlingit descent) consultant and collector for Franz Boas, noted in 1904 of the people of Yuquot: 'I never see any Body like these People for asking so a High price for there things as this People, for they say they can go to seatle or tacoma and get High Price for whatever they Bring there.' Yet there is a contradiction at the heart of this behaviour. The crucial element lies in the conceptualization of non-material rights, vital of course in Northwest Coast society, where the ownership of names, songs and performances is fundamental to the conduct of ceremonial life. In a paradoxical manner – particularly for a seemingly materialistic society – it may be the ownership of these ceremonial rights that matters more than possession of the paraphernalia through which they are expressed. In this way, then, it can be suggested that the materials collected by European explorers – stripped of meaning on acquisition – signify less to Native people today than do ceremonial regalia from later periods, which have survived with knowledge of the requisite privileges intact.

Collecting

Underlying the collecting reflex, then, there was no grand plan to acquire and preserve artefacts for a natural history cabinet. What Cook's expedition required was water, a mast and fodder for the animals. In scientific collecting it was natural history specimens that had priority. The casual and apparently inconsequential acquisition of Native artefacts occurred when, quite literally, other obligatory transactions had been fulfilled. Next to this the exchanges for furs and for natural and ethnographic curiosities were of minor significance. Yet, nevertheless, these exchanges occurred and a collection accumulated, unconsciously, and without design. Some materials were acquired as part of the process of testing and trading by the Mowachaht with the strangers. Just as the taunting of the British sailors with human flesh may have been designed as a Native experiment in defining European boundaries of taste, so some of the trade in artefacts was designed to exploit British naiveté and avarice. Best known was the occasion on which a performance was enacted with a bird mask that seemed to produce its own song. On 1 April a Native

today put up before his face an image of a bird's head & offered it for sale, at the same time shaking it up and down, while another person sitting by him applyed a small whistle to his Belly so as to collect the air by drawing the Skin round it & immitated in some measure the whistling of a bird; this being supposed to be done by some Contrivance raised the Value of it so much in the Eye of one of our collectors of Curiosities, that he immediately offered a very large price for it which was as quickly accepted…

Most other acquisitions of artefacts occurred by chance, during relatively close relations which pertained during the visit.

A second aspect of collecting was the purchase of materials for use by the crew. Mowachaht material culture was not held in contempt by the Europeans – it was appreciated and understood. Perhaps the best example of the use of a Native artefact was the occasion when an 'old North Briton of irascible spirit' broke a Native canoe down to the waterline in retaliation for theft. One of the officers, Molesworth Phillips 'who had that instant made a purchase of a bow & arrow from another Indian…let fly at the savage, with such good aim, that the arrow

136. *Chitoolth*, or whalebone club, inlaid with abalone shell from California (called 'Monterey shells') and collected in 'New Georgia' by Archibald Menzies in 1792–4. The best-known Nuu-Chah-Nulth weapon, the *chitoolth* was often carved, as here, with a Thunderbird finial. L: 57.5 cm (22.7 in).

past close to his ear, & called off his attention from the old man in the boat'. Of all materials brought away from Nootka Sound, perhaps the most important were the sea otter furs. These were collected, in theory, for protection against the severe weather expected to be encountered further to the north. But some of the crew, at least, were aware of the commercial possibilities of trade in these skins, which was later to render them so valuable in Asia. Most interestingly, while sea otter cloaks were collected in great quantity – perhaps 1,500 according to the American crew member John Ledyard – not a single example has survived in a European or North American museum, so that it is possible to say that the survival rate of collected artefacts was in some respects in inverse proportion to their utility for the crew of the expedition.

A great range of material culture was obtained by the crew in exchange for metal; beads and alcohol were rejected by the Mowachaht. The survival rate was best for weapons, of which numerous examples were collected and commented upon. The generic artefact from Nootka Sound – that which symbolizes the Native place and people – is the *chitoolth*, or spatulate club, surmounted with an eagle or thunderbird (fig. 136). This was carved from the dense jawbone of the large whales that were hunted during annual migrations to the Arctic. Other clubs combined wood and stone, and included pecked and ground stone basalt blades set as tongues in faces that were carved with exaggerated and sweeping features. A type of stone club, described in the nineteenth century as a slave killer and transformed in this century into a dance baton, consisted of a blunt wedged handle and finial carved with a bird or other crest. Metal, so much valued by the Natives, was also exchanged back to the explorers in the form of crescent-shaped knives of cold-hammered wrought iron, and also laminated iron and steel, possibly of an Asian origin.

More worthy of comment was the ceremony with which the explorers were greeted. The common feature of the welcome was a song performed by an individual of high status, who wore a conical basketry hat woven with scenes of the whaling, chanted and sounded a bird rattle, or *kuhmin*, carved from alder. It is not clear which species of bird were intended to be represented, but these may have included duck, gulls and cormorants. Performances of numerous masked dances were observed by the Europeans. Masks were noted and acquired,

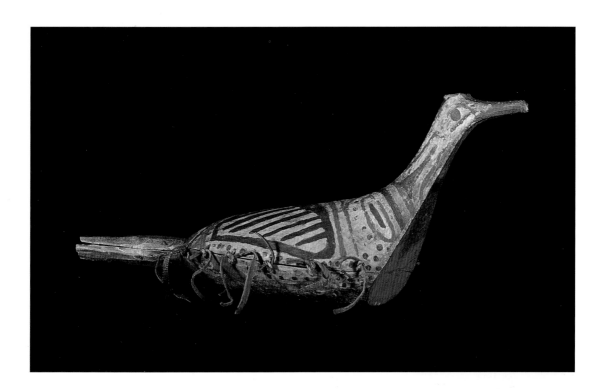

137. Eighteenth-century alderwood bird rattle in two halves secured with skin ties, of the kind used by people of high rank when greeting strangers or guests, such as Cook's expedition. L: 47 cm (18.5 in).

138. Eighteenth-century alderwood gull mask with flicker feathers and, inside, a rattle of small limpet shells which sounded when dancing, for use no doubt in the winter ceremonial. Gulls, favoured as pets, heralded the arrival of herring in the spring by shrieking, wheeling and diving over fish shoals, and so perhaps symbolize plenty. L: 37 cm (14.6 in).

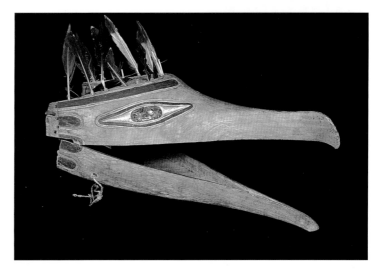

sometimes in a deliberate staged transaction, as with the bird mask above, or else in the aftermath of a ceremonial. Comments were appreciative, if not congratulatory, talking for instance of Native decorations: 'These consist of an endless variety of carved wooden mask[s] or vizors, applied on the face, or to the upper part of the head or forehead. Some of these

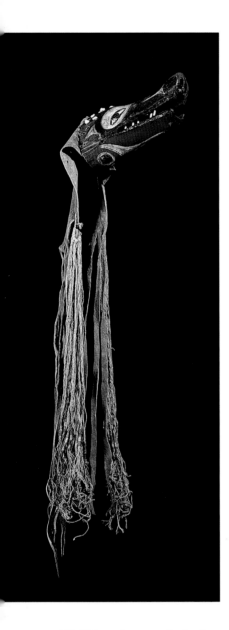

resemble human faces, furnished with hair, beards and eye-brows.' Speculation about their use was quite various: 'Whether these masks are worn as an Ornament in their Public entertain-ments, or as some thought, to guard the face against the arrows of the enemy, or as decoys in hunting, I shall not pretend to say; probably on all these occasions.' On several occasions at the beginning of the stay, on 31 March and 2 April, the ships were greeted with single chiefs in masks: 'The principal or indeed the only performer, appeared in a Mask, which was made of wood not badly carved & painted in the manner they generally do their faces, of these he had two expressing different Counte-nances which he changed every now & then.' Apart from the two or three bird masks, the only other zoomorphic mask was a wolf frontlet of cedar decorated in micaceous black paint with dentalium teeth, dentalium being an important form of wealth with some of the attributes of a currency.

Also collected were a dozen or so human face masks, which were carved of cedar and other woods and stylistically related to solid carved heads. These seem to have been brought down to Cook's cabin for a performance, probably on 22 April: 'At the time when the Captain prevaild on some strangers to ven-ture down into his Cabbin, they carrid down four wooden busts which they Placed in the Cabbin in a particular order, & also a carvd skreen work, that folded, & which stood up about the height of a fender almost all round the Cabbin…' Erna Gunther suggested that these heads may be related to the Kwakwaka' wakw *toogwid* or *toxuit* dance of the winter ceremonial (fig. 140). In one of these performances the female dancer taunts the audi-ence to kill her; this, as recorded by Franz Boas, involves an apparent beheading, which is achieved by a sleight of hand: the 'person who cuts it shows a carved human head bearing the

139. Eighteenth-century forehead frontlet of red cedar, with mica eyes, an elk-skin (?) strap with nettle-fibre ties, and dentalium-shell teeth. Such frontlets may have been worn by participants in the Klukwana, Shamans' or Wolf Dance, which was the central winter ceremonial of the Nuu-Chah-Nulth. L: 20 cm (7.9 in).

140. Wood sculpture representing a trophy head, with human hair, a skin strap for suspension and a joint underneath for fixing to a post or carved body. Warfare was in part conducted by clandestine raids with the intention of obtaining heads to bring back to the village for display. H: 33 cm (13 in).

141. Alderwood bowl in the form of a squatting woman, collected in 1778 at Yuquot. L: 26 cm (10.2 in).

expression of death which he holds by its hair. These heads are as nearly portraits of the dancer as the art of the carver will permit.' More general explanations for these heads of dead people may relate to the practice of taking trophy heads in war, and conversely also to the commemoration of high-ranking individuals.

Another group of carvings is stylistically related to the feast bowls acquired on the voyage. Most of these may have been collected at Yuquot on 22 April during the visit, already mentioned, made by Cook to obtain fodder for the animals. On this visit large housepost-like screens were sketched by Webber,

142. An alderwood bowl for drinking oil or water ceremonially, collected at Yuquot in 1778 and deposited in the Leverian Museum, 1780–1806. Two figures act as handles or supporters with open and grimacing mouths, and the bowl is decorated with vertical fluting, a design reserved for people of high rank. L: 20 cm (7.9 in).

giving rise to speculation as to their function, and particularly as to whether or not they were gods. Cook was not convinced: 'I am not altogether of that opinion, at least if they were they held them very cheap, for with a small matter of iron or brass, I could have purchased all the gods in the place, for I did not see one that was not offered me, and two or three of the very smallest sort I got.' Others, William Ellis and Lieutenant Charles Clerke, made similar comments after purchasing a 'variety of images in different attitudes' and noticing that the Natives have 'many small Images carv'd in various whimsical Attitudes'.

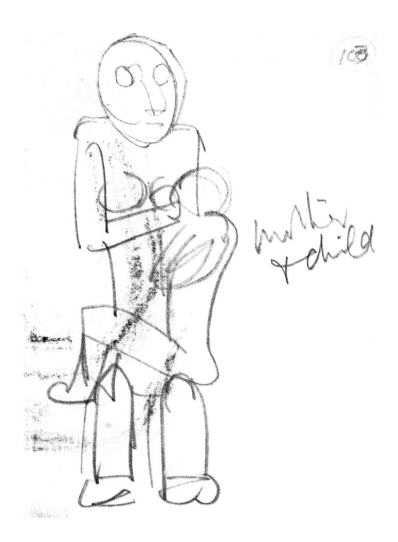

143. A sketch of a Nuu-Chah-Nulth figure by Henry Moore (1898–1986). Moore commented that the British Museum's ethnographic galleries contained 'an inexhaustible wealth and variety of sculptural achievement'.

144. One of a series of Mowachaht carvings collected in 1778 and later to become associated with Henry Moore's development of the mother-and-child theme. It was perhaps this example that he sketched. H: 28 cm (11 in).

figures are remarkable. There is a great feeling of maternal protectiveness but they are not at all sentimental. Look how one child has a finger in its mother's eye.

In a narrow sense, of course, Moore was appropriating Native ideas for the production of huge sculptures, created at vast expense to adorn the sculpture gardens of, for instance, museums of modern art, and the forecourts of corporate headquarters. This borrowing of Nuu-Chah-Nulth themes and values in Moore's work went unacknowledged, at least until the publication of the sketch from the 1920s by Alan Wilkinson in 1977. Yet in a very real sense, unbeknownst to the Mowachaht or to Moore's appreciative audience, Native values and Cook's collecting brought benefit to world aesthetics.

6 THE NORTHWEST COAST

Among the northern peoples of the Northwest Coast, the Haida, Tlingit and Tsimshian, Raven is the great fixer or trickster. Called Yetl by the Haida, he is the one who, while not strictly creating the world, transformed existing beings and places into those known today. In a Haida story earth is created by Raven out of dust on the ocean. For the Kitimaat in northern British Columbia the world was created by the Raven, Wiget, who flying over water could find no place to rest. So he dropped pebbles into the sea, and each one became an island. After land appeared, he created vegetation, animals, birds and fish. Finally, he wanted to create people but could not find the right material to do this: he tried everything, until eventually he

145. Bill Reid (1920–98), *Among the Raven and First Men*, 1980, monumental carving of the Haida origin myth in the Museum of Anthropology, Vancouver. The Raven has found a clam from which creatures emerge to create people. H: 200 cm (78.7 in).

The Northwest Coast showing the location of peoples mentioned in the chapter.

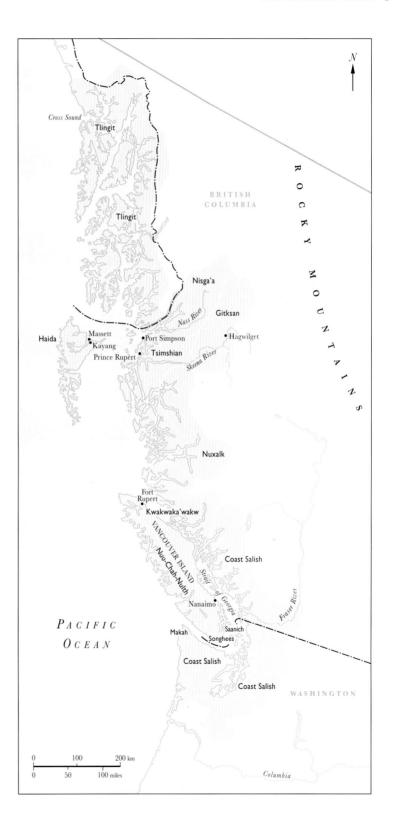

146. The Tsimshian Gerald Stewart (b. 1964) holding a speaker's staff in Bill Reid's canoe, *LooPlex*, at Clam Beach, British Columbia, 1990s. Reid was the central figure in the revival of Haida art in the third quarter of the twentieth century.

was able to make man and woman from clay and wood. For Bill Reid, the Haida artist who made a sculptural representation of the creation story, Raven finds a clamshell full of little beings when the flood recedes. These he forces out into the world, enabling them to procreate with chitons and produce the first people. A more general myth tells of how Raven created daylight, at a time when the world was in darkness, by seizing fire or letting the sun go, and frightening people into the woods and sea, where they became the animals represented by the skin clothing they wore.

The Northwest Coast is a thin stretch of land, crescent-shaped, 2,400 km (1500 miles) long and confined between the coastal mountain range and the Pacific Ocean, between California and Alaska. Archaeological research suggests that this lush coastline, with mild weather and rain forest, came to be inhabited more than ten thousand years ago. Gradually people, over many millennia, achieved specialized technical abilities to subsist effectively in the rich marine environment. Between about 4,500 and 2,000 years ago, the distinctive traits of Northwest Coast culture appeared, emphasizing particularly the year-round intensive exploitation of marine resources, first shell fish and then salmon. The abundant resources of timber and food are the product of a warm sea current and heavy rainfall. Together they have provided, until very recently, ample resources for what was

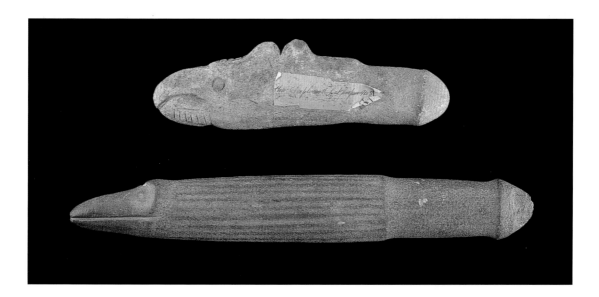

147. Two pecked and ground stone clubs originally from Tsimshian territory, one carved with what may be a fish, perhaps a salmon, the other with a bird head, perhaps a raven. Another example, from the Kitandach site in Prince Rupert Harbour, has been dated to AD 1–500. L: 25 cm (9.8 in), 38 cm (15 in).

one of the densest populations of any hunter-gatherer society. Apart from fish, shell fish and sea mammals, the land offered a great variety of foods – for instance more than forty species of fruit, such as huckleberry and salmonberry, and bulbs and rhizomes, including species of onion, fern and camas (the cambium, or inner layer of bark, was also eaten). Five species of Pacific salmon (*Oncorhynchus* sp.) may be caught as they run upstream deep into the coastal mountain ranges to spawn. These have provided a basic food supply for many millennia, once it had been recognized that a diet of pure salmon led to vitamin A poisoning. Salmon were trapped, speared and caught by trolling hooks. Other fish include steelhead trout, herring, sturgeon and vast halibut caught on recoiled hooks in the south and embellished hooks in the north; herring were collected with a spiked rake during spring spawning. Complementing fish and an array of molluscs were mammals such as deer and elk, and also marine mammals such as seal and sea lion, porpoise and, amongst the Nuu-Chah-Nulth and Makahs, the whale. As well

148. Elk-antler hand-adze (metal blade now missing) from the Columbia River region of Washington and Oregon, eighteenth or nineteenth century, collected before 1836 and carved apparently with bird and mammal spiritual helpers. This would have been used to make canoes, containers, and plank and beam houses. L: 25 cm (9.8 in).

as food, the forest provided abundant timber, particularly western red cedar for houses and canoes, alder and yellow cedar for other carvings, and bark for clothing and mats. Basketry was twined from split roots, for instance from the spruce, and from grasses and bark.

The superabundant food resources enabled a dense population to exist, connected to and organized along the waterways of the coast and major rivers like the Nass, Skeena, Fraser and Columbia. In winter Northwest Coast peoples lived in permanent village settlements away from the sea, moving out to fish camps in the summer to exploit resources as they became available seasonally. Villages were inhabited by kin groups or local residential groups, sharing common descent by lineage and/or clan. Most significant in social organization were principles of stratification and differentiation. Large villages, for instance, were divided into groups that effectively comprised chiefs or nobles, commoners and slaves, the latter captured in war. Status depended on the maintenance of wealth, through ownership of resources and through trade, and on the expression of position in potlatches, meaning literally in Chinook jargon 'give' but better translated as 'feast'.

Northwest Coast art, expressing status differentiation particularly through potlatches, provides easy recognition of this group of North American peoples, equalled elsewhere on the continent perhaps only by Plains and Southwestern peoples. Apparently simple tools – hand-adzes (fig. 148), chisels of jade or beaver teeth, basalt mauls or hand-hammers, and wood wedges – enabled the vast red cedar to be cut and coaxed into useful forms, including large canoes (fig. 146) and vast planks for building communal houses (fig. 158). Exquisite works of art – for use in feasting and performance at potlatches – were, and are, expertly carved. Potlatches have different foci: for the Tlingit and Tsimshian they are designed to mourn chiefs; for the Haidas, to establish the rights of the heir in the maternal line. This was also the case for the southern peoples of British Columbia. Among the Kwakwaka'wakw there is greater emphasis on the passing on of rights in dancing societies, in which initiates are symbolically seized by spirits who endow them with spectacular privileges. Common to these performances are the re-enactment of stories of contact between ancestors and the supernatural world, and the demonstration of

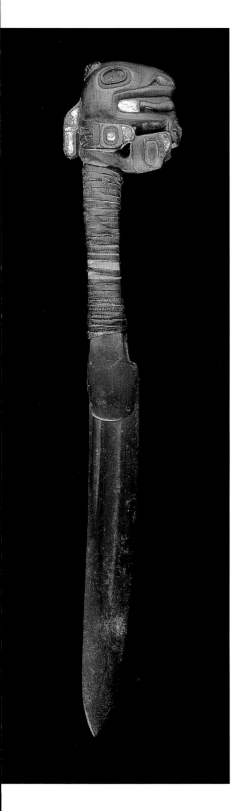

149. Northern Northwest Coast dagger with an imported European or American blade, nineteenth century. The wood finial is carved with a killer whale, inlaid with haliotis shell and consuming, or passing spiritual power to, a human figure. H: 41 cm (16.1 in).

150. Back view of a Tlingit wood-slat cuirass, or torso armour, collected on the Russian expedition of Otto von Kotzebue on the *Rurik*, 1815–18. The slats are twined together with sinew, with areas of wood left uncovered for abstract crests. H: 60 cm (23.6 in).

supernatural powers by the performers. Guests witness, and so in a sense make real, the ownership of these privileges, and for this may be paid or given goods.

Of all the aspects of Northwest Coast life, perhaps two or three related ideas are most important. First is the necessity for people always to show respect, for animals, for the natural world and particularly for elders. Only by observing and paying attention to their elder siblings, and parental and grandparental generations, would the young grow up to be competent members of their community. And only by showing respect for spiritual qualities of the natural world would raw materials be made available, whether food or wood. The late Peter Webster from Ahousaht, for instance, recorded how, when his father cut down a cedar for a canoe, he would talk to the tree as though it were a human being, asking it not to hurt him since it was going to be transformed into something of beauty and utility. Closely related to ideas of respect are those of purity, and particularly the necessity of attaining this symbolic state by abstinence, by ritual bathing and scrubbing, and by the singing of appropriate songs, all of which continue to this day. Respect is shown to food resources, particularly in the treatment of the first salmon of the season. Traditionally all salmon bones would be thrown back in the water, to ensure that they multiplied and that the fish returned. Prayers would be said, even to fish hooks: 'Hold on, hold on, younger brother.'

Art

Northwest Coast art is essentially an abstract style of applied design, adapted with highly variant meanings to three-dimensional objects. The basic characteristics of this art were defined by Franz Boas in his account of *Primitive Art* (1927), and refined by Bill Holm in *Northwest Coast Indian Art* (1965). Holm explored the intellectual nature of the art style, and effectively created a manual for use by artists. Boas characterized art with specific features. Central to the art is the use of physical aspects of animals – such as the head of a bear, teeth of beaver or the fin of a killer whale – to portray representationally a crest in an otherwise symbolic animal. The symmetrical representation of the animal is flattened and laid out so that all limbs are visible. This whole image then becomes available to wrap round a three-

151. Watercolour, 1859, by Montague William Tyrwhitt-Drake (1830–1908), showing a Coast Salish grave, probably Songhees, in Victoria harbour, Vancouver Island. The figure on the left perhaps represents a chief, and that on the right is performing an act of purification with animals, possibly minks.

dimensional object, such as a headdress or bowl. Some elements, particularly the head and tail, are given sculptural qualities, while others are painted, incised or outlined in low relief. Another characteristic is a *horror vacui*, the dislike of leaving empty space, particularly in two-dimensional artworks. These aspects of Northwest Coast art were codified by Bill Holm in the 1960s in a single set of practical principles, which he termed the 'formline' system of design. In this an abstract split design of a crest would be carved or painted on a box front, the outline in black, the secondary elements in red and occasional tertiary elements in green. While this was primarily a painted art, elements might be carved as boxes in low relief, and more rarely embellished with inlay. However, this provided a system capable of infinite variation, which could be adapted and spread across sculptural objects with an inventive freedom that could ignore the rules for two-dimensional forms.

A huge range of artefacts might be decorated with these designs. Most stunning are the big houses, the large multi-family

152. Two Coast Salish houseposts of cedar, collected by Edmund Verney and sent to England in 1863. Both posts are surmounted by owl-like figures, no doubt guardians, while the minks or weasels climbing the posts perhaps represent a purification ritual in which preserved animals were passed over a person. H: 3.5 m (11ft 6in).

153. Northern Northwest Coast chest with a telescoping lid of red cedar with shell inlay, nineteenth century, perhaps used for ceremonial paraphernalia. The central crest design is a bear with two-dimensional profiles on either side. L: 55 cm (21.7 in).

154. Haida or Tsimshian storage chest of yellow and red cedar, nineteenth century, with abstract painted and carved crest designs. The sides are constructed from a plank of wood. Cuts were made on the exterior for three vertical corners, and then steamed and bent so that the plank could be joined together with pegs or bindings at the fourth corner. L: 84 cm (33.1 in).

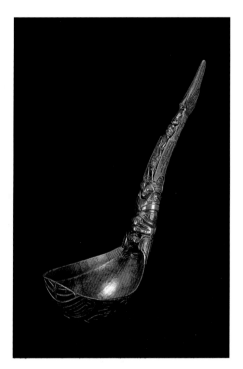

155. Haida ceremonial ladle of big-horn sheep horn, nineteenth century, British Columbia, for use at potlatches. The main figure is a large bear, whose head and paws – at the bottom of the handle – grasp the edge and whose body is spread two-dimensonally across the underside of the bowl. L: 53 cm (20.9 in).

dwellings, which might be painted with crests across the front, and have entrance doorways with large deeply carved and highly painted poles depicting stories of the occupants. These poles, misleadingly termed 'totem' poles, have nothing to do with totems, that is guardian spirits from the natural world, obtained by individuals in the Algonquian-speaking Northeast of the continent during spirit quests. Instead, the stories depicted on poles are inherited mythologies. Canoes are similarly decorated, as are the ceremonial paraphernalia for feasting. These include, for instance, large wood bowls and boxes, carved particularly of alder and used to serve salmon, other fish and, above all, 'oolachen', or candlefish grease, a thick butter-like condiment which enhances the taste of relatively dry smoked salmon. To serve this food, superbly carved wood and horn ladles and bowls would be used (fig. 155); the horn, which came from both mountain goat and big-horn sheep, was softened by boiling and carved three dimensionally with crests.

Clothing was limited, consisting of twined, shredded and usually spun cedar-bark garments, and capes and cloaks for the shoulders. These were occasionally decorated with formline designs, either painted, or created with admixtures of wool. This came primarily from the mountain goat, but probably originally also from dogs, although it is unlikely that any dog-hair blankets survive any more than there are 'Coppers'

157. John Gwaytihl at Massett (?) in the 1890s
with a different model of a house.

156. Painted wood Haida model
of the Bear House, Kayang, British
Columbia, carved for the
British Museum by John Gwaytihl
(*c.*1820–1912) in the 1890s, after the
original house had been abandoned.
The frontal pole recounts two stories,
including one about a hunter, his
mother-in-law and a whale.
H of pole: 85 cm (33.5 in).

158. Frame of the Bear House, Kayang, still standing in the late
nineteenth century; the frontal pole is now in the British Museum.
Such a house, this one the home of a lineage of the Eagle moiety,
was both a practical dwelling and the spiritual centre for the family.

159. Ivory walking stick finial in the form of beavers (?), carved by Charles Edenshaw (Tahaygen, d. 1920), perhaps the most famous Haida artist actively supplying the demand of non-Natives for Native artefacts. H: 7 cm (2.8 in).

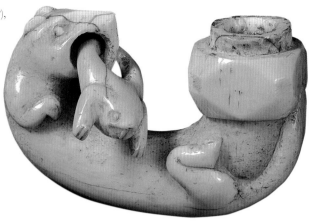

160. Carved and painted wood figure of a shaman, prepared for burial. A number of such naturalistic figures are known, perhaps all carved by Simeon Stilthda (*c*.1799–1889) from Yan for sale to collectors and missionaries. L: 57 cm (22.4 in).

161. (below) Nineteenth-century canoe model, Haida, painted with abstract formline crest designs. Technically and symbolically, such models share much with feast dishes, which were sometimes carved in the form of canoes. Seagoing canoes, up to about 21 m (70 ft) long, were vital for subsistence, trade and ceremonial activities. L: 160 cm (63 in).

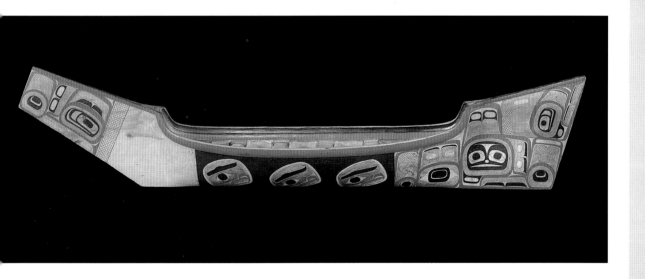

162. An eighteenth-century twined Tlingit robe of mountain-goat wool, with a pattern of white and brown diamonds crossed with yellow lichen-dyed stripes, and originally a line of sea otter skin at the neck. Sixteen of these early twined wool textiles are known from the northern Northwest Coast. 130 x 100 cm (51.2 x 39.4 in).

163. Coast Salish spindle whorl of maple, nineteenth century, used for spinning mountain-goat wool and carved with a bird of prey, carrying fish. Associated with textile production and therefore wealth creation, such images may have contributed to the process by both guarding and purifying the spinner as she worked. Diam.: 20 cm (7.9 in).

(see below) made of Native rather than smelted copper (fig. 175). Decorated twined wool textiles seem to have originated in northern British Columbia among the Tsimshian, with geometric designs derived from women's basketry. These ceremonial cloaks, originally also geometric, developed among the Tlingit in the nineteenth century into a single formalized style – the

164. Paul Kane (1810–1871), *Woman Weaving a Blanket*, 1847, watercolour showing a Coast Salish (Saanich) weaver sitting probably on a cat-tail mat, and wearing and weaving mountain-goat wool blankets. Dog fur was also said to have been used, although no surviving textile is yet known to contain it.

Chilkat blanket – in which the crests were taken from male painted designs. Textiles were complemented by furs. Although those of the sea otter were particular esteemed, many small animals were also used. Unfortunately, virtually no fur clothing has survived in museum collections, apart from a few textiles woven – in this respect only, like the hareskin clothing of the Subarctic – with strips of skin.

In terms of representation, elaborate decoration, social significance and cultural value Northwest Coast art matches that of any other, in North America and throughout the world. The revival in the art from the 1950s and 1960s onwards is partly due to the nature of the style, and the embedded social and aesthetic significance of ceremonial regalia. Surprisingly, then, many of the most valuable objects from an indigenous perspective are not necessarily the items that would have a high aesthetic value to an ethnocentric European sensibility. Instead, they have abstract qualities. Items such as eagle down and cedar bark are used in potlatches to bless and purify; they are sacred materials equivalent to the sweetgrass used in Native societies over much of the rest of North America.

The most significant of these abstract materials are Coppers, torso-shaped, shield-like sheets of copper, decorated with engraved, painted and domed or repoussé crests. In theory they are thought to have originated from riverine placer copper in Alaska – in practice all may come from sheets of smelted copper imported for trade purposes or as protective sheathing for the hulls of wood ships. On the northern Northwest Coast Coppers might be destroyed at potlatches commemorating dead chiefs. Among the Kwakwaka'wakw in the south, early in the twentieth century, they might be broken and mended at such events, each time gaining in value, up to thousands of dollars. Copper was believed by the Kwakwaka'wakw to bring light into world. Meaning 'red', it is symbolically associated with salmon, and smells like salmon, and through the colour is also associated with red cedar bark, blood and life itself. When placed the right way up in the sea there is daylight, and when upside down, darkness. In one myth the Sun comes to earth on a copper pole, the ancestors come down on copper ladders, and Raven's canoe is of copper, as is Thunderbird's house. Copper is light and can be used for curing. The Kwakwaka'wakw perhaps acquired the idea of the Copper (*tlaq*) from the Haida to the north, along with small amounts of placer metal. Coppers represent significant stores of wealth, categorized by personal name and with values running into thousands of blankets in the nineteenth and early twentieth centuries. These would be transferred between people of high rank at potlatches, for instance from a chief to his son-in-law, as the companion of the bride. At grease feasts – involving the competitive consumption and burning of oolachen, or candlefish oil – Coppers might be broken, or killed, to shame visiting lineages. Today, among some peoples, Coppers may not

165. Soapstone bowl dating to the Marpole phase of the Strait of Georgia Tradition, *c.*AD 1–900, washed up at Cowichan Bay, Vancouver Island, in 1895. This phase in the development of Northwest Coast culture is characterized by the appearance of substantial numbers of woodworking tools and artworks. H: 21.6 cm (8.5 in).

be broken, because that is equivalent to wanting the death of a rival chief. Until recently Coppers were killed with wedge-shaped stone clubs, known colloquially by their mid-nineteenth-century collectors as slave killers (fig. 174). At the centre of the concept of ownership of Coppers and other ceremonial objects there seems to be a paradox. The right to use certain names or crests is vested in individuals, clans or lineages with inherited positions. Only the use of masks or display of specific privileges by the owner is significant, and in this sense it is often the abstract right that overrides other considerations.

This artistic creativity is ancient. Earliest evidence for Northwest Coast art comes from the Fraser River region of southern British Columbia, during the Locarno Beach and Marpole phases, *c*.1400 BC–AD 400. Features of historic art, particularly round eyes with pointed lids, are seen on bowls (fig. 165). Also important at this period were skeletal details and abstract geometric forms, the combining of these features creating Northwest Coast art as seen at contact (fig. 173). The arrival of Europeans after 1774 brought an influx of metal tools – already known, of course, from trade and from the survival of metal on Asian shipwrecks brought to America on the swift Japan current. The inclusion of the Northwest Coast in the rapidly developing trade system brought metal tools for everyone, so that the carving of poles, houses and canoes, which may have been efficiently conducted with stone tools before, was speeded up, possibly allowing greater growth and elaboration of architectural and art forms.

166. Nineteenth-century mask used in the Kwakwaka'wakw winter ceremonial by the Nulthamalth, or fool dancer, an important figure who enforces correct behaviour. They are said to have very large runny noses and matted hair, and to hate cleanliness and order, despite their role in the potlatch. H: 22 cm (8.7 in).

On the southern Northwest Coast the main focus of ceremonials lies in series of rituals in which individuals of high rank are captured by malevolent spirits with cannibal or wolf-like characteristics, and then released by their families. This essential theme is endlessly elaborated, with sensational theatrical skills, and performed today, as in pre-contact times, in big houses, around flickering fire pits, with apparent tricks including the beheading of performers and the use of disem-

167. Nineteenth-century Kwakwaka'wakw mask representing Dzoonokwa, a child-eating giant of the forest, or Wild Woman of the Woods. Possessing pursed lips so that the dancer could frighten the crowd with cries of 'Ho, ho', she might, however, give young men supernatural gifts, such as a self-paddling canoe. H: 30 cm (11.8 in).

168. Nineteenth-century Tsimshian mask with articulated eyes and mouth, perhaps representing a bear, since facial hair is indicated by fur, apparently both from grizzly and black bears. This is probably a *naxnox* mask, signifying supernatural power associated with chiefly might. H: 54 cm (21.3 in).

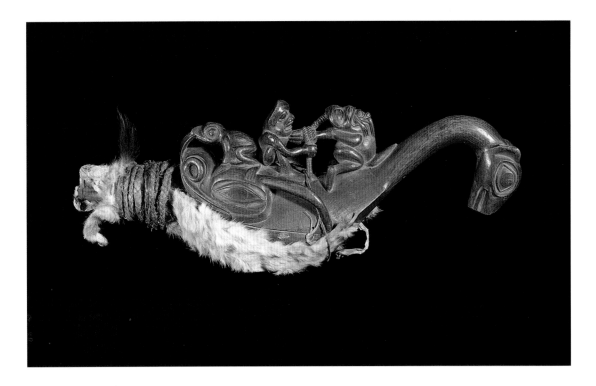

169. Nineteenth-century Tlingit shaman's rattle in the form of an oystercatcher (?) surmounted by the head of a mountain goat, with a frog on the back whose tongue is joined with that of the goat. A shaman is tying up a witch, from whose mouth a second frog emerges, probably representing the expulsion of the evil spirit. L: 35 cm (13.8 in).

170. A type of amulet known as a Soul Catcher, collected before 1867 and said to have been used by shamans to blow the soul of the patient back into the body. Traditionally assumed to be made from bear femurs, they are always carved with double heads, of esoteric meaning known only to the practitioner. L 19 cm (7.5 in).

bodied voices, costumes and vast transformational masks. In this ceremonialism Northwest Coast art was employed with more inventiveness and less formality than on the boxes and other two-dimensional flat surfaces. On northern Northwest Coast masks abstract designs sometimes cut across the features of the face, such as the mouth, symbolizing blood or food perhaps, breaking all the inherent formalized rules seen on two-dimensional artefacts. More constant is the three-dimensional treatment of the face, the smooth and realistic faces of the northern peoples, in comparison to the harsh, deeply sculptural forms, with the sharp intersection of angled planes, preferred in the nineteenth century in the southern part of the coast. And so it is often in the treatment of the face, rather than in the abstract design system, that tribal style is best identified. Of all the Northwest Coast art forms, perhaps the most

171. Three speaker's staffs from northern British Columbia, nineteenth century, of the type probably used by prominent individuals while speaking in a variety of roles; that on the right is carved with a Copper. L: 151 cm, 129 cm, 152 cm (59.4 in, 50.8 in, 59.9 in).

172. Claude Mark, Gitksan (Tsimshian) shaman, wearing a Soul Catcher and other paraphernalia including a horn crown, 1924.

malevolent, and yet captivating, is that created for Tlingit shamans in Alaska. Compelling effects are achieved by a highly plastic representation of human features, which are then distorted with the forms of spirits emerging, only to disappear or else be incorporated in the body of the mask and represented with distended mouths. A particularly disturbing feature includes the tormenting of witches or sorcerers, the process intended no doubt to force out the evil inside. These are shown especially on rattles used among the Tlingit in performances to cure an ailing individual (fig. 169). In these ceremonies elaborate necklaces or aprons of amulets would be worn, often featuring that most feared creature, the land otter, so much more important than the sea otter. Shamans were powerful figures, whose life required abstinence, and constant work with dangerous beings in order to fulfil the obligations of the craft.

European contact

Europeans arrived first from east Asia in the early eighteenth century, with Russian exploration culminating in the founding of the Russian-American Company fort at Sitka in 1799. Spanish exploration, from the south, began with the 1774 voyage of Juan Pérez to thwart other Europeans, while the British concentrated on finding the Northwest Passage and then, in unsuccessful competition with New Englanders, on the sea otter trade. Most significant was the voyage of George Vancouver in 1791–5, a much disliked martinet of a sea captain, whose lack of charisma was made up for by his exceptional abilities as a marine surveyor. He was accompanied by two scientists, Menzies and Hewett, whose collections partially survive in the British Museum. While the Spanish from 1789 attempted settlement, Vancouver remained in the boats at sea, continually sending out surveying parties, so that in three summer seasons, from 1792 to 1794, most of the coast from California to southern Alaska was mapped, to be engraved and published for all to use four short years later in 1798. Consequently, Vancouver's scientists, regarded by their captain with a healthy contempt, could collect opportunistically, particularly from Native trading, travelling or fishing canoe parties, encountered casually by surveyors. Native canoes would generally have had with them, of course, no ceremonial materials, but bows, arrows and small items of daily use. Most interesting of the symbolic materials collected by Vancouver, and commented on by every European explorer, were labrets, or lip plugs, worn from puberty by women of high status. While this feature was commented on as a reprehensible savage trait, and an indication of Native unworthiness, it was also expressive of more fundamental aspects of Native society, particularly concerning the role of women. Comments on labrets were combined with those expressing mystification at the prominence of female leaders in the matrilineal northern Northwest Coast societies, as evidenced particularly by the speeches made by women to Europeans from canoes. While the reality that nephews would succeed maternal uncles was not conveyed to explorers by the unaccustomed sight of Native women in leadership positions, they clearly understood that, at some level, these societies were radically different.

American traders, who arrived on the Northwest Coast only in 1788, quickly came to dominate the seaborne traffic with Natives in sea otter pelts. The price in China, which had been a few hundred dollars in the 1770s, was reduced by the beginning of the nineteenth century to $20 in 1802, when 15,000 pelts were exported; by 1829 the sea otter was virtually exterminated. And along with the staples of trade, metal tools and manufactured textiles came disease. Young Doctor recorded a Makah tradition that 'Boston Men' (Americans as opposed to the British 'King George's Men') buried bottles to lay claim to Neah Bay. The Makahs believed that they also buried disease, since anyone who went near the place became ill and died. The United States failed, nevertheless, to dominate the land fur trade, which from the 1790s was the preserve of Montréal-based independent traders, apart from the brief, unsuccessful venture of the American John Jacob Astor at Fort Astoria, on the Columbia, in 1811–13. Under a treaty of 1819 between the United States and Spain, territory north of latitude 42° was ceded to the US. So the vast area up to 54° 40′ was jointly administered by the United States and Britain until 1846, particularly by the Hudson's Bay Company, which, having combined with the North West Company in 1821, founded Fort Vancouver in what is now the state of Washington in 1825. Dominant on the West Coast through this period, the Hudson's Bay Company extended its remit by leasing southeast Alaska from Russia after 1839, in return for food grown on the Company's Oregon Territory farms. Ultimately this area between 42° and 49° became American, not because of the bluster of the presidential campaign of Polk in 1844 with the slogan '54° 40′ or fight', but because from 1841 overwhelming numbers of Americans streamed into the country along the Oregon Trail. It was this, rather than the American entering and naming of the Columbia River by Robert Gray in 1792 or the first crossing of the continent by Alexander Mackenzie of the North West Company in the same year, which determined the final disposition of the American Pacific Northwest. After the Treaty of Washington of 1846 the Hudson's Bay Company moved north to Victoria, which had been founded in 1843, but continued to lease the Alaskan fur trade from Russia until the 1860s. In the aftermath of Russian defeat in the Crimea, and the Hudson's Bay Company's refusal to purchase Russian America, this territory, now Alaska, was acquired by the United States in 1867. During this same period the colony of Vancouver Island was replaced in 1858 by that of British Columbia, which in 1870–71 agreed to join the Canadian confederation provided that a transcontinental railway was built.

Just as Oregon was populated by Americans, so during the 1850s and 1860s large numbers of Americans came north to the interior riverine gold-fields of British Columbia, which yielded large sums, often millions of dollars a year. Indians were affected in numerous ways, most catastrophically by the endless strains of new diseases which resulted in the further rapid decline of the population. With gold miners, coal miners and the administrators who replaced the fur traders came new technology. This ensured, for instance, the early disappearance of the Native textile industry in wool and cedar bark. Although disturbances occurred – both American and Native – there was little aggressive military activity. The Royal Engineers, for instance, were in British Columbia primarily for the surveying of the international boundary. The Royal Navy, established on Vancouver Island at Esquimault in Songhees territory until 1907, patrolled the coast and maintained peace to the overwhelming advantage of traders and settlers. Surprisingly, there are few naval collections in the British Museum, apart from one made in the 1840s and a second better-documented one presented without source in 1861 by Lord John Russell, the Secretary of State for Foreign Affairs. Much of this collection is documented to the Halkomelem, or Coast Salish, from around Nanaimo, at that time important for coal mining, since coal was required, for instance, for the Hudson's Bay Company ship, the *Beaver*, the first steamship in the Pacific.

If the Southeastern United States was colonized so that Europeans could use deerskin gloves and breeches, and the Subarctic so that people could wear felted beaver hats, then the Northwest Coast succumbed to satisfy the Chinese taste in sea otter furs. By the mid-twentieth century this had changed. From this point on, the Northwest Coast would provide Europeans with Native tinned salmon of the species colloquially called pink or humpbacked – least appreciated by Native and non-Native alike – and sheds of red cedar for European suburban gardens. From the point of view of collecting, the Native world was perceived through removed stands of carved poles. These were placed for tourists along railway lines and in public parks in Sitka, Alaska, for instance, and Stanley Park, Vancouver, as also at the British Museum. Equally popular were model totem poles, made for sale, with clan symbols and lineage stories if from British Columbia, and perhaps more often with shamanic concepts if Alaskan-derived. Today, though the salmon and forests are disappearing, new uses for primary products are continually being found. Most interesting is that for Pacific yew, *Taxus brevifolia*, the fine-grained, slow-growing timber which made superb Native bows and whaling harpoons, and is now believed to provide an efficacious essence in the treatment of cancer – truly a sacred wood.

Most significant of the cultural effects of colonization were those relating to the banning of the potlatch under Indian Acts passed in Canada between 1884 and 1951. Potlatching, deemed anti-capitalistic because of the gifting and destruction of food and other wealth, resumed in the 1950s, and was associated with a revival in art, particularly during the 1960s. The centres for this revival include the Royal British Columbia Museum in Victoria, where the Kwakwaka'wakw sculptor Mungo Martin worked; Hazelton in Tsimshian (Gitksan) territory, where the 'Ksan Association instituted a highly successful carving school; and Seattle, where Bill Holm's account of *Northwest Coast Indian Art* (1965) provided a

173. (below) A wooden grease dish or bowl in the form of an anthropomorphic figure with a human hawk-billed face, human feet and wing- or flipper-like arms, collected in 1787 by George Dixon on a fur-trading voyage, perhaps from the Haida at Kiusta. L: 26 cm (10.2 in).

174. (left) Pecked and ground basalt club carved with a human face, the eyes inlaid with abalone shell, collected as a 'dagger' at Fort Rupert in Kwakwaka'wakw territory during the 1860s. These weapons may also have been used to destroy Coppers, symbols of wealth whose value may have been counted in slaves. L: 23 cm (9.1 in).

175. A Kwakwaka'wakw chief, wearing a blanket decorated with an abalone shell-and-button representation of a crest and holding a Copper with repoussé decoration, Fort Rupert, 1894.

176. Kwakwaka'wakw wooden feast dish adorned with human (?) hair, collected by Edmund Verney in the 1860s from Vancouver Island. The large whale form supported by two human figures is no doubt representative of the host's mythic origins. The visible head may be vomiting, indicating the richness and quantity of the food. L: 76 cm (29.9 in).

177. Kwakwaka'wakw potlatch, Alert Bay, 1880s. A speaker on the pole construction to the left is calling out the recipients of presents, which were effectively given as payments for the witnessing of the privileges and position of the host.

178. (below) Kwakwaka'wakw potlatch figure of red cedar, British Columbia, nineteenth century. On arriving at a village for a potlatch, guests would be confronted by large anthropomorphic figures; some might emphasize the wealth and importance of the host through size and demeanour, while others, like this one, would caricature the features of the guests. H: 220 cm (86.6 in).

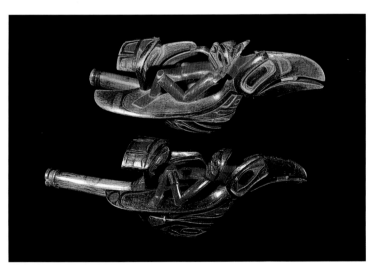

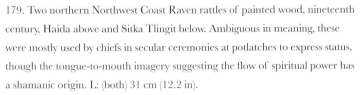

179. Two northern Northwest Coast Raven rattles of painted wood, nineteenth century, Haida above and Sitka Tlingit below. Ambiguous in meaning, these were mostly used by chiefs in secular ceremonies at potlatches to express status, though the tongue-to-mouth imagery suggesting the flow of spiritual power has a shamanic origin. L: (both) 31 cm (12.2 in).

primer for carvers and curators. Among the Haida, Bill Reid's work reinforced the carving tradition, and for the Tlingit, Nathan Jackson, associated initially with Carl Heinmiller's programme at Port Chilkoot, lead the way.

Collections from the Northwest Coast

Almost nothing from British Columbia was acquired during the period of high empire. Lord Dufferin, the Irish-born Governor-General of Canada (1872–8), was the first in that office to visit the province in 1876, acquiring carvings and other materials of which little remains. In 1885 a successor, Lord Lorne, visited British Columbia a few months before the completion of the Canadian Pacific Railway, but collected rather little. Lord Lansdowne, also Governor-General in the 1880s, seems to have been given two pairs of Haida masks, which were sold to the British Museum in 1947. In contrast to the Arctic, the Woodlands and the Plains, there was virtually no expression in England of imperial (or Native) British Columbia in commercial exhibitions or shows. British Columbia Natives were, however, quite frequently included in American exhibitions, particularly at the St Louis Exposition of 1904. The most enduring links, in Native terms, between the Royal Family and British Columbia came through the visit of the Duke of York, the future George V, in 1903, when he was given a Tsimshian frontlet, the only such item in the collection with secure documentation. Later, the Queen was presented with a carved pole created by Mungo Martin (*c*.1881–1962), the Kwakwaka'wakw, at the time of the centenary of the founding of the province in 1858. This is now in Windsor Great Park.

The main focus of the Northwest Coast collections this century has been the transfer to the British Museum of the accumulations of domestic collectors, such as Harry Beasley, acquired from smaller museums and descendants of administrators and other officials. The main exception to this should have been that of Sir Henry Wellcome, the pharmaceutical manufacturer and inventor of the tablet or pill; he wrote about and campaigned for the missionary settlement at Metlakatla, which fell out of favour in British Columbia and was transferred to Alaska. Wellcome's collection might reasonably have been expected to contain significant Northwest Coast materials, but only a few artefacts can be documented even to specific peoples.

A slightly different process emerged at the end of the nineteenth century under the leadership of Charles Hercules Read at the Museum. Nowhere else in North America was there more determined and competitive collection of Native art and material. From at least the 1870s American, German and Canadian professionals stripped, usually by purchase, the Northwest Coast of accumulated objects speaking of status and prestige. Britain was, by and large, not involved in this, apart from occasional efforts by Read at the end of the nineteenth century. A number of acquisitions were made by the British Museum from the Northwest Coast, with the deliberate intention of filling gaps, and of competing in a very minor way with the great North American, French and German institutions. Read corresponded with Charles Newcombe in Victoria, who supplied two or three items, relatively well documented, from British Columbia. Most significant was the pole from Kayang, which was purchased from Chief Wiyah (fig. 158). Originally, this pole was placed outside under the colonnade of the British Museum, only being brought into the centre of the North East Staircase after 1945. It is, with the Northwest Coast poles displayed in Washington DC, one of the best-known Northwest Coast artefacts. With this pole are two models: one is of the house (fig. 156) from which the pole would be taken, and the other is of a grave, which was supplied with a snapshot but not the name of the artist. In the 1890s Haida artists created a great range of explanatory materials for museums, to complement the heirlooms also sold in large quantities to collectors and museums. The only other artefact in the early collections by a known, in this case named, artist is an Egyptian sphinx. Carved by Simeon Stilthda in the 1870s from a woodcut in a missionary bible, this was acquired no doubt because of the virtuosity displayed in the creation of this serene and accomplished work. However, it does not represent any specific Egyptian sculpture. These few documented Northwest Coast artefacts were supplemented by a small number of additional documented artefacts, also collected by Newcombe, for the Royal Botanic Gardens, Kew, which were transferred in the 1950s. Most notable is a Haida door front, of cedar, from Tanu.

The Northwest Coast displayed

Exhibitions of Northwest Coast materials in Britain began in London in 1780, with the display of collections from Cook's Third Voyage in both the former Leverian Museum and the British Museum. George III visited the Leverian in 1780, the year of the creation of the South Seas Room, the locus in the British Museum for the collections from British Columbia and Alaska. No very substantial changes were made to the collections in the Museum, apart from the dismantling of the South Seas Room and despite the rebuilding of the premises in the 1840s, until the 1860s. Other institutions and exhibitions displayed occasional interest in the Northwest Coast. George Catlin, the American painter resident in London from 1840, is believed to have been responsible for the inclusion of a Tlingit figure at the Great Exhibition in Hyde Park in 1851 (fig. 284). It is not known where this came from nor where it went to. The 1862 International Exhibition at South Kensington included a 'Vancouver Island Court', which showed an unlabelled Tsimshian mask, and utilitarian items such as a halibut hook.

Exhibitions were regularly mounted by missionary societies for propaganda purposes and to raise funds. One of the earliest was a display in Manchester in 1870, which was recorded with drawings by A. W. Franks, and included two Coast Salish houseposts collected by Edmund Verney during the 1860s (fig. 152). A photograph of a missionary exhibition from the 1890s includes an extraordinary mixture of ill-sorted and badly displayed Canadian Native materials, including a wood carving of a dead shaman (fig. 160). This is part of the group of models, already mentioned, made in the nineteenth century for explanatory purposes. Missionary societies maintained collections for circulating exhibitions; clergy would dress up ethnically mixed materials to recount entirely false episodes of Native life. One of the most famous of these occasions was the 'Orient' exhibition in at the Royal Agricultural Hall, Islington, in 1909. One tableau featured the Northwest Coast sacrifice of a child – captured from Inuit – who was rescued at the last moment by a missionary.

While the British Museum display was without such dramatic and didactic performances, other institutions, particularly in London, showed more varied Northwest Coast materials, including the Imperial Institute, which held on loan the collection of Lord Bossom, an architect who built skyscrapers in the US during the first quarter of the twentieth century. American building regulations required that these be stepped back to allow light to the street. Bossom explained these designs by referring to the form of Mesoamerican pyramids. This interest in indigenous America extended to the accumulation of a vast Northwest Coast collection which was returned to Canada on the demise of the Imperial Institute during the 1950s. With the revival in Northwest Coast carving from 1980 onwards, artists such as Richard Hunt, Tim Paul and Nathan Jackson visited Britain and erected poles in Liverpool, Yorkshire and London. The most recent interest in Northwest Coast art was caused by British Airways, who, with their 1997 multicultural liveries for aeroplanes, included a design of a whale by the Clayoquot artist, Joe David (b. 1946). The first object attributed to the Clayoquot is a whaling hat, collected in 1792–3 during Vancouver's voyage.

7

THE ARCTIC

Through much of the eastern Arctic it is said that people were born of a woman and a dog, the woman sometimes becoming Sedna, the spirit of the sea and protector of sea animals. In a version of the story told by Uloqsaq, Copper Inuit, to Diamond Jenness, *c.*1915, the woman gave birth to Indians, white men and Inuit. In a differing Iglulingmiut (?) story, told to Knud Rasmussen by Unaleq, the first two men were created from an earth hummock; one man became pregnant and split open to give birth – everyone is descended from these two. In Alaska Raven is said to have created land and all beings that go with it.

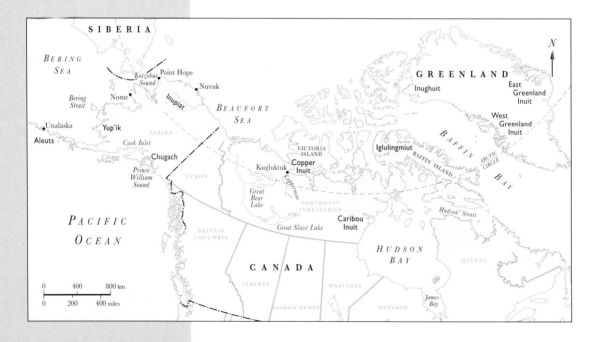

180. Nellie Hikok, Kugluktuk (Coppermine), Arctic Canada. The basic design of Copper Inuit clothing, with insets of white over the chest, has not changed since the first *amauti*, or parka, was collected during the 1850s from this nation.

181. Caribou Inuit drum, *qilaut*, with a bentwood frame and depilated caribou skin, collected in 1899. In the autumn and winter, after the main hunts, feasts and drum dances were held in a large communal snow house, featuring songs about hunting and travel or with satirical references to the abilities of others. L: 97 cm (38.2 in).

The Arctic showing the location of peoples mentioned in the chapter.

For archaeologists the early history of the Arctic, and especially of Alaska, is of particular importance, since it was across the Bering Land Bridge that the Americas were first populated 20,000 or more years ago. The cultural sequence is in the earlier stages analogous to that of the Woodlands area of eastern North America. From at least 12,000 years ago the Paleo-Arctic tradition saw big-game hunting practised over a long period when, as ice retreated, sea levels rose, and Pleistocene species of horse and bison became extinct. Between 8,000 and about 6,500 years ago the Northern Archaic tradition flourished, with more specialized tools, extensive fishing and the use of circular tents. Thereafter in Alaska a succession of very much more specialized cultures evolved, through the development of both seasonal and year-round hunting and fishing on the coast.

From around 4,000 years ago the Arctic Small Tool tradition arose on the coast, with fishing and caribou and seal hunting. It was people of this tradition who first moved eastwards through the Central Arctic to Greenland. Later cultures developed *in situ* in Alaska, while others were influenced from Asia. The Old Bering Sea tradition developed 2,000 years ago on both sides of Bering Strait, characterized by specifically Eskimoan technology. These features included the hunting of whales, walruses and seals with toggling harpoons; the use of the bow for caribou and bear, and multi-pronged spears for birds; and the use of the *umiak*, the *kayak*, the crescent-shaped *ulu* blade (by women) and the hand-drawn sled.

Most distinctive of the Old Bering Sea tradition is the curvilinear engraved art style, often incorporating zoomorphic features. Further to the north in northwest Alaska Ipiutak culture arose at around the same time 2,000 years ago, when ice conditions did not permit whaling. Ipiutak people were the first to use iron in Arctic Alaska, and created elaborate artworks, similar to those of the Old Bering Sea tradition, in a zoomorphic curvilinear style in ivory, which embellished utilitarian items such as snow goggles and harpoon sockets with features suggesting guardian spirits. At a principal site, Point Hope, evidence of some 600 houses has been found across raised beaches.

Once established in Alaska, Eskimoan cultures evolved through the internal

182. Copper Inuit *ulu* with a musk ox horn handle, Coronation Gulf, collected by P.W. Dease and T. Simpson in 1839 while exploring western Canadian Arctic shores. Of all Inuit tools, the crescent-shaped woman's knife, *ulu*, is perhaps the most significant, being used in most aspects of food and skin preparation. W: 29 cm (11.4 in).

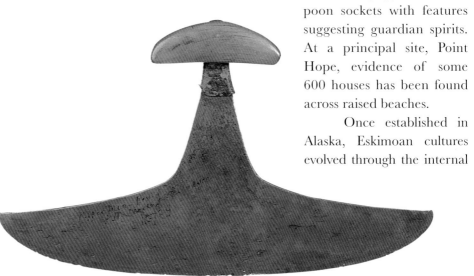

development of pre-existing technologies, external influences from Asia, and as a result of ecological change. The generalized Thule culture, arising between 1,000 and 2,000 years ago, balanced littoral and tundra hunting with exploitation of riverine resources. From north Alaska 1,000 years ago Thule people spread rapidly, over a few centuries, across the Canadian Arctic and Greenland. There Thule culture supplanted and/or incorporated the surviving Dorset peoples, descended from migrants of the Arctic Small Tool tradition, who were the first inhabitants of the central and eastern Arctic thousands of years previously. The people of the Thule culture were the ancestors of the Inupiaq-Inuktitut peoples, speaking mutually intelligible dialects of a common language and living today along the contemporary Arctic shore between Bering Strait and east Greenland. Eventually in most of the Canadian Arctic and Greenland the traditional Thule pursuit of whaling disappeared. Many elements of Thule culture, however, were also shared with the other main Eskimoan peoples, the Yup'ik speakers of both sides of Bering Strait and most of southwest Alaska, although Yup'ik and Inupiaq-Inuktitut are separate languages. The Aleuts, on the Aleutian Islands, also speak a distinct Eskimoan language, while sharing some cultural elements with other Arctic peoples.

Today there might be perhaps 200,000 Native people in the Arctic, most of whom live in Alaska, along thousands of kilometres of coastline largely beyond the tree line. In winter the sun disappears in December and returns in January leading to a prolonged period of spring, a frozen world with twenty-four-hour daylight which lasts until June. Then the ice breaks up for a brief summer, with night-time gradually returning. For both historic and contemporary Inupiat-Inuit the prime and most important subsistence activity is the hunting of seals, particularly ringed seals. These provide meat, and vitamins from liver, that would be otherwise unavailable. Perhaps most significantly seal oil was the main source of fuel for warmth. In the eastern and central Arctic oil would be pounded from seal blubber and pooled in the shallow crescent-shaped soapstone bowl, *qulliq*. Along the flat edge a line of dried moss serving as a wick would be carefully tended to provide both light and heat. Above this would be suspended a further bowl for cooking, and drying racks, all essential for the maintenance of dry clothing for hunting.

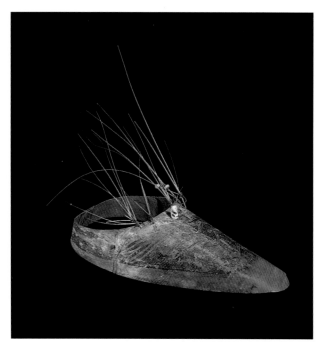

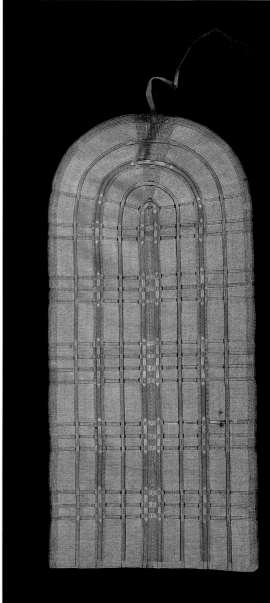

183. Painted bentwood Aleut hunting visor, decorated with sea-lion whiskers, wire-wound glass beads and ivory carvings; it was included in John Webber's portrait *A Man of Oonalashka* [Unalaska], October 1778, from Cook's Third Voyage. Such helmets protected the eyes from the glare and spray and also possessed an amuletic significance. L: 42.5 cm (16.7 in).

184. (right) Mat collected on Cook's Third Voyage, probably at Unalaska, 1778. In the eighteenth century Aleuts lived in communal semi-subterranean houses up to 61 m (200 ft) long, whose walls and shelves were lined with skin and matting of exceptional fineness twined from wild rye beach grass. L: 102 cm (40.1 in).

185. (left) Nineteenth-century wooden grease bowl, Alaska, transferred from the Royal United Services Institution Museum to the Christy collection before 1868. In the form of an unidentified, Chugach (Eskimo) mythic creature, it is, however, carved with Northwest Coast Tlingit design elements including ovoids and U-forms. L: 30 cm (11.8 in).

186. (right) Chugach twined split spruce-root hat, collected in Cook Inlet on Vancouver's voyage from a Chugach chief, possibly either Chatidooltz or Kanistooch, who were first encountered by the expedition on 26 April 1794. In Northwest Coast style, it has an abstract painted crest and an admixture of hair to the rings. H: 31 cm (12.2 in).

187. (below) Model Chugach *baidarka*, collected in 1794 by Archibald Menzies on Vancouver's voyage. Kayaks were used throughout the North American Arctic and also in eastern Siberia for hunting sea mammals; the Aleuts and the Chugach, uniquely, constructed a two- or three-man vessel, the *baidarka*, for transportation. L: 84 cm (33.1 in).

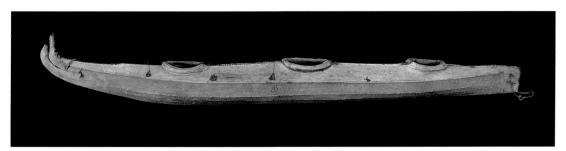

188. Nineteenth-century Aleut *kamleika* of split sea-mammal gut, decorated with skin strips and hair. Such waterproof garments, widely appreciated by European explorers as more effective than their own, are sewn with grass and sinew which swells on becoming wet, rendering the seams waterproof. W: 168 cm (66.1 in).

Many different strategies are used in the hunt for seals. They may, for instance, be obtained by stalking in the spring, as the animals bask on the ice ever alert for bears and waiting by their breathing holes. The hunter would move along the ice mimicking the actions of the seal, or in Greenland move forward hiding behind a small sled covered with a white blind or shield. Most famous and perhaps once most common was hunting actually at the breathing hole. Seals maintain systems of holes through thick ice. The hunter might build a shelter round the hole, at the bottom of which he would fit an indicator consisting of a piece of bird or animal fluff. He would then wait until this moved, indicating that the seal had returned to the hole and exhaled stale air, before striking. The draught of smelly air which would rush out of the ice was compared by the Iglulingmiut Victor Aqatsiaq, in 1987, to the hot blast of air that comes out of the tunnel when a London tube train approaches the platform.

In sea mammal hunting the harpoon is used, with a detachable shaft and a toggling harpoon-head. This is a barbed point which, on entering the animal, would catch and swivel sideways, so that the line would hold as the hunter hauled in the prey. Later in the year hunting took place from kayaks, from where the harpoon was launched with a 'throwing stick', an effective levering instrument used throughout much of the pre-contact Americas to create projectile propulsion. While the harpoons would ideally be made of wood, in the eastern Arctic, where drift wood could be an extremely rare commodity, narwhal tusks might be used. A single tusk would be honed down to a long smooth point or even, *in extremis* for the Inughuit, constructed from lengths of broken tusks tied together to form a serviceable tool – for use on land, of course, since on water they would sink.

Today Inuit continue to hunt from the edge of ice in the spring. While rifles are used to kill seals and walruses, the harpoon remains vital. Animals sink quickly, because after the end of winter they no longer have blubber to hold them up, so it is necessary to plunge a harpoon attached to a float (now usually rubber buoys) into the beast before it disappears beneath the surface. Walrus and large seal, the bearded seal particularly, are hunted in similar ways to provide thicker skin for boot soles and boats. Hunting walrus remains an enormously hazardous business in which originally the great rich beasts resting on ice were stalked from the sea in flimsy skin-covered boats. This perilous activity is amply rewarded with many kilos of sweet-smelling flesh, destined for dogs and humans alike. Beluga, or white whale, and narwhal are much appreciated for yielding succulent vitamin-C rich skin. But most precarious of all is the hunting of the giant bowhead whales. This continues today particularly in northwest Alaska by *umiak*, or open boat. The *umialik*, or leader, strikes the whale first, attaching bladders to tire it, and then despatches the creature by the severing of internal organs near the flipper.

The other animal vital to Inuit is the caribou, the deer which during the inland summer hunt provides meat and the furred skin essential for winter survival. One means of hunting caribou involved the communal stalking of animals driven on occasion between man-like figures built of dry stone and called *inuksuit* in Inuktitut. The bow, of drift wood, antler or horn, is Asiatic in origin, shared like the kayak with peoples of eastern Siberia. Another preferred method of hunting depends on driving caribou across rivers or water. The slow-swimming animals could then be despatched from kayaks with knives or lances. In the spring the diet is supplemented with eggs from migrating fowl, hunted until recently with elegant multi-pronged spears further fitted with clusters of barbed ivory prongs to pin the wings of duck and geese when launched into thick flights of the birds. Fishing, like other subsistence activities, is traditionally also conducted with sophisticated tools similar in concept and design to those of other Native communities. Most notable of these is the leister, or *kakivak*, a spear with a Y-shaped head which traps the fish on a point and between barbed arms. A number of taboos circumscribe hunting, and the preparation of caribou clothing, which must be created on the land during the autumn and before setting out on the winter sea ice. Similarly, sea mammal bones must be left in the element from which they came, thus ensuring the return of the animals.

In all of these activities transportation and travel are the vital components. In summer much travelling consisted of walking inland to caribou feeding grounds to obtain the vital end-of-season skins for winter clothing. Summer travel, and spring hunting from the floe edge, were also undertaken in large boats, the open *umiak* or woman's boat and the closed kayak. The

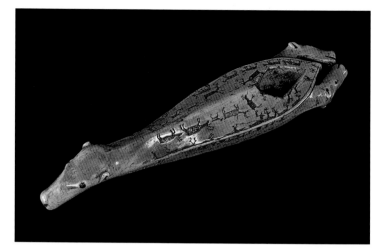

189. Nineteenth-century Inupiat ivory toggle, Alaska, in the form of a seal coming up for air. In the lower depiction the animal is shown swimming to the surface, while in the upper carving the seal is surrounded by ripples on the water surface. L: 11 cm (4.3 in).

190. Fossil mammoth-ivory arrowshaft straightener, Alaska, nineteenth century. Engraved with scenes including the hunting of geese and of swimming caribou, it is also carved with three caribou heads – caribou were principally hunted with a bow. L: 18 cm (7.1 in).

191. Model of an open, *umiak*-style Inupiat boat of skin and wood, of the type still used extensively in whaling. Collected on the Colville River by Richard Collinson on HMS *Enterprise*, 1850–55. L: 120 cm (47.2 in).

192. Inupiat dog-sled of wood, bone and baleen, collected at Nuvuk, or (Point) Barrow, by Rochfort Maguire on HMS *Plover*, 1852–5. The high bed of this type of Alaskan sled keeps soft snow and rough ice away from occupants and protects boats when being carried to the floe edge. L: 250 cm (98.4 in).

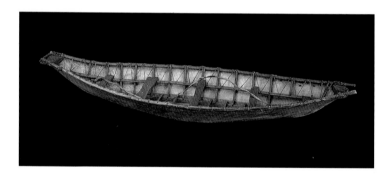

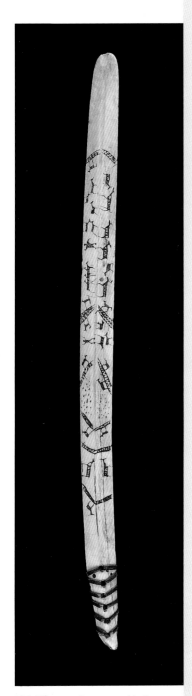

193. Nineteenth-century Alaskan snow knife with a baleen binding as a grip. The engraved scene shows caribou being driven through breaks towards a hunter. L: 42 cm (16.5 in).

kayak is constructed on the same structural principles as the violin or aeroplane – a light structure covered with a taut skin. Whereas an aeroplane skin is mechanically stretched over the plane structure, the kayak skin is pulled manually onto the drift wood structure before drying, and lightly bound with strips, for instance, of whale baleen, the very material used in nineteenth-century corsets and called whalebone. The sophistication of this vessel can be seen in several aspects of its construction. The bow, particularly in Alaska, was adapted for use at sea; in one instance, in southern and southwest Alaska, the Aleut and Pacific Eskimo used bifid or pronged prows, split to dissipate the sideways force of waves. In covering the kayak with the shaven skins of bearded seals, great care would be taken to orient the skins so that the remnant hair follicles pointed away from the water flow. This would minimize any ripples that might alert seals. Similarly, the double seaming of the skins was always finished with the seam line facing the stern – to avoid that small possibility of an extra ripple that might alert an animal.

From the sixteenth century onwards European whalers and explorers in the Arctic encountering Inuit on the sea brought them south, often by force, to perform in their kayaks for royal and other audiences, and most often to die of diseases for which they possessed no immunity. The kayaks were occasionally preserved in churches, particularly in Germany and the Netherlands. Of all Native vessels, the kayak is that most copied and manufactured in North America and Europe, both for recreational and for military use.

Dogs, dog teams and sleds constitute, like kayaks, a series of elegant contrivances for rapid transport through most of the year. While often built of wood, sleds could also be created from carefully bound and sewn pieces of whale, bear bone and ivory, tied together with seal thongs. In emergency the runners might be formed from rolls of fish wrapped in skin, frozen upright. Water, mud and ice were used to glaze the runners, which would then be scraped and polished to reduce the friction to a minimum. Before contact with Europeans whalebone or ivory was used for shoes on the runners of permanent sleds, while today nylon is employed. Nylon rope is also used on the enlarged sleds of today (pulled by skidoos, or snowmobiles, with tank-like tracks), and they continue to be flexible enabling the structure to survive the constant buffeting of movement over uneven terrain. The dog teams, hitched in a fan arrangement in the east and in parallel or tandem lines in the west, required their own specialized equipment, including, inevitably, beautiful ivory attachments, and harness and traces of bearded sealskin. In rough spring ice simple 'kamiks', or boots, consisting of rectangular flaps of skin with holes for claws and ankle ties, would be provided for the dogs.

While dogs were vital for survival before the general use of snowmobiles from the 1970s, they required an enormous expenditure of labour. Most significant was the necessity of obtaining food, which, particularly during the cold seasons, required regular hunting to provide meat. The creation of dog harness and traces requires concentration and effort. The long thongs must be carefully cut and prepared to avoid splits and tears, which would severely weaken the harness. And dog harness also required regular daily upkeep, including particularly the chewing and softening of the harness before departure every morning. Today the wild animal populations required for the upkeep of dogs are spared losses; but *in extremis* dogs could always be eaten, an option not open to those stranded nowadays because of the breakdown of mechanical transportation. Dogs, however, still provide good skin for use on boots and as parka trim, being treated as beasts of burden rather than anthropomorphized creatures in Euro-American culture. Today Arctic dogs are exported to Europe as pets, often termed Malemiuts after the Inupiaq from Kotzebue, Alaska, rather than 'huskies'. 'Husky' is originally a Canadian corruption of Eskimo, and was used in reference to people.

Houses

The Thule people in the western Arctic were based seasonally in large villages with multi-chambered dwellings. A degree of social stratification existed based on the hunting, and specifically whaling, abilities of leaders. Similar communities arose in Arctic Canada and Greenland during the Medieval Warm Period. Because of the absence of drift wood compared to Alaska, large houses were built in Canada with the ribs and mandibles of the Greenland whale, the eastern Arctic equivalent of the bowhead whale hunted in Alaska. Semi-subterranean houses of turf, the *qarmaq*, continued to be used well into

194. Contemporary snow house at Igloolik, Northwest Territories, of the type used on hunting expeditions. John Ululijarnaat, Inuit, finishing off the exterior with a knife, is wearing spring clothing including waterproof depilated sealskin boots.

this century, and indeed similar structures are still employed in a few places such as Point Hope, Alaska, as cold stores for food. The ability to trap warmth is, of course, the determining factor in the creation of homes and houses. Both turf dwellings and snow houses employ long low entrances, so that warm air is trapped in the roof of the building.

The snow house, or in an eastern Arctic dialect, *igluviga*, is the feature which most often represents the north, *iglu* itself quite simply meaning 'home'. Snow houses as represented in advertising, or in dioramas and ivory models in museum collections, epitomize the exoticism of the north. They are often shown as hemispherical structures, unstable forms suggesting a negation of standard architectural design. But in fact the reality is quite the reverse. Built of spirally ascending snow blocks, the snow house is formed, like a continuous piece of orange peel, into a parabola rather than a hemisphere, which would of course collapse. Indeed, such is the fascination for the 'igloo' and ice that the most frequently repeated public query about North America at the British Museum is the number of Inuktitut words for snow. One answer is the 107 terms for snow and ice recorded by the Nunavut Research Institute in 1989. For a snow house the blocks must be cut from hard wind-packed snow sufficiently compact to be moved, but soft enough to be cut. Originally, the tool used for this job was a graceful curved knife, *panna*, of split walrus ivory. This would be fitted with sinew- or skin-sewn handles of whalebone or antler whose porous nature

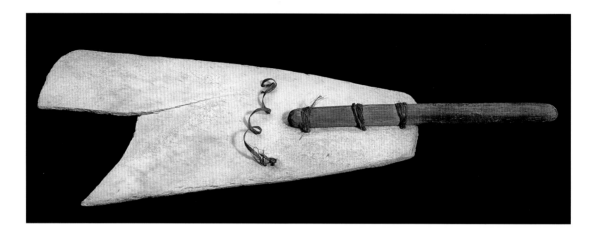

195. A nineteenth-century central Arctic snow shovel, carved from a whale scapula with a wood handle and baleen grip. Such tools were used for removing and banking snow on and around snow houses to provide additional insulation.
L: 77 cm (30.3 in).

provided a grip that contrasted with the slippery surface of the ivory. The edge of the blade would be further enhanced with a coating of ice. Once cut, the hard blocks of snow can then be fitted or faceted together using the knife to slice between blocks. Air is trapped in the hard-packed snow within the block, and in the house itself, which is entered from below, through a tunnel. Ventilation is provided through a hole at the apex of the building. The heat inside, from people and from seal-oil lamps, causes the walls to melt and re-freeze sealing the interior. The temperature might thus only rise to freezing point. During construction of the snow house the floor is excavated, leaving a

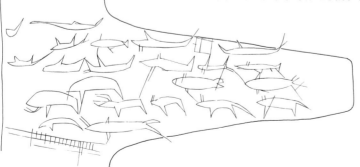

196. Engraved drawings of animals and kayaks, of amuletic significance, on the antler shaft of a Caribou Inuit man's knife, *panna*, collected in 1899. Such a knife is vital for cutting snow and for butchering animals.
L: 49 cm (19.3 in).

semicircular sleeping platform opposite the door. A porch for food is added, and windows are created from panes of clear freshwater ice. Unlike tents or regular more permanent buildings, snow houses, once they became dirty with soot, old food and the rest, could simply be abandoned. They would then be replaced with other homes, built in an hour or so, as they are still by people out hunting. In the spring the snow house may be tented on the inside, providing both protection from moisture and further insulation. In the summer tents of sealskin or now canvas are used on the land. They are also employed particularly by women in settlements for sewing, since humidity is required for the maintenance of skin flexibility outside the dry environment of contemporary central heating.

Clothing

Clothing is perhaps the supreme achievement of Arctic peoples, the vital design system on which all survival depends. Most important in all of this is the production of fur clothing for use in the winter and spring, and particularly the creation of footwear to protect the feet. Warmth, specifically hot air, moves like a liquid but upwards, so at all times it has to be trapped to provide insulation. Hunters achieve this by wearing two layers of caribou skin, one with the fur turned inwards to the skin, and the second with the fur turned outwards. So air is held between the body and the two layers of skin. At the hood the edge is finished with a ruff or fringe of fur from animals such as wolf or wolverine whose glossy hairs allow the accumulation of ice, from breath and snow fall, to be shaken away. On the feet, during the coldest part of the year, the same principles apply. Caribou skin is used because the hollow hair follicles trap insulating air. At wetter times of the year – in autumn, spring and summer – sealskin is used, depilated and oiled to provide waterproof boots, the favoured material for soles coming from bearded seals. The most notable aspect of boots is the pleating or crimping at the toe and the heel, the carefully folded material held in place with internal stitching. This avoids piercing the exterior, because that would allow moisture and cold into the boot.

Other skins, across the Arctic, are employed in great variety, both for decorative and more importantly practical

197. Drawing by Edward Adams, Assistant Surgeon on HMS *Enterprise*, showing a Copper Inuit man in 1851–2 on Victoria Island wearing a loon-bill dance cap with amulets, indicative of hunting prowess, hanging down the front of his parka.

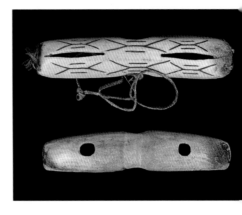

198. Two pairs of nineteenth-century antler-rind snow-goggles, Iglulingmiut and Copper Inuit. William Parry, the Arctic explorer who collected the lower pair in 1822, understood their importance and equipped his men with Inuit goggles to prevent snow blindness. W: 12 cm, 12.5 cm (4.7 in, 4.9 in).

199. Copper Inuit man's (?) dance cap, *c.*1900, sewn with strips of contrasting caribou skin and surmounted with a loon bill and ermine skin. Such headdresses were worn by influential Natives during the drum dance, in which the loon featured because of its remarkable song and courtship display. L: 24 cm (9.4 in).

200. Drawing of the burnt decoration around the eye slits of a pair of Caribou Inuit (?) wood snow-goggles, Keewatin, 1899, including scenes of hunting swimming caribou from a kayak, and using a bow and arrow. W: 12 cm (4.7 in).

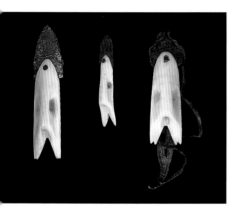

201. Three ivory harpoons, collected in 1738 in Hudson Strait, with riveted iron and steel blades, the metal obtained from fur traders or whalers. The smaller harpoon head would have been used for ringed seals, while the larger examples would have been suitable for bearded seals and walruses. L (max.): 18 cm (7.1 in).

202. Watercolour by John White of the Inuit mother and child kidnapped by Martin Frobisher and brought to Bristol in 1577. The basic form of the *amauti*, with the child in a warm capacious hood, remains unchanged today.

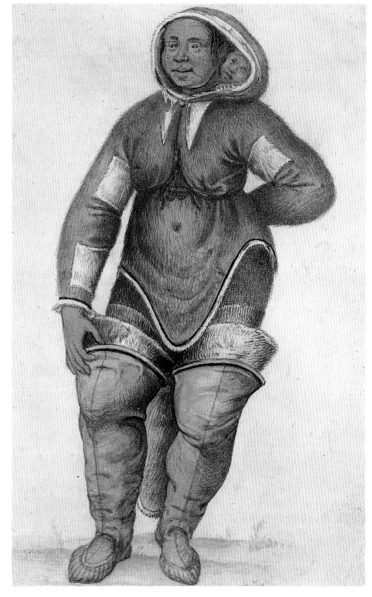

purposes. Most interesting are the materials employed for lightness, such as birdskin, and those included for waterproofing qualities. As has already been mentioned sealskin was used for waterproof footwear, but most ingenious was the use of sea mammal gut (fig. 188) sewn in strips to make parkas. From the eighteenth century onwards these were considered more effective than the European equivalents and are still preferred, for instance, by the Yup'ik-speaking peoples in southwest Alaska. Salmon skin is also used, particularly in Alaska where, cured, it provides a material appropriate for mittens and for tough but soft storage bags.

Women's clothing employs the same principles as men's, although with varied tailoring. Most significant is the *amauti*, or parka, with a capacious hood, fitted with an expanded space to carry a child. It has the additional feature of ample space across the back – giving the appearance of winged or padded shoulders – so that a child can be brought from the back to the front for nursing, without needing to leave the warmth of the mother. Another important aspect of women's clothes was the extension of leggings to create pouches for carrying items such as sewing materials. In Labrador in the eighteenth century it seems that boots were extended with a similar-shaped area as an *amauti* for carrying a baby. In many parts of the Arctic, skin clothing has today been replaced by manufactured clothing, although the design of parkas, particularly the *amauti* for women, remains basically unchanged. Skin-sewing traditions flourish for the production of particular articles such as waterproof boots, which remain more comfortable than manufactured equivalents for hunting, and caribou-skin outer clothing. When travelling on the land caribou skin is more effective against the cold than down-filled jackets, since the latter may settle into compact lumps and freeze when wet from snow and sweat.

Tools

In all of this the essential vital tool is the needle. Initially made of ivory from, for instance, the hard outer edge of a young walrus tusk, it was the implement most quickly supplanted in the Arctic as elsewhere with a metal replacement. Whether of ivory, iron or copper, needles were traditionally highly valued and so protected in carved ivory tubes, into which they were pulled on skin thongs. The *ulu*, or crescent-shaped knife, used for cutting and scraping meat and skin, remains the vital woman's tool, complemented by a variety of scrapers designed for removing fat or hair.

Many of these tools are of great tactile quality, with a plasticity of form and a deceptive simplicity of function. Men's tools include most particularly the crooked or curved-blade knife for carving, and the mouth-held drill. This last, one end held in a mouthpiece, is driven by a bow whose string, wound round the drill, is moved laterally. In Alaska the tradition of using engraving tools, particularly the drill bow, to depict hunting and other scenes flourishes, as do various sculptural schools, many associated with carving from ivory. Some of these western Arctic sculptural traditions relate to the creation of figures of amuletic significance, for instance for adorning hunting visors. In the eastern Arctic amulets might more often be formed from animal parts, such as bones, claws or beaks. Figures of humans might be employed particularly as dolls and used not as playthings but as models for the development of girls' sewing skills. In all of these things technique, though of course vital, is always insufficient without ritually appropriate behaviour and the maintenance of belief in a greater world, where respect for the animals is essential before the creatures will allow themselves to be killed, and their meat, skin and ivory to be put to useful ends.

Old World contact

Contact between the Old World and the Arctic was in many ways multi-dimensional. Trade across Bering Strait dates back 2,000 years; it ceased for a while during the Cold War in the 1940s but is now resumed. Paul Tiulana, Inupiat from King Island, recalled on a visit to London in 1985, exchanging $4 watches for walrus tusks, as these were said to be larger on the Siberian side of the strait during the 1940s. Contact with Europe dates back a thousand years to the Vikings, but ceased after Viking settlements became agriculturally non-viable, disappearing with the worsening of the climate in the fourteenth century.

In the fifteenth and sixteenth centuries new contacts arose in part because of the Newfoundland cod fishery, and in part because of the search for the Northwest Passage and mineral wealth. The three 1570s voyages of Martin Frobisher

203. Watercolour from the Sloane collection after an original by John White (?), showing Inuit attacking a British longboat off south-east Baffin Island during one of Martin Frobisher's three expeditions in 1576–8. Originally intending to discover the Northwest Passage, Frobisher was diverted into mining supposed gold ore on Kodlunarn or White Man's Island.

(1539–94) to Baffin Island symbolize the often fruitless search for northern riches. The first voyage, of 1576, resulted in the bringing to London of ore samples, later erroneously identified as containing gold. In the following two years further expeditions went out and brought home some 1300 tons of this fool's gold, a black ore, hornblende, which when heated could turn to a golden colour. This was excavated on Kodlunarn or White Man's Island in trenches which are still visible. Some of the black ore from the 1578 voyage also survives, for instance incorporated into the wall of the former Dartford Priory, Kent. This last expedition, involving 15 ships and 400 men, remains the largest European Arctic expedition ever mounted. Later exploration of the Arctic, from the seventeenth century, revolved around the exploitation of animal resources, particularly whales off Greenland and fur traded with Indians in the Subarctic, which was reached through northern waters. The Northwest Passage, the quick route to Asia, remained a chimera into the nineteenth century. The persistent search, however, brought Europeans into contact with numerous, previously unknown groups of Natives, for instance the Inughuit and Copper Inuit.

Arctic collections

Watercolours of Inuit brought to England by Frobisher are the most substantial representation of sixteenth-century Natives. Few Arctic collections, apart from Greenlandic materials now in the National Museum of Denmark, were obtained before the eighteenth century (fig. 201). The earliest Arctic collections in the British Museum were obtained by Sloane from traders who recorded their endeavours in some detail. Of the surviving material, most intriguing is a group of ivories whose moment of collection in Hudson Strait in 1738 was well recorded by the fur trader Alexander Light. Sloane seems also to have had a particularly close relationship in the 1720s with a seaman called Henry Elking, who was probably a whaling captain in Davis Strait. Elking obtained all manner of Inuit artefacts and natural history specimens, including a walrus head which he had pickled and then lent to Mr Elford's coffee house for display, only to be mortified when the walrus was returned with a loose tusk. It is easy to imagine the jovial patrons of the coffee house plunging their hands into the salt pickle to see whether the tusks were loose. Elking was very diffident about his collecting, on one occasion noting: 'I have some mens Cloaths and other Voluminous things but they not being very clean, nor handsome think not worth your acceptance, though they are at your service, upon comand, and so am I who am proud to Subscribe myself Hond. Sir, Your Most humble Servt. H: Elking South Sea Companys Dock the 5th October 1727.' Unfortunately, neither Sloane nor Elking seems to have known how to preserve fur, and so no Inuit clothing survives in the British Museum dating to before the 1820s. Sloane had other Arctic interests, for instance he obtained specimens of Labrador (?) tea 'from Hudson's bay in North America, where by the Natives it is used as a Universal Remedy made into an infusion, and drank'. He occasionally owned animals, writing in 1735 to Swiss botanist Johann Amman (1707–41) in St Petersburg about his 'small white Fox from Hudson's bay', which he kept to observe seasonal colour changes.

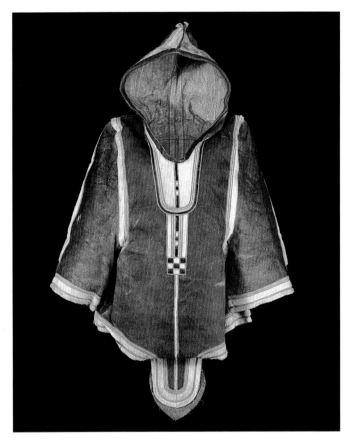

205. West Greenland child's 'kamiks', or boots, *c*.1855, of waterproof sealskin with the fur removed, in two parts – uppers and pleated sole. The uppers are of white skin with the dark outer skin layer removed, and are further decorated with appliqué skin strips. The kamik on the right has been patched. H: 16 cm (6.3 in).

204. West Greenland girl's parka of young caribou skin, with contrasting mosaicwork in white belly skin, and curved flaps, front and rear, characteristic of women's outer garments. Possibly collected by H.P. Hoppner (1795–1833) in the early nineteenth century during the search for the Northwest Passage. H: 76 cm (29.9 in).

206. *Landing the Treasures, or Results of the Polar Expedition!!!*, 1819 caricature after George Cruikshank showing the collections from Ross's 1818 expedition being transported up to the gates of the British Museum. To the left is an unhappy curator and to the right Inuit dogs with an Inuit man, probably Hans Zakaeus (see fig. 207).

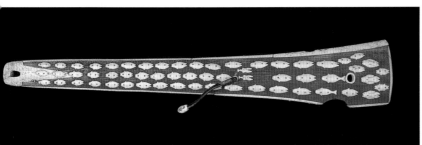

207. Inughuit sled, largely constructed of bone, ivory and wood, collected by John Ross (1777–1856) in 1818 when this group of Inuit were first in contact with Europeans. Hans Zakaeus (d. 1819), a West Greenlander, contributed sketches for the official account of Ross's voyage and acted as interpreter. L: 143 cm (56.3 in).

208. East Greenland wooden spearthrower, *ajatsit*, *c.*1900, with pegged seal-ivory plaques and edging. Used as a lever to launch, for instance, a bladder harpoon, this was the preferred weapon for hunting from the kayak, requiring only a single hand so that the other could steady the narrow craft with the paddle. L: 53 cm (20.9 in).

209. Wooden water pail, *imeq*, collected from the Ammassalik, East Greenland, *c.*1918. The rim and sides are decorated with bone and ivory plaques, which on the sides are in the form of seals and walruses.

One of Sloane's correspondents was Christopher Middleton (d. 1770), who made sixteen annual voyages to Hudson Bay for the Hudson's Bay Company in the 1720s and 1730s. He went on to look for the Northwest Passage in 1741–2, when he provided the first European maps of the west coast of Hudson Bay. Among the materials collected for Sloane by Middleton was a sample of salt from the melt water lying under ice in Hudson Strait in July 1738, noting conversely that it did not taste but could be used for cooking. Forty years later Cook's third expedition passed through Bering Strait in an attempt to find a passage from the west; that expedition acquired Inupiat, Aleut and Pacific Eskimo materials which were deposited in the British Museum in 1780. Vancouver's expedition, which in 1791–5 finally disproved that there was a Northwest Passage through the middle of the continent, also collected Chugach and other materials in 1794 along the shores of southern Alaska. After the Napoleonic wars, and the discovery of the warming of the Arctic climate by William Scoresby in 1817, the search for the Passage was resumed, but this time it was the northern route past Labrador and Greenland that was to be investigated.

John Ross (1777–1856), leader of the first of two expeditions in 1818, encountered the Inughuit in north Greenland and explored Baffin Bay. Ross's collection was presented to the Museum on his return (figs 206–7). Unfortunately, Ross had failed to enter Lancaster Sound fully, at the entrance of what was later found to be a Northwest Passage. So his results were regarded in a mixed light. His deputy William Parry (1790–1855) was then placed in charge of exploring both Lancaster Sound and, in 1821–3, northwestern Hudson Bay. Parry spent several winters with the Iglulingmiut, and his deputy G. F. Lyon (1795–1832) supplied drawings of life at Winter Island and Igloolik for engraving in the official account. Parry acquired a small representative Inuit collection for the British Museum, and employed an Inuit map in his exploration of Melville Peninsula in 1822. In the same decade attempts were made to approach the Northwest Passage from the west around Alaska. Frederick Beechey (1796–1856) was despatched in 1825 to meet a third expedition led by Parry from the west, which he did not achieve, but instead recorded much information about northwest Alaska and deposited an Inupiat collection in the Museum in 1828. One of his men, Edward Belcher

(1799–1877), a Canadian of loyalist descent, privately retained Inupiat materials on which he based the first account of 'Esquimaux' art, published at a time of growing interest in Arctic material culture for its illumination, by analogy, of the European Upper Palaeolithic. Many of these objects were presented to the British Museum by A. W. Franks in 1871.

The collections acquired during the search for the Northwest Passage are almost all associated with the Royal Navy. Very few Inuit, or Indian, items were collected by overland expeditions, because of transportation difficulties. Nothing was collected by Alexander Mackenzie (1764–1820), who first crossed the continent to the Northwest Coast in 1793. Little or nothing was brought home by the expedition of John Franklin (1786–1847) to the shores of the western Canadian Arctic during the 1820s. It was, however, the search for Franklin, after his last ill-fated expedition of the 1840s, which created the largest of the Arctic collections. This included some 600 items from across the north from west Greenland to Bering Strait. Notable among the collectors was Robert McClure (1807–73) who, on a variety of vessels, and by sledge, was recognized by Parliament as having first traversed a Northwest Passage in 1850–55. However, it was John Rae (1813–93), a Hudson's Bay Company man, who at the same time found traces of the lost expedition that enabled Franklin to be named the discoverer of the Passage. Rae, like Roald Amundsen (1872–1928), who in 1905 on the *Gjøa* was the first to sail through the Passage, followed both the subsistence and the travel practices of the Inuit. In this manner small expeditions were able to achieve greater aims than the better financed, but more ponderous naval ones.

After the locating of Northwest Passages through the Canadian Arctic, interest in exploration in the north waned. G. S. Nares's expedition in 1875–6, intended to reach the North Pole, produced the last official collection of Arctic ethnography for the Museum, for in 1880 British interests in Inuit lands were transferred to Canada. Thereafter Arctic collections were made by private explorers, such as the 5th Earl of Lonsdale in 1888–9 when fleeing scandal in England, or by traders working in the eastern Arctic as Canadian colonization proceeded during the first quarter of the twentieth century. More recently emphasis has been placed on recording contemporary material culture, particularly skin clothing, basketry, traditional tools and graphic art.

8

THE SUBARCTIC

The Chippewyan, living west of Hudson Bay towards Great Slave Lake, believe that they are descended from the first person, Woman, and Dog. According to the story as recorded by the explorer Samuel Hearne in the eighteenth century, Woman was attracted to Dog, who became man at night. She became pregnant, but before she gave birth to the first child, a giant engaged in levelling the earth and creating lakes and rivers killed Dog. He threw his entrails into the water causing them to become fish, and he also caused his flesh to become

animals, and his skin birds, so that people could hunt and eat. The first inhabitants of this region are known by archaeologists from caribou river crossings – sites for hunting that were also used as fish camps. To the east Cree origin myths tell of how man and woman were created from clay, in one version after the muskrat had brought up mud to create the earth.

210. Mary Bonnetrouge, Dene, working on quilled moccasins, Fort Providence, Northwest Territories, 1980s?

211. Dene moccasins of smoked moose skin, cloth, beaver fur, cotton and porcupine quillwork, made by Mary Bonnetrouge, 1986.
L: 28 cm (11 in).

The Subarctic showing the location of peoples mentioned in the chapter.

People moved across the Bering Land Bridge into the interior of Alaska more than 10,000 years ago; these were big-game hunters using fluted stone points for hunting similar to those employed by Paleoindians elsewhere on the continent. Gradually they moved eastwards and north into Canada. After 10,000 years ago Paleoindians were followed, or perhaps replaced, by populations with a more specialized micro-blade technology, using small stone flakes to arm tools and projectiles. Eventually, over many thousands of years, as glaciers melted and water levels receded, people moved eastwards into the Canadian Shield area around Hudson Bay. The Paleoindian peoples gradually developed Archaic stone tool kits and then, more than 2,000 years ago, acquired Woodland traits, such as the manufacture of pottery, in some areas. Ancient patterns of big-game hunting were maintained throughout the region.

The Subarctic is the largest cultural and geographic region of North America, a vast area, around 518 million hectares (2 million square miles), stretching from coastal

Labrador through to the interior and south coast of Alaska. Geographically, the Subarctic may be divided into the Canadian Shield (the horseshoe of Precambrian rock, boreal forest and tundra around Hudson Bay), the Mackenzie valley in the west, the cordillera region of the Rocky Mountains, and in Alaska the interior and coastal riverine plains. The peoples who live there, perhaps 50,000 at European contact, speak languages from two groups. In the west – Alaska, the Yukon, Northwest Territories and British Columbia – are the northern Athapaskan speakers, at contact speaking twenty-three distinct languages. In the east Algonquians, speaking languages with dialectic differences, live between the coast of Labrador, through Québec and Ontario to northern Alberta. Most of the region is described as cold snow forest, semi-arid rather than desert, with warm summer months and long winters characterized by temperatures which remain below freezing month after month.

All Subarctic peoples are big-game hunters depending particularly on caribou and moose, with very different strategies for killing the two animals. The hunting of the gregarious, and more northerly, caribou is concentrated particularly on their migration pattern, when moving between summer and winter feeding grounds. It is then that major efforts are made to obtain sufficient meat to cache for winter. One technique for hunting bison and deer, shared with southern Natives, was the use of the chute and the pound. Animals would be driven down a passage into a pound, formed of poles and of men, where they might be killed with snares and other techniques. Another ancient and much favoured late summer method of hunting, shared with Inuit and employed also in moose hunting, was to drive caribou into rivers so that they could be speared or knifed while moving slowly in the water. In winter single caribou might be driven into deep snow and killed with bows and arrows. Moose, living in the southern boreal areas of the Subarctic, are to a large extent solitary creatures, also hunted with bow and arrow, sometimes after being attracted with a birchbark horn during the rutting season, and with spears when driven into winter snow-drifts. Other animals hunted for food include bear, beaver, ptarmigan and hare. More important is fish, including trout, salmon, char and, in the central Subarctic, sturgeon, which might be speared for its thick white flesh and nutritious oil. However, in the middle of the twentieth century Ontario and

Québec Cree still depended on big game for between 50 and 80 per cent of their food.

Hunting migrant animals and fish requires a flexible mobile existence. In summer people gather along shores to hunt fish, and travel in what were previously birchbark but are now powered wood and metal canoes. In the autumn the hunting of migrating animals provided essential food, particularly important being animal skins and fat, readied for winter. After the freeze-up, mobility is resumed along frozen waterways and forest trails. The toboggan is complemented by the snow shoe, of broad form in the east but long and thin in the west. While temperatures are similar to those of the Arctic shore, this is mitigated by the plentiful supply of wood. Winter camps, therefore, are now constructed from canvas-covered ridgepole tents heated with tin stoves, though formerly skin- and birchbark-covered tents were employed in most areas. These were constructed in a variety of forms, including conical, ridgepole and domed structures. Snow and moss might be used as insulation, and fir boughs as flooring material. In the western Subarctic lodges were also built of logs. Clothing derived in the winter from the furred skins of animals; caribou in particular was used for parkas, as were the skins of small mammals such as beaver and hare. The latter, often termed rabbit, might be woven in strips into light warm garments.

Early European accounts defined Native groups, whose boundaries were delineated by drainage basins, as 'nations'. Perhaps the most important social grouping was, and is, the 'band', a group of 200–400 people who often assembled for summer and winter hunting. Ranges were rarely closely defined, and often shared by peoples with overlapping areas of usage. Leadership depended upon personal qualities and on charisma: the most important abilities were hunting proficiency and associated knowledge – ritual and practical – as well as generosity. Everything, particularly food, was shared, even though the rituals of individuals were vital for hunting success. Personal spirits guided all members of the community, and the people with most personal powers, shamans, were empowered both to prevent and cure disease, to foretell both the weather and the future, and to locate game. Male shamans might also be evil.

Underlying religion is the belief in the unity of the animal and human worlds; these operate in a strictly reciprocal

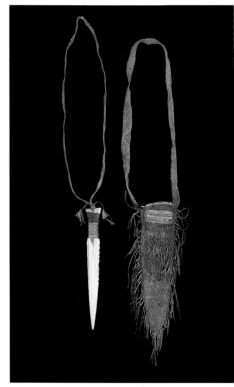

212. Heavy skin tunic, eighteenth century, made by Athapaskans or in Athapaskan style on the Northwest Coast, one of the many indications of regular trade and cultural borrowings between these two groups of people. Decorated with strips of coloured quillwork, it was probably thick enough to have acted as armour. L: 121 cm (47.6 in).

213. Two eighteenth-century Dena'ina scoops or ladles of big-horn sheep horn (?), Alaska, decorated with characteristic Athapaskan geometric designs and red ochre pigment; the left-hand example is carved with a basketry-hatted figure. Similar articles were widely used and traded on the Northwest Coast. L: 28 cm, 24.5 cm (11 in, 9.6 in).

214. Eighteenth-century Dena'ina (?) knife cut from the rind of antler or bone, and a separate ochre-dyed Dena'ina skin sheath with quillwork. The handle is wrapped in porcupine quillwork and a skin thong, also used for suspension and decorated with two amuletic appendages. L: 33 cm (13 in), 88 cm with strap (34.6 in).

215. Engraving after a sketch by Frederick Whymper, June 1867, made while surveying for a telegraph cable route through Alaska, and showing Koyukon or Tanana River Indians hunting slow-moving moose from birchbark canoes with classic Athapaskan knives.

216. 'Tourist guide on the Tanana River', 1970s. The Alaskan has in front of her a pile of embroidered fur-trimmed mittens, decorated with wool cords and tassels, and a beaded baby strap; on the right are what may be bone moose-skin scrapers.

217. Church service, Tyonek, 1970s. The Russian Orthodox Church, introduced during the Russian period in Alaska (1799–1867), remains a vital part of Native life, as here in the Dena'ina village of Tyonek, near Anchorage on Cook Inlet, where the celebrant is Father Nicolai Komkoff, an Aleutiiq from Chenega.

relationship in which animal spirits must be respected and propitiated in order to ensure that they continue to make themselves available to hunters. A hunter is successful because the animals allow themselves to be hunted. The Alaskan Ahtna, for instance, divided animals into three groups: big-game or meat-bearing animals, smaller food animals and, most importantly, fur bearers. The hunter sung and prayed before venturing on the land, and might refer to the animals by circumlocution. Purity is vital, as indeed are feelings of respect towards animals. Animal bones are burned and never given to dogs. Both the bones of beaver and fish are returned to water, so that they might be recreated. Recently hunted animals retained spiritual power, and were potentially dangerous to infants, for instance. Fur pelts retained this quality, the skins of some animals being too dangerous to bring into the home. For the Dogrib and Yellowknife in the Northwest Territories, caribou might not be attacked with sticks or stones, because it was feared that they might leave the country. A hunter fails not so much because he missed the beast but because the bear or beaver did not want to be caught, due to an act of transgression or disrespect. In all of these matters dreams provided guidance, as for instance among the Beaver in British Columbia. Dreams were the source of power, of personal spirits, of songs to use in hunting, and of guidance with specific difficulties, such as the location of game. Dreaming also provided sources for personal taboos, and for situations and actions to be avoided.

The fur trade

Native relations with the outside world have to a large extent been a product of the fur trade. In the sixteenth and seventeenth centuries initial trade in the Northeast favoured peoples like the Iroquois, who, with easy access to Europeans, were able to dominate the interior trade with other Native groups. Once fur-bearing animals had disappeared or become much reduced in New York and New England, it became necessary for European traders to move far into the interior. The French controlled access to the Great Lakes along the St Lawrence, and thence to the riverine heartland of America as far west as the Rockies. In 1670 the founding of the Hudson's Bay Company in London facilitated the creation of a shorter journey to the river routes that spread through the Canadian Shield in a great arc from James and Hudson Bays. Initially, competition ensured a degree of flexibility for Native groups. But by the Treaty of Utrecht in 1713 Hudson Bay was left to the British. The interior remained the domain of the French until 1763, although competition continued for the Hudson's Bay Company after that date in the form of independent companies – particularly the North West Company, a coalition of Scottish Montrealers and French Canadian *voyageurs* operating independently until absorption by the Hudson's Bay Company in 1821.

The demand for beaver pelts lay at the centre of the fur trade. Denuded of guard hairs, the remaining wool can be compressed to create the shiny felted material desired for top hats. This fashion and its method of manufacture remained constant until the nineteenth century when manufacturers learnt how to simulate the lustrous effect with a silk material. Indians wore beaver robes with the hair in towards the skin; after a couple of seasons of use the guard hairs fell out, so that the robes could be sold by Natives in a state ready for European use. Initially, no mechanical process was known in western Europe with which to remove the hairs: used Native pelts therefore possessed an important advantage. The fur trade was predicated on the beaver hunt. The Hudson's Bay Company used beaver as a unit of currency for accounting purposes and eventually issued coins denominated in 'Made Beaver', the value of a prime winter skin. By the 1840s the Hudson's Bay Company, moving westwards, had reached Alaska, and the Russian American Company, moving eastwards, had established itself in the interior of what was to remain Russian territory until 1867. From the discovery of gold in the Canadian Klondike in 1896, mineral exploitation became a most significant aspect of Native/non-Native relations in the north, both for Arctic and Subarctic peoples. More recently, land claims agreements reached in Alaska and Québec during the 1970s were founded on the need to facilitate the exploitation of oil and water resources.

In the eighteenth century the Hudson Bay trade was dominated, at least initially, by the Cree inhabitants of the shore, and particularly by Native trading captains. These prominent leaders travelled inland to obtain beaver in time for transportation on the annual trading voyages to Europe, before freeze-up. From the seventeenth century onwards trade rela-

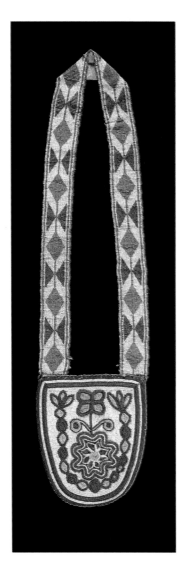

219. Watercolour by Peter Rindisbacher, 1821, showing a Cree man returning with his family to York Factory. The couple are clothed in a style probably typical of 'Home Indians', those who lived and worked around the Hudson's Bay Company post. The musket and powder horn indicate the hunter's success as a trapper.

218. Cree beaded-cloth pouch used for carrying shot or cartridges. While expressing the maker's affection for the eventual user of the pouch, the rosettes and floral designs may be associated with flowers, and so with spring and renewal. Pouch size: 20 x 18 cm (7.9 x 7.1 in).

220. 'Moose Caller', Cree man demonstrating how to attract moose with a 'moose call', a rolled birchbark instrument, early twentieth century.

221. Cree 'bitten' design of leaves and birds by Angelique Merasty, Cree, Saskatchewan (b. 1927). Created by twice folding a piece of thin birchbark and impressing symetrical forms with the teeth, this ephemeral art was once commonly practised by elders as entertainment across much of the Algonquian Subarctic. 20 x 16 cm (7.9 x 6.3 in).

222. Nineteenth-century Cree cloth hood elaborately decorated with appliqué silk ribbonwork and beadwork. Such peaked hoods, derived from aboriginal skin prototypes, were widely used from the Atlantic to central Canada by both men and women. H: 68 cm (26.8 in).

223. Cree bear-chin charm decorated with beadwork, *c.*1915. Black bears are feared and respected throughout the Subarctic; skulls may be hung in trees to demonstrate their immortality, and the tongue sinew extracted, both to placate the spirit of the animal and to silently announce a successful hunt. L: 15 cm (5.9 in).

tions were facilitated by liaisons between Europeans and Native women, creating a new group of people, country-born Métis of mixed descent. It might be assumed that these relationships were always initiated by Europeans. However, Natives were often keen to establish kin relations with rich newcomers for their own purposes. For Natives Europeans brought supplies in times of scarcity, and particularly metal products such as kettles, needles, edge blades and other tools. Such things, including wool cloth, were usually superior to those available locally. Women who were able to make wool clothes quickly could therefore devote more time to the preparation of trade pelts. Women were responsible for the production of almost all trade goods – not just furs, but also preserved foods and articles such as moose and caribou skins, birchbark, and split spruce root, or *wattap*, used for sewing canoes. But fur remained warmer than imported materials, and clothing forms such as moccasins entered general use, as did many other aspects of material culture, for instance those relating to transportation by snow shoe, canoe, pack-dog and toboggan. Competition between French and British traders ensured that the quality of European goods was maintained. In the late eighteenth century, however, fierce and unscrupulous competition between the Hudson's Bay and North West Companies encouraged the destructive consumption of alcohol by Natives in the trading process. Alcohol became quickly integrated into Native culture, both as a drink to be given away for reasons of social prestige and as a component of religious activities. Competition also arose between Native peoples for access to the Hudson's Bay Company, such as in the first half of the eighteenth century between the Cree and the Chippewyan. The most far-reaching effects, apart from those of devastating epidemics, lay in the changes to hunting and trapping patterns brought about by the fur trade.

Collections

Sloane, the founder of the British Museum, maintained a regular interest in the Subarctic and in the Hudson's Bay Company. His library included a 1684 manuscript by Pierre Esprit Radisson (*c*.1640–1710), one of the French Canadian founders of the company, and a copy of the 1670 patent and coat of arms. He maintained regular correspondence with employees of the Company to further his scientific interests. Just as Sloane obtained a rattlesnake from Virginia, so he owned a fox from Hudson Bay. The latter was kept in his garden in Bloomsbury to see whether it would change colour with the onset of winter. While only a few of Sloane's Subarctic artefacts have survived, we can see from the detail lovingly recorded in his catalogue how widely his interests ranged. He noted, for instance, that a pair of beaver skin leggings were cured by rubbing with brains. In the subsequent two centuries most of the Subarctic collec-

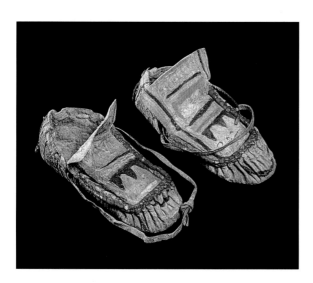

tions, whether Algonquian or Athapaskan, came through Hudson's Bay Company men to the British Museum. These were often casual donations made by people on their return to Britain. Most of the materials collected are poorly documented and consist of superbly beaded and embroidered items made by Indian women from the 'Home Guard' (Indians living and working around the trading post) for sale to whites. Few of the collections were made by prominent company personnel: there is nothing surviving, for instance, from Alexander Mackenzie (1764–1820) of the North West Company, the first person to cross the continent in 1792–3.

224. Pair of Cree or Innu model painted-skin moccasins, Sloane collection, *c.*1700; the seam between the broad vamp and puckered toe is edged with quillwork. L: 6 cm (2.4 in).

The centre of the fur trade is located around the southern end of Hudson Bay and James Bay in what is now northern Manitoba, Ontario and Québec. This is where the largest and most important fur-trading factories were established centuries ago, at the mouths of large rivers which provided routes into the hinterland by canoe in the summer for trading and by toboggan in the winter for trapping. This was the area from which Sloane's early Cree artefacts come, but it is also the area where Native art and material culture was most quickly adapted and changed. Early on winter furs were augmented and/or replaced with duffels and wool cloth; glass beads and ribbons were added to porcupine quillwork and appliqué work. Western Algonquians called glass beads 'spirit berries', *manneto menance*; red cloth provided a material analogous to that decorated with ochre, signifying power. The use of trade goods and decorative materials, including top hats and silver bands for trading captains,

225. Eighteenth-century Cree skin pouch, perhaps used to hold a pipe and smoking equipment or shot. Such containers, often decorated with horizontal strips of porcupine quillwork, remained in use by the Métis until the mid-nineteenth century, often after other elements of Native costume had been adapted to European traditions. L: 21 cm (8.3 in).

was expressive of the prestige and achievement of Native leaders. Unfortunately, very little of the costume that was used and worn in the eighteenth century survives in any collection. During the nineteenth century not much of the clothing that replaced the skin costume was collected, apart from highly decorative accoutrements. Here, in the area between Hudson Bay and the Great Lakes, styles of beadwork and other embroidery, in form related to those created in French-Canadian monastic institutions, developed and spread across the continent. For instance, the bilingual French-speaking Mohawk canoe-men from Kahnawake near Montréal, on the south side of the St Lawrence from Lachine, the centre of the Hudson's Bay Company operations, travelled across the continent to Oregon Territory in the first half of the nineteenth century. There they may have introduced contoured floral beadwork from Canada, where it still survives, for instance among the Yakima. The Iroquoian Huron created a similar tradition in the eighteenth century, embroidering moose hair on moccasins, and producing birchbark items for sale. While in appearance much of this embroidery seems to be European, meanings are more complex, centring on Native ideas both about design and the wider natural and spiritual world.

One of the most significant of the individuals involved in the mid-nineteenth-century fur trade was Donald Smith, Lord Strathcona (1820–1914), who came to dominate much of the company's activities. Yet there is a disjuncture between his position in history and the casual nature of his acquisition of the Native collection in the British Museum. Smith spent the first twenty years of his working life at posts in the Ungava or Québec-Labrador peninsula during the middle of the century. During the 1870s he made a fortune out of linking Winnipeg with St Paul, Minnesota, by rail and then devoted himself to assisting with the construction of the Canadian Pacific Railway, across Canada. Although promised to British Columbia in 1870 as part of the arrangement for joining the Canadian confederation, this was not completed until 1885. It was in the middle of the nineteenth century, while Donald Smith was a Hudson's Bay Company employee, that the fur trade came to impinge on the hunting and subsistence patterns of the Algonquian-speaking peoples once known as the Montagnais-Naskapi but now as the Innu. A primary source of food through the year comes from caribou, traditionally migrating between seasonal feeding grounds inland and on the coast, sometimes dispersed and sometimes in vast herds. The fur trade required skins from marten and other animals to be trapped at the same time, particularly in the late summer and autumn when the pelts were full, but not yet damaged, in readiness for the winter to come. These conflicting requirements, and the variation in the paths of the caribou migration, may well have periodically caused great hardship. When these difficulties were exacerbated by the inability of the fur traders to release food or ammunition on credit, the ensuing starvation may have been avoidable. Erland Erlandson, one of the earlier traders in the area, understood the Indians' dilemma succinctly. In 1833 at South River Post he recorded the problem of persuading Indians to hunt marten, when in their own cycle they should have been hunting caribou. The Indians asked Erlandson for supplies, which he was unable to grant them. The Hudson's Bay Company prided itself on firm and deliberate accounting on principles handed down from London and Winnipeg. Donald Smith was extremely careful with money, both his own and that of the Company. He was in charge of much of the Ungava region during the 1850s, which saw serious starvation, with numerous deaths occurring among the Innu population, for instance during the winter of 1856–7. It was said in a rather chilling phrase: 'No matter how poor the post might be, Donald Smith always showed a balance on the right side of the ledger.'

At this time, however, Indians depended on trade goods for convenience rather than necessity. Firearms might only be acquired by young men when they could be afforded, after many years spent learning to hunt with the bow. For many generations Natives active in the fur trade maintained skills in Native and non-Native technology so that, when shot and powder were not available, an easy return could be made to the bow, snares and traditional trapping. It must be assumed that if Natives chose to remain close to trading posts this was a conscious and rational decision, preferring the vagaries of man to those of animals. This century other views of the Hudson's Bay Company have suggested ways in which European commerce affected Native life beneficially. The western Cree, Joseph Dion, for instance, commented that Hudson's Bay Company factors always treated Natives with respect and provided food in times of need.

It would be reasonable to suppose that Donald Smith would have collected items of Innu material culture during his long involvement with them. This is not the case, though he wrote an account of the people which was destroyed by fire. The only collection of Native materials directly associated with him is a group of twenty or thirty Subarctic items, including particularly Cree beaded items – wall pockets and the like – probably made by Natives living close to fur-trading posts. He had become Canadian High Commissioner in London and acquired this material in 1902 for a bazaar, as part of a casual

obligation to provide materials for a fund-raising event associated with the Coronation of Edward VII. If this collection was
casually acquired, it was also casually presented to the British
Museum in 1936 by a favourite granddaughter Frances Kitson.
She was responsible for clearing out one of Strathcona's numerous residences, Glencoe, an occasion when other collections, of
archival records, were simply burnt.

The Museum collection includes examples of the superb
painted Innu, or Naskapi, caribou-skin coats. These derive from
pivotal moments in the Innu annual cycle when people came
together for the *mokushan* ceremony, a ritual of rebirth and
renewal, during which these fabulous painted coats were worn.
They were decorated with personalized designs intended to
ensure that the autumnal caribou migration occurred on time
and in the right position, by propitiating the caribou spirits. Like
most North American skin clothes, they were created by the
long laborious process of drying, scraping and softening in a
series of multiple, repetitive tasks that produced a soft, long-
lasting, cured skin. The painted decoration, in contrast to the
figurative work on the Plains, was women's work. A combination
of the men's role in drumming and dreaming the paths of the
animals with the women's ability to augment and develop
esoteric symbols created a dense series of meanings which
attracted the caribou. Perhaps around 150 of these coats
survive, many in British collections. Almost all are without
documentation. However, the history and itinerary of the coats
can be speculated on. They were used at the time of trading
before the caribou hunt, and after the patterns no longer possessed power, would have been suitable for disposal by the
shamans to fur-trading posts, particularly if there was a pressing
need for ammunition. In Quebec City or Montréal these coats
were probably used as exotic features in fur establishments; a
civil servant or soldier returning to London, or a tourist returning to New York, might acquire furs for his family and then also
a few extra Native-made items for a fancy-dress box for his children. There are records of the sale of artefacts such as Huron
moose-hair embroidered table cloths and twentieth-century
photographs of Inuit costume, both offered in stores alongside
more prosaic fur coats. People like the nineteenth-century surveyor Sir John Henry Lefroy, who acquired two such Naskapi
coats, may have also obtained them to use.

226. Pair of Innu women's beaded ear ornaments with silk ribbons, *c.*1915, the geometric design related to those painted on caribou skin. 15 x 9 cm (5.9 x 3.5 in).

227. Drawing by Witcamagin in crayon and pencil of men wearing painted caribou-skin coats, 26 February 1928.

228. Drawing by Tuma, Innu, in crayon and pencil, 21 February 1928, showing the hunting of caribou by birchbark canoe, using a spear and a rifle. The spear (*ashimagen*) was preferred, directed under the ribs towards the heart.

229. Joe Rich (Shushebish) demonstrating the method of using a bow and blunt arrow for small game, 1928. He is wearing a caribou-skin parka, with the fur out and the tail pointing downwards, and wrap-around moccasins with the broad decorated vamp characteristic of Subarctic Algonquian-speaking peoples.

230. Peenamee fleshing a caribou hide with a heavy wood-handled scraper, 1928.

231. Eighteenth-century painted caribou-skin coat. The Innu believe that men and caribou, the principal food source, are brothers; if the caribou spirit is neglected then people will starve, and the hunter dies. The women who created these coats have interpreted their husband's dreams of animal souls in bright colours. H: 115 cm (45.3 in).

Perhaps the most significant collector to have had a direct effect on the Native peoples of the Subarctic was Henry Christy (1810–65), the banker and textile manufacturer, whose generosity and collecting instincts transformed the collections of the British Museum during the 1860s. In the middle of the nineteenth century Christy introduced to his family firm in Cheshire machinery for weaving silk to replace the matted beaver felt with which, hitherto, top hats were covered. At this time seamless silk hats were very fashionable, worn by Prince Albert, the Prince of Wales and by President Lincoln. This would have had two effects on the Native Canadian population: firstly, it would have cut the demand for beaver, which might either have reduced the income of Natives dependent on the fur trade or else forced them to trap alternative fur-bearing species. Secondly, it would have allowed the beaver population to recover. In fur-trade parlance, when the beaver had been exterminated in an area, it was said that it had been 'beavered out'. In the twentieth century areas continued to be beavered out until the 1920s, when it was recognized that this resulted in the decline of trade and starvation. Slowly, conservation schemes were introduced to reluctant Natives and the even more reluctant Hudson's Bay Company, for instance by James Watt at Rupert House, Québec. Christy visited Native communities in the Great Lakes, and acquired Native materials during the 1850s; his collection included a fine moose-skin coat, but unfortunately little is documented.

Most typical of the collectors of Subarctic material, and most representative of material culture, is the collection made by the Hudson's Bay Company trader, E. B. Renouf, in eastern Hudson Bay, particularly at Great Whale River, or Poste-de-la-Baleine, where he was stationed from 1913 to 1916. This includes Inuit, Cree and Innu materials created by the Native peoples of this area of Rupert's Land, which had became Nouveau Québec in 1912 (figs 218, 226). Renouf collected a series of beaded pouches and ornaments, subsistence tools, and a number of charms. Unfortunately, he wrote rather little, apart from one or two short articles in the Hudson's Bay Company magazine *The Beaver*, including one about kayaks. The charms include an ochre-painted bear chin (fig. 223) and a stuffed goose head, testifying to the close surviving relationship between people and animals. The bear is respected for its nature – some bones are ritually preserved in trees. The role of geese is rather different. As migrating birds they appear in flocks in spring and autumn, particularly the former, when they presage food and plenty. In the eighteenth century the Hudson's Bay Company came to depend on spring geese to relieve end-of-winter food shortages, and in employing Indians in the hunt, drew them away from the seasonal interior caribou chase. James Isham (*c.*1716–61) first observed the Goose Feast in 1743, in which each person tackled a whole roasted bird, with a prohibition on breaking any bones. Among Québec Cree observances continue. In 1975 John Blackned, from Rupert House, recorded how the head of his first goose, traditionally hunted with bolas and bows, was stuffed with down and decorated with beads. The bones were wrapped in birchbark and hung up. After death the goose head would act as a grave marker. Similar observances are recorded in the nineteenth century for the Plains Crees, far to the west in Saskatchewan, where the first goose of each season would, provided that the bones were not yet broken, be ceremonially eaten. Bird meat, like fish and other flesh is dried. As well as owning numerous birchbark vessels, Sloane acquired food for his collection 250 years ago. This included

A preparation made of the Flesh of the Wild Goose & Deers Marrow. Used by the Indians near Hudgson bay for foode The Geeses flesh is dry set before a fire & then passed thro' a Snow Shoe the Deers marrow warm'd into wch. the Flesh is put to bring it to a consistancy & then put into their Rogans or Olagans [birchbark dishes].

In 1987 two Crees, Emma Schecapio and Flora Mianscum, came from Québec to London to set up a Cree tent at the Museum of Mankind (the Ethnography Department of the British Museum). They brought dried fowl with them, from which models were copied, for use in *The Living Arctic* exhibition.

Most important of other Subarctic traditions is that of birchbark, especially the creation of canoes, which were made from light malleable bark of the paper birch laid down in hull-shaped depressions, built up over wood thwarts and keel, sewn with split root and caulked with spruce gum. Birchbark is also used in numerous other ways: as a form of wrapping paper; as a basis, with curled tension, for decorative belts and garters: and, above all, as a serviceable material for containers, sewn like the

232. Dene quilled jacket of manufactured cloth and smoked caribou skin, made by Stella Martin and embroidered with quillwork by Sarah Hardisty, Wrigley, Northwest Territories, for Expo '86 in Vancouver. H: 60 cm (23.6 in).

233. Late nineteenth-century Athapaskan bag of woven caribou rawhide strips, edged with moosehide strips and decorated with wool tassels, Mackenzie River area, Northwest Territories. Such bags provided light flexible containers for carrying equipment and perhaps especially game, the openwork netting allowing circulation of air. L: 59 cm (23.2 in).

234. Coiled spruce-root basket, the rim decorated with dyed goose (?) quills, Slavey, 1850s. Such containers were widely made by Athapaskans for many purposes, including cooking – when wet, the fabric swelled and became watertight – and although replaced by metal containers soon after European contact, Alaskan Athapaskans still weave them. Diam.: 20 cm (7.9 in).

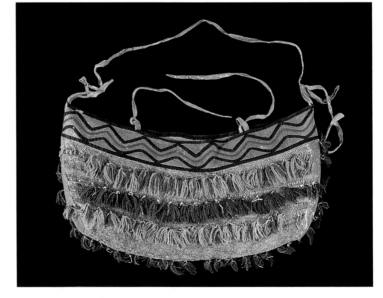

235. Birchbark container, 1860s, with wood rim, tight stitching of split root, and skin thong handles. Athapaskan peoples in the interior of British Columbia, such as the Chilcotin and Wet'suwet'en (Carrier), are noted for the scraped decoration on the exterior. Here the geometric design may relate to porcupine quillwork. H: 20 cm (7.9 in).

236. Caribou-skin model of a Gwich'in hunter in summer costume with the all-in-one trouser moccasin and beaded shirt or tunic, from the collection of Lord Lorne, before 1887. The facial paint would have been worn by a chief on significant occasions connected with ritual or the fur trade. H: 45 cm (17.7 in).

237. Coloured engraving, 1820s, after a sketch by Robert Hood (1797–1821) of Akaitcho, or Big Foot, a Yellowknife (Copper) Indian leader, with his son at Fort Providence, Northwest Territories. His clothing reflects both the fur trade and traditional usage. Akaitcho guided Sir John Franklin's 1820–22 expedition to the Arctic coast.

canoes with split roots and decorated with porcupine quillwork. Birchbark also provides an ever present material for drawing – for the design of scrolls in the Ojibwa Medicine Societies, for bitten designs impressed in folded birchbark with teeth, and for the creation of maps. Subarctic bark canoe types, still made of birchbark by the Algonquins and Attikameks, are also built of wood, for instance by the Huron in Québec. Similarly the flat bed toboggan used in the Subarctic is recreated in southern factories and sold worldwide. In addition, and perhaps mostly obtained from the Subarctic, there are the snow shoes, or *racquettes* of French explorers, with their elegant geometric bentwood frames, filled with light taught webbing woven out of raw gut or skin so that, like the skin covering of Inuit boats, they would dry to tightness, enabling people to pad across soft forest snow.

The western Subarctic

While clothing and decorative traditions are separate and distinctively different in the western Subarctic, categories of surviving material culture are in many ways equivalent to those further to the east. Museum collections reflect the highly mobile life styles: nothing is large, heavy or particularly permanent. Summer clothing, as material for Europeans to acquire and keep, was, peculiarly in view of the climate, much preferred to that made for winter. Just as in the Ungava Peninsula caribou summer coats were collected, so the shirts and full costumes created by the Dene in the Northwest Territories and Alaska were also largely summer clothes. Superbly prepared and tailored, thin caribou-skin moccasin leggings and long shirts, which were created and embellished with porcupine quillwork, seeds, glass beads and dentalium shells, could be packed up and transported down, say, the Porcupine and Yukon rivers to coastal Alaska, or to Hudson Bay and the Great Lakes.

Most distinctive, and in a sense iconic, of northern Athapaskan art are the steel knives made after the arrival of the fur trade in the nineteenth century from files and other tools introduced by the Russian, American and Hudson's Bay Companies. These are usually decorated with scroll finials to the handle,

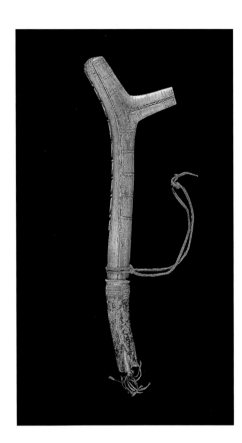

238. Athapaskan caribou-antler club, Alaska, before 1850, decorated with incised geometric designs, porcupine quillwork and beads, and with a fitted grip of skin. Originally there would have been a metal point set in the projecting tine for despatching wounded game, killing bears and hand-to-hand combat. L: 53 cm (20.9 in).

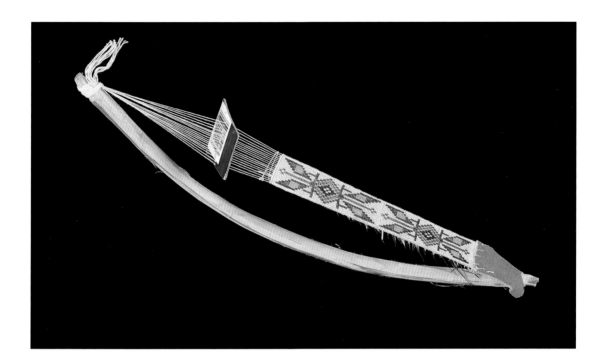

239. Slavey bow loom used for weaving strips of quillwork as appliqué decoration, created by Mrs M. Phillip, Fort Providence, *c.*1986, from a bent stick strung with sinew warps. Quilled strips of this form could be applied to clothing, belts and garters of skin. L: 37 cm (14.6 in).

similar in outline to the double-curve motif used in much beadwork and other decoration as far east as the Maritime Provinces and Maine (fig. 215). The idea of creating weapons in this way was also used on the Northwest Coast and represents only one of a series of traditions shared by the two groups of people. Another shared trait was the employment of large antlers as clubs, a feature both of the Tsimshian on the Northwest Coast and the Ingalik and other peoples in the interior of Alaska and the Yukon (fig. 238).

Moose skin in the western as in the eastern Subarctic was, where available, the preferred material for moccasins, being thick and relatively waterproof, so that it could be worn in winter with layers of fur and, later, of woollen blanket or felt. The smoking of the skin helped protect the moccasins against mould and decay. Porcupine quillwork reached its finest expression in the Subarctic, particularly among the Athapaskans of the Northwest Territories, Yukon and Alaska. Furthermore, this tradition continues today without break, particularly amongst people such as the Slavey. Most interesting of the techniques used is perhaps that of the bow loom, with a bent stick to provide the tension between sinew warps woven with wefts containing the finest quillwork ever achieved.

9 THE CANADIAN PLAINS

The Canadian Plains, or prairies, present a varied landscape similar in many ways to the American grasslands to the south. However, they effectively constitute an intermediary zone between the Subarctic boreal forests and the grasslands to the south, with forested waterways extending through much of the provinces, particularly Saskatchewan and Manitoba. In the

US the Plains are drained by the Missouri, Mississippi and tributaries, whereas in Canada the Saskatchewan river, also flowing from the Rockies, connects northwards with Hudson Bay through Lake Winnipeg.

The buffalo and horse

All Plains peoples depended until the 1870s on the great herds of buffalo, or more correctly bison, whose range originally extended through the Great Plains, east to the Appalachians, and into the Subarctic. These great animals were looked after by spiritual ancestors and, when treated by Natives with due respect appropriate to their sacredness, were hunted to provide physical sustenance and raw materials for the creation of a wide variety of worldly possessions, including clothing, housing and tools. During the eighteenth century the lives of Woodlands and Subarctic peoples were radically affected by the acquisition of the horse, which arrived from the south, having originally been introduced by the Spanish to southern Plains and Great Basin peoples in the seventeenth century. First Nations have their own alternative stories and accounts of how horses originated. According to a Blackfoot myth a poor boy embarked on a vision quest. Water Spirit gave him a mallard on a rope, which as he lead it home turned into a horse. In another, Piegan version the horse was given by the Sun to a child as a toy. Later, Morning Star gradually made the horse real. He called to it four times: at first it moved its legs, then its tail, then its ears, before finally shying, and then standing still to command. Other stories suggest, perhaps accurately, that the horse was acquired from the Shoshone, originally from Utah.

Before the arrival of the horse, the dog provided the main means of transport. The Blackfoot term *ponokomita*, or elk-dog, indicates that it was a beast of burden like the dog and as large as an elk. Sometimes it was used as a pack animal, and more frequently as a creature to pull a travois, an A-shaped bound framework of poles, onto which possessions could be loaded for transportation during the annual cycle of movement in search of game. Later the travois was adapted to the horse, which meant it could be used for greater cargoes, including, for instance, transportation of the infirm.

Hunting buffalo presented enormous difficulties before

The Canadian Plains showing the location of peoples mentioned in the chapter.

240. Late nineteenth-century beaded pad-saddle constructed from two hour-glass-shaped pieces of skin sewn together to form, together with a cushion of buffalo or dog hair, or perhaps grass, an effective pillow protecting horse and (male) rider. 44 cm x 56 cm (17.3 x 22 in).

the appearance of the horse, requiring much stealth, medicine and communal techniques, for instance in the creation of large fenced pounds into which the animals could be driven and killed. Alternatively, the buffalo might be driven over cliffs, a technique invented in Blackfoot belief by a mythic figure called Blood Clot. Discipline was vitally important in the hunt, to ensure for instance that individuals did not alarm the buffalo before the hunt started. Punishments for transgression were severe and included beatings and the destruction of property. As one would expect, different seasons produced different attributes in the buffalo. Young beasts, and certainly not old bulls, were preferred for eating, and the meat was deemed best at the end of the summer season of grass fattening. Early summer animals were required for soft dressed skins, clothes or tipis (for which six female skins might be required), while thick-haired winter skins were needed for the fur trade. Short bows and arrows were the preferred method of hunting, three arrows perhaps being required to bring an animal down. Bows were more effective than muskets but not breech-loading weapons. The anthropologist John C. Ewers has estimated that an average buffalo cow might provide 180 kg (400 lb) of meat, enough for 1.4 kg (3 lb) per person per day in a family of eight for sixteen days. In the 1880s beef rations, provided by the authorities after the buffalo were gone, were set at 700 g (1 1/2 lb) a day, supplemented with small quantities of other food. Because of the necessity of transportation from kill site to camp, light butchering, and the selection of the choicest parts, was practised. The tongue and ribs were perhaps the parts most favoured.

The advent of the horse, never as common on the northern Plains as in the south, brought northern and eastern peoples onto the Plains, who were now more easily able to exploit the rich buffalo herds. Some peoples such as the Blackfoot had always lived on the Plains, while others such as the Crees and Ojibwas moved south and west with the increased hunting opportunities. The use of the horse may have increased the wealth and ability of Plains people to elaborate their spiritual and material culture. It lead to new modes of warfare, in which 'counting coup', for instance, or touching or taking something from the enemy, such as horses, might be commemorated by pictographic records depicting events, including the role of war medicine, in their achievement. Annual ceremonies grew in significance once hunting became a simpler matter. In any case, whereas forest people had for thousands of years come onto the Plains to hunt, the advent of the horse allowed northern peoples to remain there permanently, bringing with them, for instance, northern-style conical tipis, now created more easily and at an increased size from the more readily available buffalo skin.

The horse changed Plains society irrevocably, altering many aspects of technical and cultural experience. Whereas the dog is a meat-eater and can be relatively easily protected from the cold in winter, the horse requires great pastures and some

241. Native sketch of bison hunting, *c*.1890–1910, perhaps Blackfoot in origin. The arrow is aimed just behind a front leg so that, as the beast runs, it will work its way into the internal organs of the buffalo and bring it down.

protection from the elements. Sheltered valleys needed to be found throughout the winter, as well as food; and knowledge of grasses and barks was required to ensure the horse's survival. Inner cottonwood bark, for instance, was an important winter food for the horse. In winter, ground would be cleared of snow to find grass because the horse, with its relatively compact undivided hoof, unlike the splayed caribou hoof, could not easily paw away snow to find food. Moreover, whereas the dog had little spiritual significance for the northern Plains people, the horse acquired religious importance, associated with Morning Star and with Duck, spirits of the upper world. The horse always required appropriate spiritual treatment. Knowledge in medicine and in practical things, such as the manufacture of saddles, stirrups and all the other paraphernalia, had to be quickly and expertly learned. While, of course, the whole horse complex is Spanish (or Moorish) in origin, many distinctive traits – such as use of the bit, spurs, branding and side saddles – were rejected. Because horses were scarce and valuable they needed to be protected against raiding and prevented from wandering. Ownership by sight, rather than mark, was important. Ewers

identified, from Blackfoot informants, ten different types of
horse, which were adapted to specialized tasks and could be categorized by function: (1) the buffalo hunting and war horse, (2)
the winter hunting horse, (3) the ordinary saddle horse, (4) the
travois horse, (5) the pack horse, (6) the tipi pole dragging horse,
(7) the race horse, (8) the stud, (9) the brood mare and (10) the
lead mare in a grazing herd.

Trade

In this movement of people during the last few hundred years
the ancestors of contemporary Plains people met the northernmost representatives of the agricultural Mississippian peoples of
the Lower Mississippi. The northernmost horticultural villages
where this happened, those of the Mandans and Hidatsas, were
at the centre of a great trading network. Agricultural produce
would, in particular, be traded for that of the hunt, including
clothing. As well as trade goods, of course, religious ideas, such
as that of the war between the upper and lower worlds, so prevalent amongst the Mississippians, also moved outwards across the
Plains. With trading contacts, and the movement of religious
ideas, great networks of ritual kin relations arose, through
schemes of adoption and classification. This enabled reciprocal
dealings in trade and food giving, maintained as a vital element,
for instance, both then and now, in 'give-aways' at pow-wows.
Trade was the central component of relations between First
Nations' people on the Plains and Europeans. The French, based
in Lower Canada, and specifically Montréal, sent out explorers
far to the west along riverine systems in the late seventeenth and
early eighteenth century. The network of British fur traders
extended inland from Hudson Bay. Along those routes came a
variety of goods, but particularly firearms, metal kettles and
tools, and later cloth. Just as in the east, where the Iroquois
became significant middlemen, scouring the Ohio country for
fur, so too did Cree and Plains Ojibwa bands on the northern
Plains. The development of European trade in the eighteenth
century inevitably brought epidemics, smallpox, for instance,
reducing Plains populations by half in the 1780s. As elsewhere,
the apparent benefits of technical innovations were undercut by
the effects of disease and by the arrival after 1850 of ever
increasing numbers of immigrants of European descent.

242. Blackfoot war shirt and leggings, *c.*1840–60, Alberta or Montana, decorated with painted designs including Thunderbirds, bison heads and horses, probably representing a combination of religious images relating to specific exploits of the unidentified owner. Shirts were constructed from two rear halves of deerskins. L: 150 cm (59.1 in).

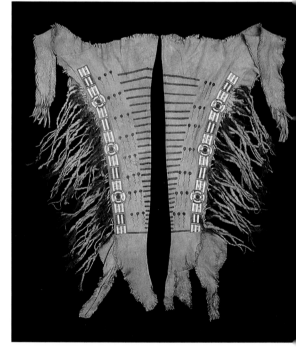

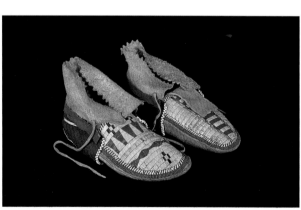

243. Blackfoot (?) side-seam moccasins, *c.*1840–60, Alberta or Montana. The abundance of quillwork is extremely unusual, as is the asymmetrical form, which suggests a self-directed design of religious significance and of possible Crow origin. L: 23 cm (9.1 in).

244. Blackfoot single-skin leggings, *c.*1840–60, Alberta or Montana, with copious amounts of ermine or weasel fur. The weasel is considered very dangerous for its size, and Scarface, a legendary figure, was said to have received a weasel-tail costume, in theory similar to this one, from the Sun. L: 114 cm (44.9 in).

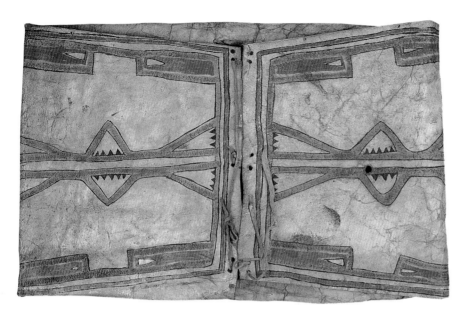

245. Parfleche, Blackfoot, *c.*1860. Parfleches are rectangular rawhide containers, particularly used in the nineteenth century for holding 'pemmican' – ground dried bison meat mixed with fat and berries. This food was vital in the fur trade, where a high calorie diet was required by canoe men. 41 x 48 cm (16.1 x 18.9 in).

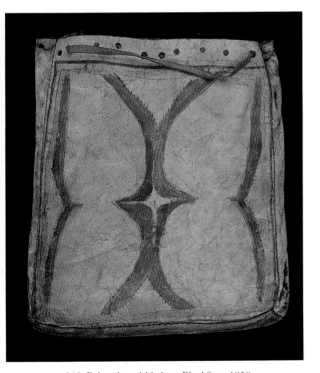

246. Painted rawhide bag, Blackfoot, 1850s, perhaps of the type used by women for multiple purposes, including transportation and storage of skin dressing tools, and for gathering berries and vegetables. 47 x 42 cm (18.5 x 16.5 in).

247. Dick Bad Boy, Blackfoot, *c.*1906–11, gathering hay in Alberta.

The Blackfoot, a principal people of the northern Plains, straddle the international boundary, in both Alberta and in Montana, where they are known as Blackfeet. Dominating much of the northwestern Plains, they were able to acquire significant wealth as represented by growing horse populations. The possibility of social differentiation arose between rich hunters with many horses and those with none. Before the arrival of the horse everyone had equal access to the hunt, although individuals had specific skills and appropriate medicines which might make them exceptional leaders in the chase. Now wealth could be accumulated, and in the middle of the nineteenth century a rich Blackfoot might own forty horses. While the emphasis on sharing – particularly meat from the kill – remained a basic tenet of Blackfoot society, it also became the practice for horses to be loaned out to people not so well endowed. In this respect the effect of the arrival of the horse on the Plains was in some slight way analogous to the role of the arrival of the stirrup in medieval European society, for in permitting the better exploitation of the animal and the development of social divisions, the introduction of the stirrup lead in Europe to the feudal system. Poor Plains people might no longer be able to hunt, with the activities of mounted hunters driving away game from the reach of those on foot. As agriculture developed during the 1880s on both Canadian and American Plains, rather different horses were required. Draught animals were supplied in both countries for ploughing, either to interbreed with Indian ponies or to supplant them. Then from the 1890s cattle ranching began to replace the earlier emphasis on horse rearing.

The Métis

The mixed heritage population of Canada was just that, but while most of the Native aspect of the heritage was Cree and Ojibwa, the European part was widely based, but including particularly people of French Canadian descent. The other significant European component was Scottish. The Métis originated with the fur trade, particularly because fur traders and *voyageurs* took Native wives, creating a group of bi-cultural country-born people of mixed descent. They developed after 1821 into a semi-independent group focused on the Red River in southern

248. Peter Rindisbacher (1806–34), *A Halfcast and his Two Wives*, *c.*1825–6, watercolour, showing three Manitoba Métis, all wearing a mixture of Native and non-Native costume; the man's clothing includes a frock coat of wool or skin, Assomption sash, a shot pouch, skin leggings and moccasins.

Manitoba. In that year the Hudson's Bay Company took over the operations of its Montréal rival, the North West Company. As a result, it was able to dispense with 60 per cent of the work force, or 1200 people. Many of these set themselves up on the Red River, mixing hunting, stock keeping and trapping.

In the middle of the nineteenth century these groups of people were given a social cohesion by adopting a shared, semi-settled life style based on the Roman Catholic church, the use of French and Indian languages (such as Mitchif, a true pervasive mixture of Cree and French), and the pursuit of seasonal activities already mentioned at the interface between the Plains and the Woodlands. Most significant of all occupations was the hunt for bison, from which was produced 'pemmican' – dried meat mixed with berries and fat – for Red River settlers and fur traders, providing a vital source of food and income in the event of crop failure. The bison (or buffalo) hunt took place at the end of the summer, when Métis in Red River carts – of wood and rawhide, without metal – would set out in their hundreds (fig. 257). The

249. Back of heavy moose-skin (?) coat, Métis, mid-nineteenth century, elaborately decorated with porcupine quillwork and impressed painted designs that seem to include four men and three animals, perhaps cows or bison and probably of religious significance. H: 130 cm (51.2 in).

winter hunt to obtain hides covered in thick wool was directed at trade with Americans at Fort Union and later St Paul. From 1815 to 1830 between 26,000 and 200,000 buffalo skins were exported annually. Perhaps the most interesting aspect of these extraordinary peoples is that the Native element of their heritage combined both Plains and Subarctic elements: they were fiercely independent, bison-hunting horsemen and incidentally also trappers, selling both meat and fur into a wider global economy. The cornerstone of all this was, of course, the labour of women, in preparing the pemmican and in the endless laborious work of drying, curing and scraping skins. Métis men depended on the women for wealth creation: successful men took more than one wife.

The Hudson's Bay Company and the Canadian Confederation

During the 1860s and 1870s the Métis life style, often carica-tured by Europeans as carefree, was first threatened and then overtaken by the general colonization of the Canadian prairies.

250. European-made steel knife with a thread-embroidered skin-covered birchbark sheath, Métis, Manitoba, mid-nineteenth century, from the collection of Sir George Simpson (*c.*1786–1860), who, as governor of the Northern Department of the Hudson's Bay Company, was responsible for the fur trade monopoly. L: 46 cm (18.1 in).

In this the crucial event was the debate about the exploitation and relinquishment of the rights of the Hudson's Bay Company, estab-lished in 1670, to the vast areas of Rupert's Land. This extended through the present Prairie Provinces south to the US border, and north into the Northwest Territories. Two expeditions in the late 1850s went out to survey the territory, one Canadian inspired, the other British financed. Both surveys dis-cussed Native affairs and proclaimed the agri-cultural and mineral riches of these territories – but it was the latter message rather than prior Native rights which was remembered. Then in 1863 a group of British investors, the International Financial Society, took control of the Hudson's Bay Company, with the intention of realizing a speedy profit through the sale of Rupert's Land to the Canadian government. This did not happen; instead, in 1869 Rupert's Land was transferred by the Company to the Canadian government, with-out reference to aboriginal peoples, for £300,000 rather than the £5,000,000 which had earlier been expected. However, the Hudson's Bay Company was allowed to retain areas around settlements and 5 per cent of the fertile belt of prairie agricul-tural land, near to the proposed route of the continental railway. These were gradually sold off, yielding, it is said, some $96 mil-lion between 1891 and 1930, as a result of the great agricultural boom which began in the 1890s to draw millions of European immigrants to the Canadian west. By 1914 the Hudson's Bay Company derived more profit from real estate and retail trade than from the fur trade. Also, in the aftermath of the American Civil War demand for buffalo increased – not so much for the delicious tongues, nor the fine winter robes, but for the tough

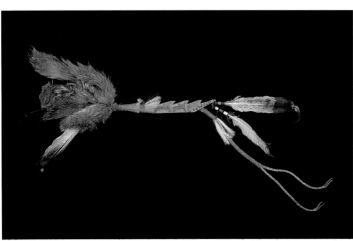

251. Smoked skin shirt belonging to Mékaisto, or Red Crow, Blood, 1880s, decorated with large beaded rosettes on the chest and back, possibly representing Thunderbirds, and with beaded bands on the arms and hair fringes. H: 97 cm (38.2 in).

252. Portrait of 'Three Western Chiefs' by Park & Co., Brantford, with Red Crow in the centre wearing the shirt shown in fig. 251, and the interpreter Jean L'Heureux (1831–1919) at the back, photographed at the time of the unveiling of the memorial to Joseph Brant, 1886.

253. Riding crop, collected from Little Shield, Blood, Alberta, 1890s. The war medicine decoration, including feathers and painted and carved figures of horses on the handle, was no doubt designed to assist in war, an important general element of which was horse raiding. L: 105 cm (41.3 in).

254. The Duke of Windsor (1894–1972), when Prince of Wales, as Chief Morning Star, an honorary Nakoda or Stoney chief, photographed in 1919. The prince was also given the famous name Red Crow by the Bloods, as was the present Prince of Wales in 1977.

255. Skin and cloth vest or waistcoat, collected from Charging Behind, Blood, Alberta, 1890s, and decorated with all-over beadwork in the stepped geometric designs characteristic of the northern Plains. H: 60 cm (23.6 in).

256. Skin dress, collected from Little Ears, Blood, Alberta, 1890s, with characteristic Blackfoot-style yoke of appliqué beadwork in lazy stitch, with additional appliqué decoration to the skirt. H: 120 cm (47.2 in).

leather used in machine belts in the industrializing United States. This, above all, cut away the mainstay of Métis and First Nations life on the Plains.

The Canadian Confederation of 1867 was in effect a union of Ontario, Québec and the Maritime Provinces, as a safeguard against American encroachment, and for Québec in part a strategy to ensure the protection of religion, language and law. The financial and other arrangements originated in a conference in Quebec City in 1864, and were passed into law in 1867 in the British North America Act. No reference was made to First Nations, although importantly the Federal government was made responsible for the Natives and for reserves. The Act enabled the Confederation to expand to include other parts of British North America, including Manitoba in 1870, and British Columbia, which also agreed to join Canada in 1870–71, provided that a railway to the Pacific was built by 1883. The Red River region in southern Manitoba, with a population in the 1860s of 10,000, mostly Métis, was at the centre of this process, which, as the Hudson's Bay Company relinquished control of Rupert's Land, came under threat from new English-speaking colonists, mostly from Ontario. The Canadian government had sent in surveyors which seemed to threaten existing Métis land-holdings.

At the centre of the resistance to this process was the great, but controversial, Métis leader, Louis Riel (1844–85). Trained as a priest and a lawyer in Montréal, he demanded full negotiations between the Métis and Canada over the terms of entry for Manitoba into the Confederation. The issue was forced by his seizure in 1869–70 of Fort Garry, the centre of Red River settlement. While the Canadian government conceded many of the issues relating to land, education and bilingualism, Riel, in allowing a rebellious Ontario Ulsterman, Thomas Scott, to be executed, ensured his own exclusion from government and exile to the United States. One important aspect of the Manitoba Act was the setting aside of nearly 570,000 hectares (1.4 million acres) for Métis occupation in units of 97 hectares (240 acres) or, as an alternative, the payment of a certificate (scrip) of $240, on the assumption that 0.4 hectares (1 acre) was worth a dollar. Riel fled to Montana where he worked as a teacher. During the 1870s, however, the failure of the government to speed land allocation to the Métis, the disappearance of the bison and the arrival of new settlers added new grievances to old. Many Métis had moved to Saskatchewan, where the recognition of Métis land rights had been very slow. Riel returned from Montana, more in the guise of a prophet, of the kind earlier represented elsewhere on the continent, than of a military leader. His short-lived rebellion of 1885, supported by a few Plains Crees, ended in military defeat and in his trial and execution, effectively a martyrdom to his people. Native participation in the rebellion was exaggerated by the government and employed to impose a restrictive policy on the Indians. Neither underlying injustices nor prejudices were solved in this process, and remain an issue today in a continuing political process pursued by various Métis organizations.

257. 'Red River Carts...constructed wholly of wood' in Minnesota during the 1870s. Such vehicles, epitomizing the successful melding of European and Native technology, were used in north–south trade from Manitoba to Minnesota.

Métis art

Métis material culture was an all-encompassing facet of nineteenth-century prairie life, expressing a combined Native and European Canadian culture not paralleled in the United States. Many of the most significant artefacts, such as the York boat,

258. Skin shirt, Métis, Manitoba, mid-nineteenth century, European in design but in most details – materials, construction and quillwork decoration – Native. Such shirts were trade items much prized by Canadians and Europeans. H: 92 cm (36.2 in).

259. Nineteenth-century multicoloured Assomption sash, fingerwoven of manufactured yarn. These important trade items, named after the Québec town where many were made, were used by Métis as belts, and also on occasion as tumplines, ropes and dog harness. L without fringe: 184 cm (72.4 in).

the birchbark canoe and the Red River cart, were vital components of the maintenance and development of the fur trade, and then of the Métis and European settlements. The birchbark canoe, paddled by French Canadian *voyageur*s, by Mohawk from Kahnawake and by Métis, dominated the inland waterways of the northern continent in the middle of the nineteenth century. The York boat, a Hudson's Bay Company innovation, built on European and specifically Orcadian principles, was similarly powered. The Red River cart (fig. 257), in origin French or Scottish, brought people and supplies north from Minnesota and the United States to the Canadian Prairies. Similarly, housing and clothing styles reflected a combination of European and Native styles, but while Native aspects of architecture are, of course, poorly preserved, those related to clothing survive in museum collections in profusion.

Métis individuality and pride was expressed through their decorated dog teams and carts, and in their bright expressive clothing styles. These last were created by women for their husbands. Dress clothing often consisted of tight-fitting military-style coats, in skin or wool cloth, including the capote, or blanket coat, some of which might be adorned with multi-coloured porcupine quillwork, beadwork or silk embroidery in a variety of styles associated with Native forms and with the Roman Catholic, French-Canadian education of women in floral embroidery, then given Native meaning. Most evocative were the vivid multicoloured Assomption sashes, braided or woven by hand, which were used by men as belts. These almost certainly combined Native techniques and European materials for textiles. The other main features of male costume, and therefore also of collections in museums, are foot and leg gear: the leggings were again created from wool cloth or more often skin, and brightly decorated in Plains style with vertical strips of quillwork and complementary fringes. Or, alternatively, trousers were tailored in skin and decorated in European and/or Native style for use in seasonal dances and celebrations. Moccasins, ephemeral creations regularly replaced, along with a wide variety of watch pockets, wall pockets and items suitable for use in urban homes, are the main nineteenth-century creations of these people, sold in large numbers through the fur-trading network. More elaborate products, such as dog harness, decorations and toboggans, and the superb saddlery – for instance the light pad-saddle used in the hunt – are less often found in museum collections.

In this as in so much else, what is actually retained and commemorated in museum collections is only a random, and highly artificial, selection of the materials that were available 100 or 150 years ago. In contrast, women's dress, with an emphasis on long Victorian skirts and dresses, and tartan shawls, was, surprisingly, apparently both simpler and more purely European in style. Yet in a sense, since these garments were expensive to acquire, they expressed the success of the male hunter in trapping and trade, and indicated a degree of balanced reciprocity in male and female dress – men were dressed with traditional feminine skills, and women wore imported items acquired with money that demonstrated male trading and trapping prowess.

Treaties in the United States and Canada

Treaties are negotiations. One of the definitions of to 'treat' is to manipulate, and it can be said that Europeans manipulated situations in North America to achieve, usually explicitly or implicitly, designated ends. One view of treaties is that they are agreements between equals recognizing the status quo; so, for instance, by the 1783 Treaty of Paris Britain recognized the fact of American Independence. But seldom were Natives on an equal footing with those sent to make treaties. And the Native idea of treaties is rather different, of course. In a contemporary Native view, that of Pete Standing Alone, the word used by the Blood (a section of the Blackfoot) for treaty, *innaihtsiini*, means the parties 'must achieve a common purpose'. Properly speaking, for Natives treaties or agreements originated in the pre-European situation in meetings, whose form was by no means homogeneous, incorporating in the Northeast much speech-making and the exchange of wampum, especially in New York and New England. To the west an important component was the calumet ceremony, in which pipes – for peace – were smoked to cement understandings between independent sovereign peoples. In both of these events there were religious over-tones, missing from the making if not the celebration of European treaties. There are also a number of different views about Native participation. In the first and most prevalent interpretation Indians are seen as being powerless, helpless peoples at the mercy of Americans and Europeans. This disadvantage was compounded by language, cultural and behavioural differences – incomplete or incompetent translation of treaty terms, for instance – and by factionalism either within individual tribes or First Nations, or between independent peoples. And of course these differences were always exploited by the superior powers.

However, this view of the powerlessness of Indians is in some cases an over-simplification. As mentioned, Native peoples regularly conducted political relations with other peoples. Also, in the fur trade, a dominant economic activity throughout much of the continent for hundreds of years, Indians held considerable if not pre-eminent power over isolated groups of Europeans in the Subarctic and interior. Negotiations and trade agreements, which possessed many aspects of treaties, bore this in mind. Natives were competent middlemen, well able to handle and indeed manipulate competition, being fully aware of the benefits of both competition and reciprocity. Occasionally, of course, Indians held the upper hand militarily. Pontiac's Revolt in the 1760s was occasioned, in part, by the British ending of French payments to Indians. The Proclamation of 1763, by which even today Indians have the right to hunt and fish, as they always have done, may have been brought about by British altruism or, in the alternative view, by the determination of the colonial authorities to avoid another wide-ranging revolt of this kind.

Treaties grew out of payments for land, which again can be seen in two contrasting lights – as mortgage payments towards purchase or as perpetual annuities. However, it can be reasonably argued that for Native people they have a religious aspect, conferring on these agreements the sacred qualities associated with a close relationship to the land. Or in an alternative view they are seen as a sort of Indian Magna Carta, fundamental documents to be negotiated and manipulated in a process continuing today. In the European view of law in the sixteenth century uncultivated land was regarded as empty and available for occupation by others: it was this idea that allowed Europeans to acquire land. Nevertheless, the British preferred to pay for their land, if only to calm consciences. By the Royal Proclamation of 1763 only the Crown could purchase land from Indians, who were regarded as possessing the right of occupancy in all areas not covered by cessions and by prior purchases. In the US a series of trade and intercourse laws in the early nineteenth century legislated in a similar manner to prevent intrusion onto Indian land. Until the American Revolution the main ideological thrust against Indians was not military but religious: Indians were to be saved and civilized, and once settled, had no need for the land, particularly in view of the catastrophic long-term decline in population. After the American Revolution ideas of economic and social progress came to the fore – Indians were to be assimilated and civilized. As this happened, the thrust of treaties was less to make peace, which usually existed in any case, and more to acquire land. The most definite statement of the early evolutionary view was provided by Thomas Jefferson, who pointed out in the 1820s that progress could be conceived in spatial as well as temporal terms: as you moved east from the Rockies towards the great cities of the coastal United States, the country became more progressive and (in the nineteenth-century sense) civilized.

Up until 1871 the United States made 371 treaties and fought perhaps forty wars against Indians. It is sometimes said that on only one or two occasions, for instance the Cherokee removal in 1837–8 and after the Santee Sioux revolt of 1860s, was land directly taken away as a consequence of military action. One British Canadian view is that, unlike the United States, Canada behaved with humanitarian vision, particularly in the minimization of military force. The end result was, however, much the same, and so today Canadian First Nations may view the process of alienation of their territory as being no less unacceptable than the apparently more bloody pattern of events in the United States. Eleven treaties were signed in Canada from 1871, and there was one war, as mentioned, the North-West Rebellion of 1885 under Riel. However, these treaties were almost all made in circumstances in which the Euro-Canadians were all powerful – very seldom was there actual need to use military force. Most American treaties followed invasions by settlers into Native territories. Conversely, the post-1871 Canadian Treaties have a modern and contemporary aspect. They were designed to extinguish First Nations rights, mostly in advance of

260. Pitikwahanapiwiyin, or
Poundmaker (*c*.1842–86), Plains
Cree. He is holding a small personal
pipe for everyday use and has a
Hudson's Bay Company blanket
draped over his shoulder.

261. Soapstone elbow pipe with wood
stem, Plains Cree, Saskatchewan,
collected by Elgin Morell from
Poundmaker on his surrender at
Battleford, 26 May 1885; Morell was
part of the column of Lieutenant-
Colonel W.D. Otter who received
the surrender. L: 20 cm (7.9 in).

settlement, railways and mineral exploitation from Ontario
through to eastern British Columbia. The last treaty, Treaty 11
of 1921, arose because of the discovery of oil at Norman Wells
in the Northwest Territories. This was followed half a century
later by the James Bay and Northern Québec Agreement of
1975. This, although not called a treaty, was in a sense exactly
that, in that First Nations' rights had to be both entrenched and
curtailed before the great James Bay hydroelectric project could

proceed. The Alaska Native Claims Settlement Act of 1971 was similarly vital, to enable the 1960s discoveries of oil on the North Slope of Alaska to be exploited. Today the treaty process has restarted in northern and western Canada.

Canadian treaties were often requested by First Nations themselves, who recognized, of course, the tragic significance of the disappearance of the buffalo, and the arrival of Canadian settlers from Ontario with the railway. With these demands came an understanding of the importance that farming would hold for Indians, and so requests for implements, stock and grain were made. The allowances granted by the Canadian government varied between treaties, but included clothing allowances, lump sum payments for chiefs, annuities of $4 or $5 per adult and $15–25 for chiefs and headmen. Reserves were to include between 65 and 259 hectares (160 and 640 acres) per family. Unfortunately, such provisions were only fitfully and incompletely implemented, so that farming supplies were inadequate, and the 1880s programme of ideal farms with instructors failed. In the 1890s further hindrance was placed in the way of Indian farming, with a licensing system for the sale of all produce, and prohibitions on movement – on contacts, for instance, between Canadians and Indians. As immigration became significant, land sales from reserves were enforced, to provide homesteading farms for Europeans. During the First World War, as farming became mechanized, credit was unavailable to Indians; after 1918 returning veterans were provided with further homesteads, sometimes from Indian land.

Red Crow (*c.*1830–1900) was head chief of the Blood (Kainai) tribe of the Blackfoot Confederacy from 1870. As a successful warrior he was involved in thirty-three raids against neighbouring peoples including the Crows and Plains Crees. In 1874 Red Crow welcomed the arrival of the North-West Mounted Police to restore order, and he recognised early on the awful reality of the disappearance of buffalo in 1879–80. He remained loyal to Canada during the North-West Rebellion in 1885. The Prime Minister, John A. MacDonald, rewarded him and other loyal chiefs with a tour of eastern Canada. There Red Crow attended the unveiling of the monument to Brant, or Thayendanegea (*c.*1742–1807), the Mohawk leader who had remained loyal to Britain during the American Revolution (figs 251–2). Red Crow also visited the Mohawk Institute near

Brantford and returned to the Blood Reserve a strong propo-
nent of education for Indians. However, although baptised a
Roman Catholic, Red Crow retained his Native religion and
spent the last years of his life fighting the attempted suppression
of the Sun Dance. He became a successful farmer, growing
grain and vegetables, and in 1894 accepted an offer from the
government to exchange prized horses for fifteen cattle, part of
a programme that led to the establishment of profitable ranching among the Blood in southern Alberta.

Whereas Red Crow and Louis O'Soup (see p. 250) successfully maintained Native roles in the new state, Poundmaker (figs
260–61) was unable to resolve the impossible contradictions
inherent in leadership of the Plains Crees after the Treaty signing.
Discontent arose from 1833 onwards because of the reduction in
the farming equipment and livestock promised to the Indians,
which coincided with Métis unrest. Poundmaker's Crees were
joined by others, particularly the Nakodas (Stoneys), who were
early involved in the Métis action at Duck Lake during the
North-West Rebellion in 1885. Since leadership depended on
consensus, Poundmaker was unable to stop his people sacking
Battleford after the Indian agent culpably failed to release rations.
As a result, even though in subsequent skirmishes Poundmaker
prevented his followers from killing retreating soldiers, he was
tried for treason and sentenced to three years in jail.

The Sun Dance

Just as the 1763 Royal Proclamation codified Indian law to that
date, so the Indian Act of 1876 codified Canadian laws. One
aspect of the Indian Act was that provisions could be easily
amended, thus giving Indian Commissioners substantial
powers. From a cultural point of view the 1885 Indian Act,
which prohibited the potlatch on the Northwest Coast, was crucial in providing the model for the prohibition of the Plains Sun
Dance in 1895. Both prohibitions remained on the books until
the 1950s, although they were not generally enforced.

The Sun Dance was the primary ceremonial occasion of
Plains peoples, performed in July or August with a series of
events lasting several days. Often an individual acted as host,
providing food and making gifts, in order to ensure his and the
people's good health. It acted as a means of re-animating or

recreating nature and the world. Large numbers of people came together, after spending much of the rest of the year dispersed in hunting grounds. The occasion served to express the rebirth of common tribal interests, to provide a forum for tribal politics, and to renew the rank of chiefs. At the centre of the ceremony was a lodge built of poles, around which young men danced, as part of a series of vow-fulfilling ordeals. One of these included gazing at the setting sun, hence the name Sun Dance. No drinking was allowed, hence the alternative name for the ceremony, Thirst Dance. The explanation for the Canadian banning of the Sun Dance lies in the idea that it was wasteful to give away goods, as in the potlatch, and in a dislike for the extravagance so exhibited, for the waste of time and for the other supposed evils which might occur when a large number of First Nations' people were gathered together. One aspect that was particularly disliked by Euro-Canadians was that it provided a forum for elders to tell stories about their war exploits, horse raids and hunting to younger men no longer able to pursue these activities.

Métis and Plains collections

The earliest documented Canadian Plains collection in the British Museum was acquired from a soldier, Major George Seton (1819–1905). He was also an artist, trained in creating panoramas for military purposes, and thus interested in recording what he saw. He served in the Royal Canadian Rifles from 1853 to 1858, the last two years stationed at Fort Garry, Manitoba (Rupert's Land), at the behest of the Hudson's Bay Company who had requested protection from supposed American and Native threats. At the end of his posting he participated in the British and Canadian exploring expeditions discussed on p. 235.

Another participant in the British exploring expedition was a French scientist, Eugène Bourgeaux (1813–77), who also obtained, entirely incidentally, one or two First Nations' objects including a drum and songboard. A significant example of the professional collector, he was described by Sir William Hooker as 'the prince of botanical collectors'. He seems to have become interested in his profession while tending his father's herds in the French Department of the Hautes-Alpes. In 1857–8 he

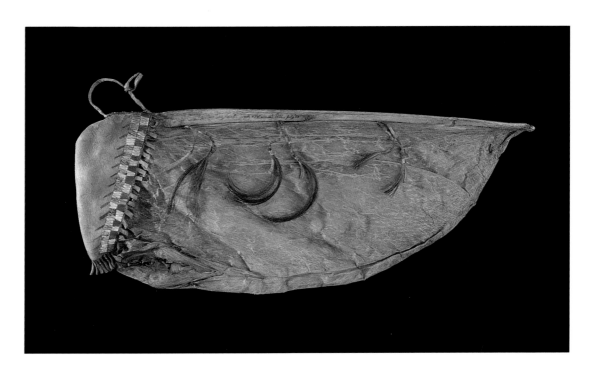

262. Cree bag or pouch, Canadian Prairies, 1850s, constructed from a pelican bill and decorated with dyed quill embroidery in folded-line technique. Bags of this type were made and used by women to hold domestic kit, such as materials for quillwork or sewing. 45 cm x 18 cm (17.7 x 7.1 in).

accompanied the British expedition of John Palliser (1817–87), during which he made collections for the Royal Botanic Gardens, Kew. Unfortunately, Bourgeaux never wrote anything, and indeed seldom documented his collections on this or subsequent expeditions, such as that to Mexico during the French period of the 1860s. Bourgeaux's impact on the Canadian Plains was much greater than the collection of one or two artefacts would suggest. He drew to the attention of the British government the great fertility of the Canadian Plains – Rupert's Land – for both arable farming and ranching. Of course, if he had not made this observation, then no doubt someone else would have done so, and the end result – agricultural settlement – would have been the same. At the same time Palliser emphasized in his report the necessity of making proper provision for the Native population before the buffalo disappeared, and indeed before opening the land for European settlement.

While in Rupert's Land Seton made a small ethnographic collection, including two parfleches (fig. 245) and a Cree bag (fig. 262). Somewhat later, a less well documented group of material was collected by Lord Lorne (1845–1914), when Governor-General (1878–83) of Canada. Some of these artefacts were obtained on a visit he made to the prairies in

1881, while others seem to have been obtained from Plains leaders on a visit made to Ottawa and the east in 1885. One of the costumes belonged to Louis O'Soup (*c*.1830–1913), the noted Plains Ojibwa or Saulteaux leader. He wore this superb shirt (fig. 264) when addressing Lord Lorne on 19 August 1881 at Fort Qu'apelle, Saskatchewan. The speech, complaining about the treatment of his people, was incompletely translated and summarized so as to omit complaints. He was presented with a Waltham watch by Lorne, who in turn was presented with the costume which he subsequently sold to the British Museum. O'Soup, whose name means Back Fat – the prized fat of moose – devoted most of his life to trying to persuade the Canadian government to honour Treaty 4 in detail. In 1911, in his eighties, O'Soup was one of a delegation of nine leaders that went to Ottawa to complain:

> For many years we have put our children to school and there is not one yet that has enough education to make a living… They go to their parents for a start and their parents have nothing to give them, and the young men is reported as lazy. But he has nothing to scratch the ground with, and cannot farm.

Although brought up to be a noted moose hunter, O'Soup was also, incidentally, an excellent pioneer farmer on the prairies: in 1888 at the Broadview Fair he won first prize for the best dairy cow, first prize for the best three-year-old steers and a special prize for the fattest steer. He also grew wheat. But, because of federal restrictions on Native farming, he stopped farming and changed reserve. Lord Lorne's few objects are complemented by a group of around eighty items collected during the 1890s by a Ration Issuer, F. Dean-Freeman, on the Blood Reserve in Alberta (figs 253, 255–6).

263. Sydney Hall (1842–1922), journalist and artist for the London *Graphic*, drew this picture of Louis O'Soup wearing his full ceremonial costume in August 1881, and then had him sign the drawing with his mark, a moose (?), at the bottom right.

264. Blue wool shirt of Louis O'Soup, Blood. The shirt, which was given to the Governor General Lord Lorne in 1881, is adorned with panels of beadwork, surrounded by beaver skin and edged with coloured cloth tape and bunches of dyed horse hair. H: 65 cm (25.6 in).

THE AMERICAN WEST

Whereas the Canadian Plains were approached through the Great Lakes and from Hudson Bay, the American West was explored from the east and south after the Louisiana Purchase of 1803. Traders, surveyors and the military moved north from New Orleans, up the Mississippi, and west and northwest down the Ohio to the Mississippi-Missouri

Part of the American West showing the location of peoples mentioned in the chapter.

265. Uren Lernard from Warm Springs, Oregon, in contemporary pow-wow costume and wearing a hair roach with feather pendants at the All-Idaho Indian Expo, Boise, 1990. Such headdresses, originating among the horticulturists of the Missouri, are widely used today on the pow-wow circuit, celebrating Pan-Indian values, as in the Grass Dance.

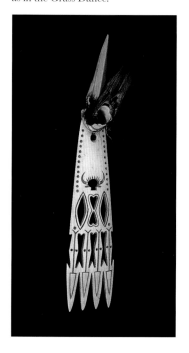

266. Elk-antler or bison-bone roach spreader (for spreading deer hair across the head), decorated with incised arrows, cut-out bison headdress, red and black pigment, woodpecker scalp and mandible (?), collected by Duke Paul of Württemburg from the Oto chief Isch-nan-uanky near the Platte River (?) on 18 September 1823. L: 33 cm (13 in).

rivers. This vast territory, to be much augmented in the 1840s by war and by treaty, was that about which in July 1845 John O'Sullivan (1813–95), the New York journalist, employed the apt but unfortunate phrase 'manifest destiny' in a debate about the annexation of Texas. It was, he said, 'our manifest destiny to overspread the continent allotted by Providence for the free development of our yearly multiplying millions'. This sentiment prevailed through the rest of the nineteenth century as an explanation for the Euro-American peopling of the West. By the 1890s the continental United States had been effectively occupied by the Americans, and the physical, if not cultural, frontier between Natives and non-Natives had virtually disappeared.

Plains peoples: horticulturists and hunters

The great American Plains extend 3,200 km (2,000 miles) from Texas north to Canada, and west some 800 km (500 miles) from the Mississippi-Missouri rivers to the Rocky Mountains. As in Canada, European and European-American fur traders were the first to move onto the northern Plains, where they encountered horticulturists and bison hunters, particularly those speaking Siouan and Caddoan languages. While much of the High Plains consists of semi-arid grasslands, occupied by big-game hunters since Paleoindian times 10,000 years ago, the riverine peoples moved north along the Missouri during the last millennium. There, rich flood-plain land was available for farming for a variety of peoples. Along the Missouri and Mississippi, and their tributaries, lived settled tribes, for instance the Pawnee in Nebraska, and the Mandan, Arikara and Hidatsa to the north. They combined the growing of maize, beans and squash with the seasonal hunting of buffalo. Large villages were constructed of domed circular lodges, of wood and earth, not entirely dissimilar in structural principles to the sod and whalebone dwellings of the North American Arctic.

Around these settled peoples lived nomadic hunters. Of these, those known collectively as the Sioux are the most familiar, if only for the long-flowing war bonnets of swept-back eagle feathers. Divided into seven peoples speaking related languages, the eastern Sioux or Santees occupied parts of Minnesota in the early nineteenth century and are known as the Dakotas. The Yanktons, or Nakotas, are the central group, and the Tetons, or Lakotas, make up the western Sioux – both groups inhabiting the states of North and South Dakota. Sioux, derived through French from *Nadowe-isi-w*, the Ojibwa word for 'snake' or 'enemy', is a non-preferred term but provides an effective name which encompasses all these allied peoples, independent but sharing a varied culture. Like other hunters, they moved west onto the northern Plains with horses and guns, where they became the dominant force for much of the nineteenth century, eventually reaching as far west as Wyoming and Montana. Fully equestrian by 1760, the western and central Sioux came to dominate the horticultural riverine peoples – the Arikaras, Mandans and Hidatsas on the Upper Missouri. These peoples, numbering like the Sioux in tens of thousands around 1800, controlled the fur trade while living in well-fortified villages. Devastated by epidemics, particularly of smallpox, in the first third of the century, they lost their pre-eminence to the High Plains hunters.

Initially, relations with the United States were friendly – Lewis and Clark recognized the Sioux as the dominant force on the Missouri in 1804 – but the decline of the fur trade, in which they participated, and the arrival of settlers made conflict inevitable. Within twenty years of the removal of Southeastern peoples in the 1830s, while the Cherokees and others were rebuilding their farms and nations, America had expanded westwards with the acquisition of Texas, much of Oregon Territory, northern Mexico and California. White settlers now crossed the continent and Indian country: Plains peoples were isolated no longer. Before the Civil War (1861–5) segregation of Indians and Americans was the rule – after the Civil War assimilation, in conjunction with ever increasing numbers of railroads, was seen as desirable: the first transcontinental railroad was completed in 1869 and was rapidly followed by three more. During the 1850s a series of meetings, intended to protect surveyors, migrants moving west, and farmers, resulted in agreements and treaties, many of which were later to be broken.

Little Crow's War of 1862 in Minnesota exemplifies such events. Converted to farming and to Episcopalianism, the Dakota Sioux leader, Little Crow, or Taoyateduta, recognized the inevitability of American settlement and signed treaties. Much of the monetary payment promised by the treaties went to traders and to people of mixed descent, who used political connections in Washington, rather than kin relations, to their advantage in business and in land dealings with Dakotas. Little Crow was eventually forced onto the offensive by the failure to provide the promised rations during the summer of 1862. 'The money is ours', he said, 'but we cannot get it': the Indian agent would not release supplies without payment. Some 500 settlers were killed before the army resumed control, and thirty-eight Indians were hung. Little Crow fled to Canada, where he asked for assistance, pointing out the help given the British in the War of 1812 and finding out, as Sitting Bull was to later, that this counted for relatively little. After returning home, Little Crow was killed the following year, while picking raspberries, for a bounty of perhaps $75 offered by the state of Minnesota for scalps.

The loss of western Sioux lands occurred through a similar process of attrition. Again early negotiations with the United States proved to be ineffective. Two treaties at Fort Laramie, Wyoming, were crucial, the first, of 1851, promising discussion and friendship with the Lakota Sioux and other Plains peoples. This was particularly important in relation to the building of forts and trails through Lakota territory. The second treaty, of 1868, guaranteed the Great Sioux Reservation – South Dakota west of the Missouri river – more than 10.1 million hectares (25 million acres). Also, under Red Cloud's influence the US agreed to the abandonment of the Bozeman Trail and American forts along the Powder River. All of this was reversed during the 1870s, when the discovery of gold in the Black Hills lead to the intrusion of gold miners and, subsequently, the destruction of George Armstrong Custer by Crazy Horse and Sitting Bull at the Battle of the Little Big Horn, Montana, in 1876. After the Custer defeat Sitting Bull was driven into Canada, and Crazy Horse surrendered the following year, 1877. As a result large reservations, such as the Great Sioux Reservation of 1868, were radically reduced in size. A second aspect of the campaigns against Indians lay in hysterical hatred, which in part gave rise to massacres. One such occasion was the Sand Creek Massacre of 1864, when a force under John M. Chivington massacred much of Black Kettle's Cheyennes or, as they call themselves, Tsistsistas, following their settlement in Colorado. Similarly, the Battle of Wounded Knee, and the killing in 1890 of more than 200 Sioux of Big Foot's Band after they had surrendered, arose in part because of general fears of the effects of the Ghost Dance. This manifestation of a messianic religion, inspired by the Paiute prophet, Wovoka, promised a return of the Sioux world as it existed before the arrival of Americans.

Historians have suggested that in the period 1866–91 the US army fought 1,040 engagements with Indians. Less than 1,000 Americans died, whereas 4,371 Indians were killed out of a population of 200,000–300,000. More important than these controversial figures, with relatively few deaths from the action of the army in comparison to the great losses of the Civil War, was the erosion of the subsistence base of the Indians. Most significant of all was the sheer force of the numbers of people moving into the West. As the buffalo disappeared, the land was enclosed with newly invented barbed wire, patented by Joseph F. Glidden in 1874. Subsequently for Native nations there was no choice but to submit to confinement in the reservations, and to depend on self-reliance and on the rations and the goodwill of Americans. Before European contact there are likely to have been as many as 10 million or more buffalo in the US and Canada. These were first depleted and then nearly exterminated in the nineteenth century for a number of reasons. Initially, Indians used them to provide robes for domestic use, preferring young female animals for thin skin and tender meat. After the Civil War buffalo competed with ranch animals, and particularly after 1870 older male beasts provided the thick skin required for industrial belts employed in American industry. The extermination of buffalo was also regarded as having what was then regarded as the beneficial affect of forcing Natives to farm.

Further to the south a similar process enveloped, for instance, the Osages, living in Missouri and northern Arkansas. First contacted by the French, whom they called Heavy Eyebrows, in the seventeenth century, they came to dominate surrounding peoples through successful diplomatic and trade relations, in a manner analogous to that of the Iroquois and Sioux. In the nineteenth century, from 1808, in a series of devastating treaties, the Osages came to be confined to a relatively small area of what is now northeastern Oklahoma. By 1875 the buffalo had disappeared, but in that year a couple of thousand Indians harvested 50,000 bushels of maize, 20,000 bushels of wheat, and had already built hundreds of houses and planted orchards. The Osages, unlike many other Native peoples, were also able to retain some control of mineral rights, in this case oil, discovered in 1897. By 1925 headrights (annual individual royalty payments) reached $13,200, more than £100,000 a year to-day; during the Depression this income disappeared, and only recovered to the 1920s figures during the 1970s.

Allotment and Native farmers

In 1871 Congress removed the full sovereign nation status of Indian peoples: no more treaties were signed. As Indians declined in numbers, through disease and cultural attrition, condemned apparently by race to the savage or barbarian stage of evolution, assimilation – into the wider American world – became intellectually respectable. The Dawes or General Allotment Act of 1887 was the principal instrument of this movement. The

267. Crow dress of wool decorated with elk teeth and bone replacements, the number of teeth probably indicating the husband's hunting prowess and acting as charms for longevity. Plains dresses were once made from one skin, but in the nineteenth century fuller dresses, preferable for riding, were constructed from two skins. L: 113 cm (44.5 in).

268. (below) Mid-nineteenth-century northern Plains robe. War exploits decorating men's robes were openly discussed, but the abstract geometric designs on women's robes, of mythological origin and sometimes protective function, were seldom explained. The design here with a pair of horns suggests an abstract buffalo form. 180 x 150 cm (70.9 x 59.1 in).

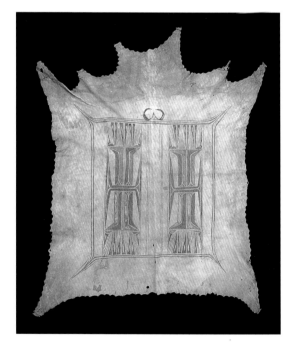

269. Elk-antler club from the eastern Plains, first half of the nineteenth century. The distal end of the blade is set with four screws. L: 50 cm (19.7 in).

270. Painted rawhide horse ornament and armour, possibly Crow, brought to England by Bryan Mullanphy, 1825. Ornaments of this kind were used in pairs, one on either side of the saddle; the geometric decoration of the few surviving examples no doubt possesses esoteric, probably protective, significance. 90 x 60 cm (35.4 x 23.6 in).

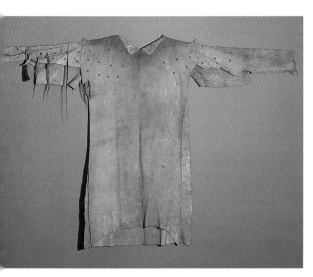

271. Skin shirt that may have belonged to Bull Bear, or Mato-Tatanka, a signatory to the first Sioux Treaty with the US in 1825, probably collected in 1829–31. Painted with red pigment and black circles, the neck is edged with white beads, and the arms with horse hair locks. H: 105 cm (41.3 in).

272. 'Post recently destroyed', Wounded Knee, South Dakota, c.1972. The site of the last military action by US forces in 1890, Wounded Knee was occupied on 27 February 1973 by the American Indian Movement bringing national and international attention to Native issues. The date is now recognized as a tribal holiday by the Oglala Sioux Nation.

273. 'Funeral of Gabriel Two Eagle, a Viet Nam Hero', 1970s. The Lakotas and other Native peoples are a significant element in the US armed forces. Most famous perhaps was the participation during the 1940s of the Navajo 'Code Talkers', who used elements of their language to provide secure communication for US forces.

274. Unfolded rectangular painted rawhide parfleche, c.1825. Such articles were made by women for storing and transporting food and dress. After the laborious process of skin preparation the interior surface was sized, often with a glutinous wash made from skin scrapings, and the design painted, largely with mineral pigments. 67 x 51 cm (26.4 x 20.1in).

Act represented an unholy alliance between those who wanted Indian country for American settlement and liberals who saw assimilation as the best means of ensuring the survival of Indians. Land could be allotted in 65-hectare (160-acre) sections to families; Indians then became American citizens after twenty-five years. Inevitably, land was alienated – when debts, for instance, forced sales away from Native farmers. 'Surplus' land – even though confirmed as Indian under treaties – could then be opened for white allotment and settlement. The moneys thus raised were held in trust and returned to the government against administrative and other expenses. Education was one of these expenses, symbolized by the boarding school, particularly that at Carlisle, Pennsylvania (1879–1918), founded by Captain Richard Henry Pratt to turn Natives into Euro-Americans. General Allotment, too, encapsulated an ambiguous view: if Indians really were dying out, then reservation land would be absorbed naturally into the greater whole. But of course if Indians were to multiply and make an adjustment to American life, as was to happen in the twentieth century, then land for the increased future generations would no longer be available. The underlying presumption was usually that Plains people did not make good farmers. After the arrival of Americans, reservations and Indian Agents, new crops were introduced. These included, for instance, the seemingly foul-smelling potato which the Hidatsas preferred to grow for sale rather than eat. A more fundamental American idea was that the prairie rather than river flood-plain should be farmed. The highland was, however, harder to cultivate and less satisfactory than lower-lying ground, drying out too quickly and, eventually, as Americans were to find out, creating dust-bowl conditions from time to time. Tobacco was grown everywhere. Among the Hidatsas, for instance, old men grew the plant, using, for instance, a buffalo rib to dig the earth, and it was old men who smoked most. It was recognized that smoking affected the lungs, and stopped people being able to run effectively.

As mentioned, from an intellectual point of view the determination to assimilate Plains Indians was based on an evolutionary view of social development. Hunters would become farmers, and farmers would reach civilization. Gradually, however, through the work of anthropologists in the later nineteenth century, particularly Franz Boas (1858–1942), cultural relativism,

275. 'Harry Door, Crow Indian, farming', *c*.1910.

and the recognition of cultural individuality, came to replace racial and evolutionary schemes of human development. At the same time the growth of conservation movements, and the recognition that Indian peoples, particularly in the Southwest, had survived and would even prosper, reversed assimilationist sentiment. While Indians were granted citizenship in 1924, it was only during the depression, with John Collier's Indian Reorganization Act of 1934, that the continuing damage brought about by Indian allotment was ended. Education was for the first time oriented towards Indians, and schools were instructed to end the ban, dating from the 1880s, on the use of Indian languages in schools. In 1935 the founding of the Indian Arts and Crafts Board gave recognition to the importance of art in cultural survival. After World War II, however, in part because of prevalent anti-communism, New Deal ideas faded and were replaced by a determination to end the reservation system. The Klamath and the Menominee reservations, for instance, were terminated during the 1950s, and in 1953 the states were given civil and criminal jurisdiction over Indian peoples. Nevertheless, a significant degree of sovereignty remains, enabling, for instance, Native nations to set up highly successful gambling establishments across the United States.

Contact and collecting on the American Plains

In the first half of the nineteenth century the United States assumed control of the Plains west of the Mississippi. In 1800 the Spanish had returned power to the French, who in turn, under Napoleon, had sold this Indian country to President Jefferson. This, the Louisiana Purchase of 1803, provided funds for the French to continue the war in Europe. Jefferson, even before this acquisition, was involved in the organization of perhaps the most famous of a long series of US exploring, later surveying, expeditions. Under the leadership of Jefferson's secretary, Meriwether Lewis (1774–1809), and William Clark (1770–1838) the US Corps of Discovery explored the northern reaches of the Louisiana Purchase. They travelled from St Louis up the Missouri, across the northern Plains and down the watershed of the Columbia to the Pacific in 1804–6. Both were much aided by Natives along the route, and Clark subsequently devoted much of the rest of his life to relations with Indians, especially as Superintendent of Indian affairs at St Louis from 1822 to 1838. Clark also possessed a rich collection, or cabinet, of Native curiosities, perhaps the first such museum in the American West. With these and with his time he was generous, especially in respect of the amateurs who were most responsible both for gathering artefacts and creating early records of western Native peoples during the first half of the nineteenth century. One such person was Duke Paul von Württemburg (1797–1860), a naturalist in the Humboldtian tradition, who amassed vast natural history collections from his travels between the 1820s and the 1850s, particularly in North America.

In May 1823 the duke arrived in St Louis for the first time, where he was welcomed by William Clark and René Auguste Chouteau (1749–1829), who in his youth, in 1764, was a founder of this still part-French city. Duke Paul visited Clark on several occasions, once when he was receiving a delegation of Potawatomis, lead by Stream-of-the-Rock, who was there to complain to the superintendent about the depletion of game and fish along the tributaries of the Illinois. This took place in a large hall full of Indian curiosities, one of which, a calumet, is recorded as having been given to the duke (fig. 276). This is said to have come from the North West, a designation suggesting that it may possibly have been acquired on the Lewis and Clark expedition in 1804–6. Other articles were obtained by the duke during his summer journey travelling north up the Missouri.

The process of the acquisition of collections is seldom very well documented, even by diarists such as Duke Paul. In September 1823, however, the duke visited an Oto village near the Platte River, Nebraska. He wrote extensively about the earth lodges of these farmers, their size, construction, contents

276. Calumet from the northern Plains, possibly Mandan, with a catlinite pipe bowl, and stem and (reversed) pendant of bald eagle feathers quill-wrapped and adorned with horse hair. Given to Duke Paul of Württemburg by General Clark in 1822–4, this may have been collected during the first American crossing of the continent in 1804–6.
L: 113 cm (44.5 in).

and divisions. He visited that of a chief, Isch-nan-uanky, who had travelled to Washington and met President James Monroe two years earlier. The Indian brought out, as a special honour, leather cushions for the duke to sit on. The European presented him with many different kinds of 'wares' and in return received all sorts of articles of the kinds that 'warriors value most highly'. These included the chief's own head ornament, consisting of a roach constructed from the tail hair of deer, which the duke recorded as worn on a largely shaven head and indicating the status of the wearer, particularly his right to have a 'say in council decisions'. While unfortunately this is unlocated, the roach spreader (fig. 266), which he described as a 'comb of bison bone' was included in the collection purchased for the Museum in 1868. In addition, a large group of artefacts was made available for bartering, but the duke was obliged to be very selective

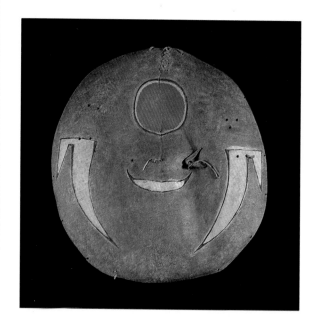

277. Buffalo rawhide shield, possibly the example collected by Duke Paul of Württemburg in September 1823 from a Pawnee chief identified as Schakè-ru-leshar. The design, perhaps representing the sun and moon, would have come from a vision and acted as protection in war and horse raiding.
Diam. of shield: 58 cm (22.8 in).

278. Sketch of the war exploits portrayed on the soft tanned skin cover of the Pawnee shield (left).

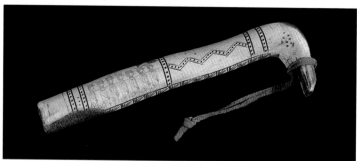

279. An elk-antler adze used in preparing skin, collected in 1822–31 perhaps from the Omahas or Otos. This example, from which the blade is missing, is incised with geometric decoration and images of soldiers with headdresses, or shakos, commonly worn *c.*1800–1812 by, for instance, the British Light Infantry. L: 31 cm (12.2 in).

280. Pawnee woman and child in a cradleboard, with the Morning Star picked out in brass studs, photographed on the road to Fort Kearny in the 1860s (?) by an unidentified photographer. Fort Kearny, Nebraska, was a military post (1848–71) on the Platte Route during the California Gold Rush.

281. Cradleboard, carved from cottonwood and painted with the design of the Morning Star surrounded by rainbows or other celestial phenomena, possibly collected in September 1823 from a Pawnee village on the Wolf branch of the Platte river. L: 93 cm (36.6 in).

in order not to deplete his own trade goods. Some of the unlisted domestic Oto items (fig. 279) may also have been acquired on this occasion.

On 26 September the duke visited the Skidi or Wolf Pawnees, where he was made welcome by Ta-rare-kak-schà, which he translates as the Axe, and from whom he seems to have obtained a bow. Pawnee religion and medicine were explained to him in some detail, along with the significance of sacrifices made to the Morning Star. Two days earlier the duke had visited a Grand Pawnee village, where he may have obtained articles decorated with the Morning Star, Sun and Moon (fig. 281). The role of stars was also explained to Alice Fletcher at the beginning of the twentieth century by the Pawnee James Murie: 'First of all was Tiráwa-atius, the power above all and over all, the father of all things. Then came the lesser or under powers; these were given places in the heavens; they are in stars…' The Pawnee 'were organized by the stars; these powers above made them into families and villages and taught them how to live…' Duke Paul probably acquired a Pawnee shield at this village (fig. 277), sold to him by two men and a woman acting in concert. This shield includes representations of two separate events: the rawhide shield itself is painted with a depiction of the personal war medicine of the owner, medicine that would provide supernatural help in war – particularly in horse raiding and in counting coup, that is the system of graded honours obtained, for instance, by touching an enemy. The cover of the shield (fig. 278) is painted with realistic pictographs depicting the war exploits of the original owner, including counting coup with lances and seemingly also horse raiding. Such shields and covers originated in pre-horse times but continued to be important, although they were not necessarily used by mounted warriors, both because they were heavy and unwieldy and because they offered no protection against firearms.

Buffalo robes provided more extensive surfaces on which war exploits could be recorded. A mid-nineteenth-century northern Plains example in the British Museum's collection depicts eight or more war exploits (fig. 282). The owner is certainly portrayed eight times, each time with a straight-up eagle-feather bonnet; in the middle and on the left he is shown with a calumet, indicating leadership in a war party. There are also

282. Sketch of war exploits painted
on a soft tanned buffalo hide,
northern Plains, collected before
1868. 220 x 75 cm (86.6 x 29.5 in).

283. Detail of a Yanktonai Winter
Count associated with Blue Thunder,
showing some of the 119 pictographs
for each winter from 1785 to 1901.
The sitting buffalo represents the
death of Sitting Bull and so must
indicate the winter of 1890–91.
Overall dimensions: 90 x 112 cm
(35.4 x 44.1 in).

four depictions of much enlarged scalps, shown with paths connecting the owner to the dead, scalped enemy. On the middle right is a shield, painted red with green stars, again representing the personal medicine of the owner. On the left-hand side the

284. The US display at the Great Exhibition, London, 1851. Plains and Northwest Coast figures, probably supplied by George Catlin, are here juxtaposed with the sensational sculpture of *The Greek Slave*.

warrior is depicted capturing a woman dressed in green, and above them he is shown in a separate incident sheltering behind his horse, wounded in the leg, and shooting arrows. A final significant detail lies in the claw-like necklace worn by the owner, suggesting a bear or eagle connection with his name. Such symbolism, and the use of synonyms and metonyms for events, is combined with personal medicine in the iconography of war on other shirts. A final and important record using the same iconographic system is the Winter Count (fig. 283), in which years are symbolized by the depiction of one single event for each year. Originally, these too were executed on skin, although in the reservation period other materials, such as flour-sack cotton, came to be used. The British Museum Winter Count, associated with but probably not by the Yanktonai or Nakota Sioux, Blue Thunder, is one of these.

285. Yellow Calf (d. 1938), Arapaho, Wyoming, 28 September 1927, then aged sixty-seven, wearing a feather bonnet and cloth shirt.

286. Yellow Calf's feather bonnet, constructed of the immature tail feathers of a golden eagle, the tips decorated with hair symbolizing scalp-locks. Such flaired headdresses, constructed as here over a skull cap with a beaded front band, were originally representative of war honours. H: 75 cm (29.5 in).

There are very few later groups of documented artefacts from the American Plains in the British Museum. Most surprising, perhaps, is that there is nothing that can be securely documented to collection by the Pennsylvania lawyer-turned-painter, George Catlin (1796–1872). Catlin, after seeing an Indian delegation in Philadelphia, determined to devote his life to recording the disappearing way of life of the western Indians. From 1830 to 1836, initially with the assistance of the by now elderly William Clark, he travelled the western Plains sketching Indians, recording their lives and making collections. In the late 1830s he mounted an exhibition in New York and then took the show to England, where he remained, more or less, for thirty years and where he published his life works. While in London, he created at the Egyptian Hall in Piccadilly during the 1840s what amounted to the first proto-Wild West shows, employing tableaux vivants and groups of touring Ojibwas. It was through this medium, the Wild West show, that Europeans learnt at first hand about Plains Indians, in a manner no longer available today. While these entertainments enhanced and replaced pre-existing stereotypes of Indians with new visions of feather-bonneted savages, they also made available across much of Europe one authentic view of Siouan life. The first Wild West show, that of the much mythologized Buffalo Bill, or William F. Cody (1846–1917), came to London in 1887 to perform at an American exhibition at Earls Court in Queen Victoria's Jubilee year. Enormously successful, this show and subsequent return visits, in 1891, 1892 and 1903,

287. Water jar, Acoma, nineteenth century. Most Pueblo pottery is constructed by coiling, which creates robust serviceable vessels, and then decorated with highly sophisticated, often abstract designs based on representational forms, such as the parrots shown here, of which beaks and tails remain. Diam: 25 cm (9.8 in); H: 25 cm (9.8 in).

288. 'Showcase Acoma', window display of pottery, including water jars, and on the left a canteen, 1970s. Both mould- and hand-made pottery remain vibrant traditions, including particularly vessels decorated with the precise geometric designs made famous by Lucy Lewis.

289. Water jar, Zuni, nineteenth century. From about 1700 Zuni pottery has been decorated with matte mineral and carbon paints over a white slip that covers most of the body. Designs, including a semi-realistic deer with a heartline from mouth to heart, and a duck, are executed in broad horizontal bands. Diam: 35 cm (13.8 in); H: 26 cm (10.2 in).

290. 'Waiting for a bus', 1970s. The Native woman is dressed in a highly decorated, crushed velveteen skirt and shirt, which are nineteenth century in origin but remained popular, particularly among the Navajo.

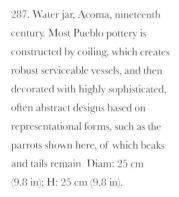

291. Tala-wipiki, Lightning *katsina* doll, received from the Smithsonian Institution in 1891. *Katsinam*, who are benevolent spirits, here relating to rain, live among the Hopi during the winter and first part of the year. Dolls, their physical embodiment, are given to children on ceremonial occasions to elicit good behaviour. H: 28.5 cm (11.2 in).

292. First Phase Chief Blanket, Navajo, *c.*1800–1850, a form widely traded in the West and onto the Plains. Originating with a shoulder blanket, a series of styles evolved in the nineteenth century from this simple but elegant tapestry-weave form, which employs natural white and brown wool with indigo-dyed stripes. 133 x 178 cm (52.4 x 70.1 in).

293. Textile woven in naturally dyed handspun wool by Barbara Jean Teller Ornelas, 1985. During the first quarter of the twentieth century a number of regional styles developed, many of them, such as this one called Two Gray Hills, associated with trading posts. 63 x 40 cm (24.8 x 15.7 in).

were much blessed with royal patronage. The first command performance was held on 11 May 1887. Black Elk recorded his experience of this occasion fifty or sixty years later. Calling the queen 'Grandmother England', he remembered her saying, 'I wish that I had owned you people, for I would not carry you round as beasts to show to the people'. Shows of this kind, while seemingly exploitative, also enabled Indians to escape both reservations and, for Ghost Dancers after Wounded Knee, prison, as well as to re-enact traditional ways at the same time as earning a living. The last of the major shows in London was that of the Miller Brothers 101 Ranch, which appeared in 1914 at an exhibition celebrating a century of peace between the US and Britain. At the outbreak of war the Ranch's horses were commandeered for the Western Front, and the performers left to return home as best they could.

The Southwest of the United States

Pivotal to Native North America are the contemporary peoples of the Southwestern states, Arizona and New Mexico, that border Mexico. It was here that the first evidence of early people, the Paleoindians, was excavated during the 1920s (figs 1–2). It is here that the oldest continually occupied communities in North America, the Hopi villages, are situated. Most significantly, it was here that early farming traditions in the United States first began perhaps 5,000 years ago. Maize and squash were introduced from central Mexico, and grown in gardens as additional food sources employed to complement the hunting and gathering of wild resources in this ecologically diverse area. Only in the last millennium before Christ did agriculture became fully established. Beans were introduced at this time, and perhaps also cotton, although cotton was only widely grown after AD 700. The technology of weaving and of the manufacture of ceramics also came from Mexico. Several of the pre-contact cultures in the Southwest have been well documented by archaeologists. These include the Hohokam, Mogollon and the ancient Puebloans formerly called the Anasazi. The Hohokam and their likely modern descendants, the O'odham (Papago and Pima), are flood-plain agriculturalists along the Gila river in southern Arizona. The Mogollon, in the mountainous southern half of New Mexico and neighbouring Arizona and Chihuahua, were the first farmers, while the ancient Puebloans, in northern New Mexico, had established large villages 1,000 years ago. These consisted of complexes of multi-storeyed, interconnecting, stone-built rooms incorporating the ancient but by then highly stylized pit-house, or *kiva*, as a chamber for social and ceremonial occasions. The eleventh-century Pueblo Bonito, in Chaco Canyon, New Mexico, was the largest community with perhaps 650 rooms built on five levels. Most notable is the manner in which water was (and is) managed among both ancient and modern Puebloans in order to maintain a viable agriculture in a desert environment.

From about AD 1100 the Mogollon and Puebloan farmers in northern New Mexico suffered a series of disasters, which resulted in rapid population decline. Drought was probably a major aspect of this catastrophe, but it may have been associated with over-intensive agriculture. The Mogollon peoples disappeared, absorbed by the ancient Puebloans who moved north to form larger communities in the wetter periphery of the Colorado Plateau, particularly along the Rio Grande Valley. When Francisco Vásquez de Coronado entered this valley in 1540, he found more than a hundred Puebloan villages. Following Spanish exploration, colonization was formally begun by Juan de Oñate in 1598. With the Europeans came the introduction of new plants and animals, tools and architecture. In New Mexico, as in California later, missionary efforts were in the hands of the Franciscans, who were initially successful, claiming 60,000 converts in 1630. It was here also that the most significant Native rebellion occurred, the Pueblo Revolt of 1680–92. This was aimed at ending the missionary system, most Spaniards being driven out rather than killed.

Some time in the last millennium, the Puebloan peoples were joined in the Southwest by Apachean speakers, people of northern Athapaskan language and descent. Originating in the Canadian Subarctic they had migrated south, big-game hunting through or along the Rocky Mountains and eventually making their home in the mountainous regions of what is now Arizona and New Mexico. Called Apache (from the Zuni designation for Navajo) and Navajo (from the Tewa words for 'wide valley field'), the Navajos were originally designated the Apaches de Navajò by the Spanish in the seventeenth century. Both contemporary Apaches and Navajos refer to themselves by the same or similar basic designation for man or people: *Diné* (Navajo) and, for instance, *Ndé* (Chiricahua and Mescalero Apache). The similar, Canadian Subarctic self-designation of northern Athapaskans is Dene. The Navajos, unlike the Apaches, adopted farming, hence their name. Sheep rearing became important, especially after the Pueblo Revolt when Puebloan peoples sought refuge from Spanish reprisals among the Navajos, who utilized Puebloan technology and traditions such as weaving. Horses, introduced particularly in Spanish stock-rearing enterprises around Santa Fe, spread through trade and raiding to

294. Navajo belt of leather, second half of the nineteenth century, originally worn by men, with eight domed *concha*s (literally 'shells') made from silver coins decorated with punched and stamped designs round the edges, cut-out diamond centres for the strap, and a silver buckle. L: 100 cm (39.4 in).

295. *Apache Necklace*, 1990, by the Apache/Navajo sculptor Bob Haozous (b. 1943), made of silver, turquoise, ivory and human hair. Employing conventional jewellery techniques, the sculptor transcends the prettyness of Anglo-American aesthetics by referring, in the gorget-like plaque, to male and military symbolism, scalp-locks and Native trophies. L (without hair): 42 cm (16.5 in).

Apachean peoples, and thence onto the Plains and Plateau at the end of the seventeenth century. Navajos themselves tell varied, rather different stories, of great elaboration and complexity, about their origins in their own land in the Southwest. They arrived on earth after travelling through up to fourteen superimposed, subterranean, flat or hemispherical worlds. In each of these worlds figures like the First Man, First Woman and Coyote struggle to live peacefully, and when they failed, destruction occurred; at each stage they moved upwards from below to another layer closer to the surface of the earth, where eventually a ceremonial 'hogan', or house, was built, in which the Navajo world was created.

In the 1840s the United States occupied Santa Fe and claimed the Southwest. This conquest did not pass unchallenged, particularly by the Apaches and Navajos, who continued raiding. Eventually, pacification was achieved, brutally, by removals: 7,000 Navajos were sent on what is called 'The Long Walk' east to Bosque Redondo, New Mexico, where they remained until 1868. Military operations against Apaches continued into the 1880s, with defeated, and also friendly, Indians sent to Fort Marion, Florida, and then to Oklahoma. Just as the arrival of the Spanish in the seventeenth century brought rapid and

296. *Clarence's Truck*, 1997, by the Navajo jeweller and sometime rodeo rider Clarence Lee (b. 1952), made of silver, coral, tiger's eye and turquoise. The highly detailed Chevrolet truck of the 1950s – the decade when motorized transportation replaced horses – also contains references to scarce water both in the water butt and the use of turquoise.
L (of truck): 5 cm.

297. 'Santa Fe craft selling', Palace of the Governors, 1970s. The Native vendor from Santa Domingo, wearing a *concha* belt, has a wide variety of shell and stone necklaces on display as well as silver bracelets and rings, all created for the tourist market.

fundamental cultural as well as political change, so Mexican independence brought American influence. This came initially through trade along the Santa Fe trail from Kansas City, then through military activities, and finally with the arrival of railroads from 1879. Despite this turbulent history, Southwestern Native peoples have been well able to determine what aspects of foreign influences and material culture they are willing to incorporate into their own traditions. Expressive religions helped maintain a deep-rooted sense of place, enabling artists to infuse diverse traditions – whether basketry, weaving or jewellery – with a vigorous sense of continuing identity. So, with the arrival of the railroad and then tourists from the 1890s, artistic production joined subsistence farming as a major source of income, particularly for women in the creation of pottery and textiles. After 1900 silver jewellery from Mexican sources, adapted by Navajo men while confined in Bosque Redondo, became important as a trade item. For the Zunis, ancient jewellers, silver and turquoise work grew to be commercially important from the 1930s, as also happened with Hopi cut-out overlay work in the 1940s.

298. Fritz Scholder (b. 1937), a Native California artist, in his southwestern studio, 1970s. Apparently hanging from the rafters is a Coyote trickster figure, suspended as in Sun Dance self-mortification rituals and wearing a textile with the swastika-like Navajo whirling-logs design abandoned by Navajo weavers during the 1940s.

Few collections, field or otherwise, came to the British Museum. In the late nineteenth century the British Museum conducted exchanges with the Smithsonian Institution, through which the first few dozen items, mostly of pottery and figures, or *katsinam*, came to the Museum. The next major accessions came in the 1920s, when the head of the Department, T. A. Joyce, made a small collection in the Southwest, and in the 1940s, when two exchanges were set up with the Denver Art Museum, through which the Department acquired an initial group of Navajo textiles, including a First Phase Chief Blanket (fig. 292).

Adair, John. *The Navajo and Pueblo Silversmiths*. Norman: University of Oklahoma Press, 1944.

Amsden, Charles Avery. *Navaho Weaving: Its Technic and History*. Albuquerque: University of New Mexico Press, 1949.

Angulo, Jaime de. 'Pomo Creation Myth', *Journal of American Folk-Lore*. 48(189): 203–62.

Axtell, James. *The Invasion Within. The Contest of Cultures in Colonial North America*. New York and Oxford: Oxford University Press, 1985.

Axtell, James. *After Columbus*. New York: Oxford University Press, 1988.

Barrett, Samuel A. 'Pomo Bear Doctors', *University of California Publications in American Archaeology and Ethnology* 12(11), 1917: 443–65.

Barrett, Samuel A. 'Pomo Myths', *Bulletin of the Public Museum of the City of Milwaukee* 15, 1933.

Benson, William R. 'The Stone and Kelsey Massacre on the Shores of Clear Lake in 1849', *Quarterly of the California Historical Society* 11(3), 1932: 266–73.

Billington, Ray Allen. *Land of Savagery, Land of Promise. The European Image of the American Frontier*. Norman: University of Oklahoma Press, 1981.

Biolsi, Thomas and Larry J. Zimmerman. *Indians and Anthropologists. Vine Deloria, Jr., and the Critique of Anthropology*. Tucson: University of Arizona Press, 1997.

Birket-Smith, Kaj. *The Eskimos*. London: Methuen & Co, 1936.

Black, Lydia T. *Glory Remembered. Wooden Headgear of Alaska Sea Hunters*. Juneau: Alaska State Museums, 1991.

Blomberg, Nancy J. *Navajo Textiles. The William Randolph Hearst Collection*. Tucson and London: University of Arizona Press, 1988.

Boas, Franz. *Primitive Art*. New York: Dover Publications, 1955.

Bonar, Eulalie H. *Woven by the Grandmothers. Nineteenth-Century Navajo Textiles from the National Museum of the American Indian*. Washington DC: Smithsonian Institution, 1996.

Brody, Hugh. *Living Arctic. Hunters of the Canadian North*. London: Faber and Faber, 1987.

Brose, David S., *et al. Ancient Art of the American Woodland Indians*. New York: Harry N. Abrams, 1985.

Brown, Jennifer S. and Robert Brightman. *"The Orders of the Dreamed"*. St Paul: Minnesota Historical Press, 1988.

Brownstone, Arni. *War Paint*. Toronto: Royal Ontario Museum, 1993.

Bunzel, Ruth. *The Pueblo Potter: A Study of Creative Imagination in Primitive Art*. New York: Columbia University Press, 1929.

Carlson, Roy L. *Indian Art Traditions of the Northwest Coast*. Burnaby: Archaeology Press, Simon Fraser University, 1983.

Carter, Sarah. *Lost Harvests*. Montreal & Kingston: McGill-Queen's University Press, 1990.

Cirillo, Dexter. *Southwestern Indian Jewelry*. New York: Abbeville Press, 1992.

Clutesi, George. *Son of Raven, Son of Deer. Fables of the Tse-shaht People*. Sidney: Gray's Publishing Limited, 1967.

Coe, Ralph, T. *Sacred Circles*. London: Arts Council of Great Britain, 1976.

Cole, Douglas. *Captured Heritage: The Scramble for Northwest Coast Artifacts*. Vancouver: Douglas & McIntyre, 1985.

Damas, David, ed. 'Arctic', *Handbook of North American Indians* 5, ed. William C. Sturtevant. Washington DC: Smithsonian Institution, 1984.

Dawson, Lawrence E., and James Deetz. 'A Corpus of Chumash Basketry', *Annual Reports of the University of California Archaeological Survey* 7, 1965: 193–276.

DeMallie, Raymond J. ed. *The Sixth Grandfather. Black Elk's Teachings Given to John G Neihardt*. Lincoln and London: University of Nebraska Press, 1984.

Dilworth, Leah. *Imagining Indians in the Southwest*. Washington DC: Smithsonian Institution Press, 1996.

Drucker, Phillip. 'The Northern and Central Nootkan Tribes', *Bureau of American Ethnology Bulletin* 144, 1951. Washington DC: Smithsonian Institution.

Duncan, Kate C. *Northern Athapaskan Art. A Beadwork Tradition*. Seattle: University of Washington Press, 1989.

Edmunds, R. David, ed. *American Indian Leaders*. Lincoln: University of Nebraska Press, 1980.

Efrat, Barbara S. and W.J. Langlois. 'Nu·tka. Captain Cook and the Spanish Explorers on the Coast' *Sound Heritage*, 7(1), 1978.

Efrat, Barbara S. and W.J. Langlois. 'Nu·tka. The History and Survival of Nootkan Culture' *Sound Heritage*, 7(2), 1978.

Erffa, Helmut von and Allen Staley. *The Paintings of Benjamin West*. New Haven and London: Yale University Press, 1986.

Ernst, Alice Henson. *The Wolf Ritual of the Northwest Coast*. Eugene: University of Oregon Press, 1952.

Ewers, John C. 'The Horse in Blackfoot Indian Culture with Comparative Material from other Western Tribes', *Bureau of American Ethnology Bulletin* 159, 1955. Washington DC: Smithsonian Institution.

Feder, Norman. *Art of the Eastern Plains Indians: The Nathan Sturgis Jarvis Collection*. Brooklyn: The Brooklyn Museum, 1964.

Feest, Christian F. *Native Arts of North America*. London: Thames and Hudson, 1980.

Fitzhugh, William and Aron Crowell, eds. *Crossroads of Continents*. Washington DC: Smithsonian Institution Press, 1988.

Fleming, Paula Richardson and Judith Luskey. *The North American Indians in Early Photographs*. New York: Harper and Row, 1986.

Fleming, Paula Richardson and Judith Lynn Luskey. *The Shadow Catchers. Images of the American Indian*. London: Laurence King, 1993.

Ford, Clellan S., ed. *Smoke from their Fires*. New Haven: Yale University Press, 1981.

Garratt, John R. *The Four Indian Kings*. Ottawa: Public Archives of Canada, 1991.

Gayton, Anna H. and Stanley S. Newman. 'Yokuts and Western Mono-Myths', *University of California Anthropological Records* 5(1-110), 1940.

Glenbow Museum. *The Spirit Sings*. Toronto: McClelland and Stewart, 1987, 2 vols.

Gough, Barry M. *Gunboat Frontier*. Vancouver: UBC Press, 1984.

Gunther, Erna. *Indian Life on the Northwest Coast of North America*. Chicago: University of Chicago Press, 1972.

Gustafson, Paula. *Salish Weaving*. Vancouver and Seattle: Douglas & McIntyre and University of Washington Press, 1980.

Hail, Barbara A. and Kate C. Duncan. *Out of the North. The Subarctic Collection of the Haffenreffer Museum of Anthropology Brown University*. Bristol: Haffenreffer Museum, 1989.

Halpin, Marjorie M. *Totem Poles: An Illustrated Guide*. Vancouver: University of British Columbia Press, 1981.

Harper, J. Russell. *Paul Kane's Frontier*. Austin and London: University of Texas Press, 1971.

Hauptman, Laurence M. and James D. Wherry. *The Pequots in Southern New England*. Norman and London: University of Oklahoma Press, 1990.

Hawthorn, Audrey. *Kwakiutl Art*. Seattle: University of Washington Press, 1979.

Heizer, Robert F., ed. 'The Luiseno Creation Myth', *Masterkey* 46(3), 1972: 93–100

Heizer, Robert F., ed. *The Destruction of the California Indians*. Santa Barbara and Salt Lake City: Peregrine Smith Inc., 1974.

Heizer, Robert F., ed. 'California', *Handbook of North American Indians* 8, ed. William C. Sturtevant. Washington DC: Smithsonian Institution, 1978.

Heizer, Robert F. and John E. Mills. *The Four Ages of Tsurai*. Trinidad: Trinidad Museum Society, 1991.

Helm, June, ed. 'Subarctic', *Handbook of North American Indians* 6, ed. William C. Sturtevant. Washington DC: Smithsonian Institution, 1981.

Herem, Barry. 'Bill Reid: Making the Northwest Coast Famous', *American Indian Art Magazine*, 24(1), 1998: 42–51.

Hill, Sarah J. *Weaving New Worlds. Southeastern Cherokee Women and Their Basketry*. Chapel Hill and London: University of North Carolina Press, 1997.

Holm, Bill. *Northwest Coast Indian Art: An Analysis of Form*. Seattle: University of Washington Press, 1965.

Holm, Bill. *Spirit and Ancestor*. Seattle: Burke Museum and University of Washington Press, 1987.

Honour, Hugh. *The European Vision of America*. Cleveland: Cleveland Museum of Art, 1975.

Hudson, Travis and Thomas C. Blackburn. 'The Material Culture of the Chumash Interaction Sphere', *Ballena Press Anthropological Papers*, 1982–7: 25–8, 30, 31.

Indian and Northern Affairs, Canada. *Inuit Art Section. Catalogue of Services and Collections*. Ottawa, 1984.

Institute of Early American History and Culture. 'Indians and Others in Early America', *The William and Mary Quarterly*, Third Series 53(3), 1996.

Issenman, Betty Kobayashi. *Sinews of Survival*. Vancouver: UBC Press, 1997.

Jonaitis, Aldona, ed. *Chiefly Feasts*. New York: The American Museum of Natural History, 1991.

Joppien, Rüdiger and Bernard Smith. *The Art of Captain Cook's Voyages*, Vol. 3. New Haven and London: Yale University Press, 1988.

Kew, J.E. Michael. 'Sculpture and Engraving of the Central Coast Salish Indians', *University of British Columbia. Museum of Anthropology Notes* 9, 1981.

King, J.C.H. *Artificial Curiosities from the Northwest Coast of America*. London: British Museum Publications, 1981.

King, J.C.H. *Thunderbird and Lightning*. London: British Museum Publications, 1982.

King, J.C.H. 'Woodlands artifacts from the studio of Benjamin West 1738–1820', *American Indian Art Magazine* 17(1), 1991: 33–47.

King, J.C.H. 'Sloane's Ethnography', *Sir Hans Sloane*, ed. Arthur MacGregor, pp. 228–44. London: British Museum Press, 1994.

King, J.C.H. 'Vancouver's Ethnography', *Journal of the History of Collections* 6(1), 1994: 33–58.

King, J.C.H. 'Franks and Ethnography', *A. W. Franks: Nineteenth-Century Collecting and the British Museum*, ed. Marjorie Caygill and John Cherry, pp. 136–59, 346–51 and pls 13–16. London: British Museum Press, 1997.

Krech, Shepard. *A Victorian Earl in the Arctic. The Travels and Collections of the fifth Earl of Lonsdale 1888–9*. London: British Museum Publications, 1989.

Kroeber, Alfred L. 'Handbook of the Indians of California', *Bureau of American Ethnology Bulletin* 78, 1925. Washington DC: Smithsonian Institution.

Kroeber, Alfred L. *Yurok Myths*. Berkeley: University of California Press, 1975.

Krupat, Arnold. *For Those Who Come After*. Berkeley: University of California Press, 1985.

Leroux, Odette, *et al.*, eds. *Inuit Women Artists. Voices from Cape Dorset*. Vancouver: Douglas and McIntyre, 1994.

Lévi-Strauss, Claude. 'The Art of the Northwest Coast at the American Museum of Natural History', *Gazette des Beaux Arts*, 24, 1943: 175–82.

Lévi-Strauss, Claude. *The Way of the Masks*, trans. Sylvia Modelski. Seattle: University of Washington Press, 1982.

Lottinville, Savoie, ed. *Paul Wilhelm, Duke of Würtemburg. Travels in North America, 1822–1824*. Norman: University of Oklahoma Press, 1973.

Lippard, Lucy. R., ed. *Partial Recall. Photographs of Native North Americans*. New York: New Press, 1992.

MacDonald, George F. *Haida Monumental Art*. Vancouver: UBC Press, 1983.

McDonnell, Janet A. *The Dispossession of the American Indian 1887–1934*. Bloomington and Indianapolis: Indiana University Press, 1991.

McLendon, Sally. 'Pomo Baskets. The Legacy of William and Mary Benson', *Native Peoples*, 4(1), 1990: 26–33.

McLendon, Sally and Judith Berman, eds. 'Exhibition on Pomo Indian Weavers and Basketry', *Expedition* 40(1), 1998.

Macnair, Peter L., Alan L. Hoover and Kevin Neary. *The Legacy*. Victoria: British Columbia Provincial Museum, 1980.

Marshall, Ingeborg. *A History and Ethnography of the Beothuk*. Montreal and Kingston: McGill-Queen's University Press, 1996.

Mason, Otis Tufton. 'Aboriginal Indian Basketry: Studies in a Textile Art without Machinery', *Report of the U.S. National Museum, Smithsonian Institution, for the Year 1902*, pp. 171–548. Washington DC: Government Printing Office, 1904.

Mathiassen, Therkel. 'Material Culture of the Iglulik Eskimos', *Report of the Fifth Thule Expedition 1921–24*, Vol. 6(1), 1928.

Mignon, Molly R. and Daniel L. Boxberger, eds. *Native North Americans: An Ethnohistorical Approach*. Dubuque: Kendall Hunt Publishing Co., 1997.

Mooney, James. 'Myths of the Cherokee', *Annual Report of the Bureau of American Ethnology*, 19, pp. 3–548. Washington DC: Smithsonian Institution, 1898.

Moses, L C. *Wild West Shows and the Images of American Indians 1883–1933*. Albuquerque: University of New Mexico Press, 1996.

Neel, David. *The Great Canoes*. Vancouver and Seattle: Douglas & McIntyre and University of Washington Press, 1995.

Nunez, Theron A. 'Creek Nativism and the Creek War of 1813–1814', *Ethnohistory* 5, 1958: 1–47, 131–175, 292–301.

Oakes, Jill and Rick Riewe. *Our Boots. An Inuit Women's Art*. Vancouver and Toronto: Douglas and McIntyre, 1995.

O'Neale, Lila M. 'Yurok-Karok Basket Weavers', *University of California Publications in American Archaeology and Ethnology*, 32, 1932: 1–184.

Ortiz, Alfonso, ed. 'Southwest', *Handbook of North American Indians* 9 and 10, ed. William C. Sturtevant. Washington DC: Smithsonian Institution, 1979, 1983.

Owsley, Frank L. 'Prophet of War: Josiah Francis and the Creek War', *American Indian Quarterly* 9(3), 1985: 273–93.

Penney, David W. *Art of the American Indian Frontier*. London: Phaidon, 1992.

Phillips, Ruth B. *Patterns of Power*. Kleinberg: The McMichael Canadian Collection, 1984.

Powers, Stephen. *Tribes of California*. Berkeley: University of California Press 1976 (first published 1877).

Ray, Arthur J. *I Have Lived Here Since the World Began*. Toronto: Lester Publishing and Key Porter Books, 1996.

Rogers, Edward S. 'The Material Culture of the Mistassini', *Bulletin 218*, Anthropological Series 80, National Museum of Canada, Ottawa, 1967.

Secakuku, Alph. *Following the Sun and Moon, Hopi Kachina Tradition*. Flagstaff: Northland Publishing, 1995.

Silverberg, Robert. *Mound Builders of Ancient America*. Greenwich: New York Graphic Society, 1968.

Squier, E.G. and E. H. Davis. 'Ancient Monuments of the Mississippi Valley', *Smithsonian Contributions to Knowledge* 1, 1848.

Summers, R.W. *Indian Journal*. Lafayette: Guadalupe Translations, 1994.

Suttles, Wayne, ed. 'Northwest Coast', *Handbook of North American Indians* 7, ed. William C. Sturtevant. Washington DC: Smithsonian Institution, 1990.

Swanton, John R. 'The Indians of the Southeastern United States', *Bureau of American Ethnology Bulletin* 137. Washington DC: Smithsonian Institution, 1946.

Swidler, Nina, *et al.*, eds. *Native Americans and Archaeologists. Stepping Stones to a Common Ground*. Walnut Creek, London and New Delhi: Sage Publications, 1997.

Taylor, Colin F. *The Plains Indians*. London: Salamander Books, 1994.

Teilhet-Fisk, Jehanne and Robin Franklin Nigh. *Dimensions of Native America: the Contact Zone*. Tallahassee: Florida State University, Museum of Fine Arts, 1998.

Thompson, Judy. 'The North American Indian Collection. A Catalogue', *Jahrbuch des Bernische Historichen Museums*, 53/5 for 1973/4, 1977.

Thompson, Judy. *From the Land. Two Hundred Years of Dene Clothing*. Hull: Canadian Museum of Civilization, 1994.

Torrence, Gaylord. *The American Indian Parfleche*. Des Moines and Seattle: Des Moines Art Center and the University of Washington Press, 1994.

Trigger, Bruce G. 'Northeast', *Handbook of North American Indians* 15, ed. William C. Sturtevant. Washington DC: Smithsonian Institution, 1978.

Trigger, Bruce G. and Wilcomb E. Washburn. *The Cambridge History of the Native Peoples of the Americas*, Vol. I (2 parts). Cambridge and New York: Cambridge University Press, 1996.

Trimble, Stephen. *The People. Indians of the American Southwest*. Santa Fe: School of American Research Press, 1993.

VanStone, James W. 'Material Culture of the Davis Inlet and Barren Ground Naskapi: The William Duncan Strong Collection', *Fieldiana. Anthropology*, NS 7, 1985.

Varjola, Pirjo. *The Etholén Collection*. Helsinki: National Museum of Finland, 1990.

Wade, Edwin L. and Rennard Strickland. *Magic Images: Contemporary Native American Art*. Tulsa and Norman: Philbrook Art Center and University of Oklahoma Press, 1981.

Wardwell, Allen. *Tangible Visions*. New York: The Monacelli Press, 1996.

Washburn, Wilcomb E., ed. 'History of Indian-White Relations', *Handbook of North American Indians* 4, ed. William C. Sturtevant. Washington DC: Smithsonian Institution, 1988

Webster, Peter S. *As Far As I Know. Reminiscences of an Ahousat Elder*. Campbell River: Campbell River Museum and Archive, 1983.

Weigle, Marta and Barbara A. Babcock, ed. *The Great Southwest of the Fred Harvey Company and the Santa Fe Railway*. Phoenix: The Heard Museum, 1996.

Whiteford, Andrew Hunter. *Southwestern Indian Baskets. Their History and Their Makers*. Santa Fe: School of American Research Press, 1988.

Whiteford, Andrew Hunter. *I am Here. Two Thousand Years of Southwestern Indian Arts and Culture*. Santa Fe: Museum of New Mexico Press, 1989.

Wilkinson, Alan G. *The Drawings of Henry Moore*. London: Tate Gallery Publications, 1977.

Wright, Barton. *Kachinas. The Barry Goldwater Collection at the Heard Museum*. Phoenix: W.A. Krueger Co. and the Heard Museum, 1975.

Wright, Ronald. *Stolen Continents*. Toronto: Penguin Books, 1993.

PHOTOGRAPHIC CREDITS

Illustrations are listed by figure number. All photographs of objects in the British Museum, which were supplied by the Museum Photographic Service, are indicated by the following departmental abbreviations:

Ethno   Ethnography
PD   Prints and Drawings
PRB   Prehistoric and Romano-British Antiquities

1. PRB 1962.12-6.137
2. All rights reserved, Photo Archives, Denver Museum of Natural History
3. Ethno (l. to r.): Sl 1373; Sl 1254; Sl 886; Sl 885; Sl 2089
4. Ethno S.343
5. Ethno S.340
6. Ethno Library
7. Ethno S.540
8. Ethno S.257
9. Ethno S.276
10. Ethno S.266
11. Ethno S.574
12. Ethno S.324
13. Ethno S.513
14. Ethno 1903.7-11.1
15. Ethno S.331
16. Ethno Library
17. Courtesy of Richard Pirko
18. Courtesy of Richard Pirko
19. Courtesy of Richard Pirko
20. Courtesy of Richard Pirko
21. Ethno 1854.6-6.1
22. Ethno 1884.1-1.1
23. Ethno S.332
24. Ethno S.315
25. PD
26. Ethno Q85 Am 21.a+b
27. Ethno 1929.12-16.7
28. Ethno Dc.13
29. Courtesy of the National Gallery of Canada
30. Ethno Library
31. Ethno 6976
32. Courtesy of National Archives of Canada, C87698
33. Ethno LL.3
34. Ethno Sl.1730
35. Ethno Sl.758
36. By permission of the British Library
37. Courtesy of The Chase Manhattan Library and Archives

38. Ethno 1949.Am 22.119
39. Ethno 1878.11-1.625
40. Ethno Sl.203
41. Ethno Db.2
42. Ethno Dc.44
43. Ethno Library
44. Ethno Library
45. Ethno 1983.Am 37.1
46. Courtesy of J.C.H. King
47. Courtesy of National Anthropological Archives, Smithsonian Institution, NAA 51-11
48. Ethno Sl.573
49. Ethno Library
50. Ethno Sl.1532
51. Ethno 1921.10-14.84
52. Ethno 1986.Am 18.117
53. Ethno Am 1977, loan 01.3 (Stonyhurst College)
54. Ethno Am 1977, loan 01.2 (Stonyhurst College)
55. Ethno 1993.Am 9.1
56. Ethno Q78.Am 39
57. Ethno 1921.10-14.102
58. Ethno Dc.76
59. Ethno 2598
60. Ethno 1949.Am 22.169; 1949.Am 22.170
61. Ethno 2575.a+b
62. Ethno 1977, loan 01.51 (Stonyhurst College)
63. Ethno Dc.80
64. Ethno 1944.Am 2.219
65. Ethno 1982.Am 28.20
66. Courtesy of National Anthropological Archives, Smithsonian Institution, NAA 361, 199-4
67. Ethno 2144
68. Courtesy of the National Gallery of Canada
69. Ethno 1991.Am 9.1
70. Ethno 1991.Am 9.4
71. Ethno 1991.Am 12.1.a+b; presented by M. and E. Sosland
72. Ethno Library
73. PD
74. PD

75. PD
76. PD
77. PD
78. PD
79. Ethno Sl.1368
80. Courtesy of Peabody Museum, Harvard University (H. Berger)
81. Courtesy of Peabody Museum, Harvard University (H. Berger)
82. Ethno Sl.1237
83. PD
84. PD
85. Ethno Library
86. Ethno 7479.i
87. Ethno 7479.d+e
88. Courtesy of National Anthropological Archives, Smithsonian Institution, NAA 45837-C
89. Courtesy of J.C.H. King
90. Ethno 1980.Am 32.1
91. Courtesy of National Anthropological Archives, Smithsonian Institution, NAA 1044-A
92. Courtesy of National Anthropological Archives, Smithsonian Institution, NAA 44550-C
93. Ethno 1977.Am 28.13
94. Ethno Library
95. Ethno Sl.1218
96. Courtesy of the Museum of the Cherokee Indian, Cherokee, NC
97. Ethno NWC.68
98. Courtesy of National Anthropological Archives, Smithsonian Institution, NAA 41886-S
99. Ethno Q87.Am 27
100. Ethno Van.168; Van.169
101. Ethno Van.198
102. Courtesy of Dugan Aguilar
103. Courtesy of Huntington Library
104. Courtesy of National Anthropological Archives, Smithsonian Institution, NAA 43114-A
105. Courtesy of National Anthropological Archives, Smithsonian Institution, NAA 43114, 165
106. Courtesy of Santa Barbara Mission Archive

Library, Santa Barbara, California.
107. Ethno Van.157
108. Courtesy of Santa Barbara Museum of Natural History
109. Ethno Library
110. Ethno Van.204; Van.205
111. Ethno Van.196
112. Ethno NWC.46
113. Ethno 1910-124
114. Courtesy of Huntington Library
115. National Museums of Scotland 1950.112; 1950.112A
116. Courtesy of National Anthropological Archives, Smithsonian Institution, NAA 76-15815
117. Courtesy of Huntington Library
118. Ethno 8182
119. Courtesy of Dugan Aguilar
120. Ethno Library
121. Ethno: 2004.
122. Ethno: Q72 Am 62.
123. Ethno 6222
124. PD
125. Ethno Library; courtesy of Hupquatchew, Ron Hamilton.
126. Ethno 1949.Am 22.229
127. Ethno NWC.89; NWC 88; NWC.67
128. Ethno 1981.Am 25.56
129. Courtesy of National Anthropological Archives, Smithsonian Institution, NAA 56759
130. Ethno 1842.12-10.37
131. Ethno 1949 Am 22.85
132. Ethno Library (Edward Curtis)
133. Ethno NWC.53
134. Ethno 4138
135. Ethno NWC.57
136. Ethno NWC.41
137. Ethno NWC.28
138. Ethno NWC.55
139. Ethno NWC.71
140. Ethno NWC.58
141. Ethno NWC.9
142. Ethno 1971.Am 5.1
143. The work illustrated on p. 144 is reproduced by permission of the Henry Moore Foundation from p. 103, Notebook 3, 1922–4.

144. Ethno NWC.64
145. Courtesy of
   J.C.H. King
146. Courtesy of
   David Neel
147. Ethno 6782; 1979.Am
   10.1
148. Ethno 1950.Am 9.1
149. Ethno S.1310
150. Ethno 1929.12-18.2
151. Ethno Library
152. Ethno 1944.Am 2.393;
   Q87.Am 5
153. Ethno 1920.10-14.1
154. Ethno 1944. Am 2.197
155. 1949.Am 22.82
156. Ethno 1898.10-2.1
157. Ethno Library
158. Ethno Library
159. Ethno 1971.Am 9.2
160. Ethno 1944.Am 2.131
161. Ethno +228
162. Ethno NWC.51
163. Ethno 6809
164. Courtesy of Stark
   Museum, Orange, Texas
165. Ethno 1896.1-25.1
166. Ethno 1944.Am 2.145
167. Ethno 1949.Am 22.63
168. Ethno +217
169. Ethno 1949.Am 22.111
170. Ethno 1939.Am 11.1
171. Ethno 1949.Am 22.86;
   +5335; + 5336
172. By permission of the
   Canadian Museum of
   Civilization, Québec,
   Canada, 59800
173. Ethno NWC.25
174. Ethno 6784
175. Courtesy of National
   Anthropological Archives,
   Smithsonian Institution,
   NAA 42975-E
176. Ethno 1944.Am 2.134
177. Courtesy of National
   Anthropological Archives,
   Smithsonian Institution,
   NAA 38582-D
178. Ethno 1949.Am 22.125
179. Ethno +5931; 2233
180. Courtesy of Tessa
   Macintosh
181. Ethno 1900.4-11.18
182. Ethno St.748
183. Ethno NWC.3
184. Ethno NWC.24
185. Ethno 1630
186. Ethno Van.190
187. Ethno Q78.Am 11

188. Ethno 1842.12-10.46
189. Ethno 1855.11-26.231
190. Ethno 1936-1
191. Ethno 1855.11-26.79
192. Ethno 1855.11-26.354
193. Ethno 1949.Am 22.19
194. Courtesy of Bryan and
   Cherry Alexander
195. Ethno 1883.1-11.1
196. Ethno 1900.4-11.30
197. Courtesy of the Scott
   Polar Research Institute
198. Ethno 1855.11-26.458;
   1824.4-10.12
199. Ethno 1903.6-15.1
200. Ethno 1900.4-11.38
201. Ethno Sl.1933.8;
   Sl.1933.15; Sl.1933.18
202. PD
203. PD
204. Ethno 1990.Am 12.1
205. Ethno 1855.11-26.281
206. PD
207. Ethno Q80.Am 1
208. Ethno 1941.Am 1.4
209. Ethno 1967.Am 3.1
210. Courtesy of Tessa
   Macintosh
211. Ethno 1987.Am
   2.13.a+b
212. Ethno 1982.Am 28.21
213. Ethno NWC.31;
   NWC.33
214. Ethno Q72.Am 46;
   2630
215. Ethno Library
216. Courtesy of National
   Anthropological Archives,
   Smithsonian Institution,
   NAA 32, 492-9
217. Courtesy of National
   Anthropological Archives,
   Smithsonian Institution,
   NAA 45, 475-3
218. Ethno 1921.10-4.170
219. Courtesy of the
   National Archives of
   Canada C1917.
220. Courtesy of National
   Anthropological Archives,
   Smithsonian Institution,
   NAA 56963
221. Ethno 1989.Am 21.6
222. Ethno 1984.Am 7.1
223. Ethno 1921.10-4.181
224. Ethno Sl.202
225. Ethno 1921.10-14.98
226. Ethno 1921.10-4.185
227. Courtesy of the Field
   Museum, Chicago

228. Courtesy of the Field
   Museum, Chicago
229. Courtesy of the Field
   Museum, Chicago
230. Courtesy of the Field
   Museum, Chicago
231. Ethno 1963 Am 5.1
232. Ethno 1987 Am 2.1
233. Ethno 1959.Am 7.7
234. Ethno 2647
235. Ethno 1566
236. Ethno 1887.12-8.17
237. Ethno Library
238. Ethno 1949.Am 22.149
239. Ethno 1986.Am 13.2
240. Ethno 1949.Am 23.1
241. Ethno Library;
   presented by M. and E.
   Sosland
242. Ethno Q72.Am 14.d
243. Ethno Q85.Am 33.a+b
244. Ethno Q72.Am 14.a+b
245. Ethno 1982.Am 28.18
246. Ethno 1989.Am 28.19
247. Courtesy of the
   Provincial Archives of
   Manitoba
248. Courtesy of National
   Archives of Canada,
   C46498
249. Ethno 1954.Am 5.965
250. Ethno 1944.Am
   2.203.a+b
251. Ethno Q83.Am 288
252. Courtesy of the
   Brantford Historical
   Society, Ontario
253. Ethno 1903-102
254. Ethno Library
255. Ethno 1903-32
256. Ethno 1903-31
257. Courtesy of National
   Anthropological Archives,
   Smithsonian Institution,
   NAA 98-10100
258. Ethno 1985.Am 13.1
259. Ethno 1936.10-20.40
260. Canadian Pacific
   Archives, image number
   A.4263
261. Ethno 1928.10-12.5
262. Ethno 1982.Am 28.13
263. Courtesy of National
   Archives of Canada,
   C12947
264. Ethno Q72.Am 17
265. Courtesy of Kenny
   Blackbird
266. Ethno 5216
267. Ethno 1930.20

268. Ethno 1982.Am 28.20
269. Ethno Q87.Am 15
270. Ethno 1977, loan 01.6
   (Stonyhurst College)
271. Ethno 5203
272. Courtesy of National
   Anthropological Archives,
   Smithsonian Institution,
   NAA 357, 337-8
273. Courtesy of National
   Anthropological Archives,
   Smithsonian Institution,
   NAA 349, 342-12
274. Ethno 1977, loan 01.16
   (Stonyhurst College)
275. Courtesy of National
   Anthropological Archives,
   Smithsonian Institution,
   NAA 98-10101
276. Ethno 5200
277. Ethno 5202
278. Ethno 5202
279. Ethno 5210
280. Ethno Library
281. Ethno 5196
282. Ethno 917
283. Ethno 1942.Am 7.2
284. Courtesy of the
   Victoria and Albert
   Museum
285. Ethno Library
286. Ethno 1939 Am 22.1
287. Ethno 1888.5-17.1
288. Courtesy of National
   Anthropological Archives,
   Smithsonian Institution,
   NAA 229, 124-6
289. Ethno 1888.5-17.7
290. Courtesy of National
   Anthropological Archives,
   Smithsonian Institution,
   NAA 227, 193-12
291. Ethno 1891.6-12.24
292. Ethno 1948.Am 17.21
293. Ethno 1985.Am 18.1
294. Ethno 1923.12-14.1
295. Ethno 1997.Am 12.2
296. Ethno 1997.Am 12.19
297. Courtesy of National
   Anthropological Archives,
   Smithsonian Institution,
   NAA 275,174-5
298. Courtesy of National
   Anthropological Archives,
   Smithsonian Institution,
   NAA 257, 175-3